The Fourth Amendment in Flux

The Fourth Amendment in Flux

THE ROBERTS COURT, CRIME CONTROL, AND DIGITAL PRIVACY

Michael C. Gizzi
R. Craig Curtis

University Press of Kansas

© 2016 by the University Press of Kansas
All rights reserved

Published by the University Press of Kansas (Lawrence, Kansas 66045), which was organized by the Kansas Board of Regents and is operated and funded by Emporia State University, Fort Hays State University, Kansas State University, Pittsburg State University, the University of Kansas, and Wichita State University

Library of Congress Cataloging-in-Publication Data
Names: Gizzi, Michael C., author. | Curtis, R. Craig, author.
Title: The fourth amendment in flux : the Roberts court, crime control, and digital privacy / Michael C. Gizzi, R. Craig Curtis.
Description: Lawrence, Kansas : University Press of Kansas, 2016. | Includes index.
Identifiers: LCCN 2016000656| ISBN 978-0-7006-2256-6 (hardback) | ISBN 978-0-7006-2257-3 (paperback) | ISBN 978-0-7006-2258-0 (ebook)
Subjects: LCSH: Searches and seizures—United States—Cases. | United States. Supreme Court. | BISAC: LAW / Constitutional. | POLITICAL SCIENCE / Constitutions.
Classification: LCC KF9630 .G59 2016 | DDC 345.73/0522—dc23
LC record available at http://lccn.loc.gov/2016000656.

British Library Cataloguing-in-Publication Data is available.

Printed in the United States of America

10 9 8 7 6 5 4 3 2 1

The paper used in this publication is recycled and contains 30 percent postconsumer waste. It is acid free and meets the minimum requirements of the American National Standard for Permanence of Paper for Printed Library Materials Z39.48-1992.

Contents

Preface, *vii*

PART I

1 Explaining the Roberts Court's Fourth Amendment Jurisprudence, *3*

2 Setting the Stage, *25*

3 The Burger Court and the Rise of a Jurisprudence of Crime Control, *42*

4 The War on Drugs and the Triumph of the Rehnquist Court, *61*

PART II

5 The Roberts Court in Flux, *81*

6 The Jurisprudence of Crime Control on the Roberts Court, *101*

7 Reining in the Excesses of Crime Control, *120*

8 Toward the Future, *143*

Notes, *161*

List of Cases, *171*

Index, *175*

Preface

We set out to write this book on the Roberts Court and the Fourth Amendment after a multiyear collaboration on a variety of related projects. Both of us have long been fascinated by the Fourth Amendment, and by how the law has developed over the past fifty years. We began our work together writing on the law of vehicle searches, and had been particularly interested in the judicial impact of *Arizona v. Gant*, the Supreme Court decision in 2009 that modified the law of vehicle searches incident to arrest. When we first approached Chuck Myers at the University Press of Kansas, it was with the idea of writing a book on *Arizona v. Gant*. We were so pleasantly pleased when Chuck suggested that we think bigger, and consider a book on the broader issues of the Fourth Amendment during the Roberts Court and, in particular, the role that technology was playing in shaping changes in the law. This occurred prior to the Supreme Court's decision in 2014 in *Riley v. California*, mandating warrants before police could search a cell phone. Chuck's foresight with regard to this key issue is greatly appreciated.

The process of doing the research and writing the book has been extraordinarily rewarding for us both, enhancing our teaching and giving us a sense of making a real contribution to the state of knowledge in the discipline. It is our hope that our readers will be better equipped to make sense of the work of the Court, the persistent conflicts stemming from the war on drugs, racial profiling, the use of deadly force, and the enduring debate in this country over the proper balance between personal freedom and societal order.

No project of this magnitude could be done entirely on our own. We want to thank Chuck Myers for the support and encouragement he has provided throughout the process of writing and refining our argument. Steve Wasby encouraged us to develop the initial book proposal, and has provided good advice throughout the project. Craig Hemmens and Michael Palmiotto took the time to read and review the entire manuscript. We appreciate their support for the project. Ethan Boldt and Bill Wilkerson both read early parts of the manuscript and provided insights into making the book better. We also want to thank Robert Demke for excellent copy editing. Jane Raese, Kelly Chrisman Jacques, and Michael Kehoe made the production and marketing processes painless.

Michael Gizzi would like to thank Dr. Jacqueline Schneider, chair of the Department of Criminal Justice Sciences at Illinois State University, for supporting my work on the project, and for leading a department that provides a supporting environment for research. Several colleagues provided support and patiently listened to explanations of the book's thesis as it developed. Ralph Weisheit, Jason Ingram, and Cara Rabe-Hemp were particularly helpful. As coordinator of the graduate program, Jason Ingram provided extra graduate assistance support. My graduate assistant, Mia Gilliam, was very helpful in conducting related research on the Rehnquist Court. Students in my criminal procedure course read early drafts, and helped me refine the argument through teaching. Several students completed independent study projects tied to the book's argument. My graduate law and society students challenged me to defend my arguments and, in the process, made the book much better.

The Illinois State University Office of Research and Sponsored Programs provided grant support for a related project on building a digital search and seizure archive of materials from the papers of Supreme Court justices. Much of that work was extremely valuable in writing the first half of this book. The librarians at the Manuscript Division of the Library of Congress were very helpful during my multiple trips to Washington, DC, exploring the development of search and seizure law during the Burger Court years. John Jacob, archivist at the Lewis F. Powell, Jr., Archives at Washington and Lee University Law School, was extremely helpful in facilitating a research trip to the archives.

Finally, my wife, Julie, and son, Nick, were supportive throughout the development of the book, and showed great patience when I was preoccupied by writing the book, or was headed to the Coffee House in Uptown Normal for yet another two-hour session of writing. Their constant support means more than I can ever acknowledge.

Craig Curtis would like to thank his department chair, Mark Gobeyn, and his dean, Chris Jones, for their support for this project, including the granting of a sabbatical leave that allowed me to devote my entire attention to research and writing for the fall semester of 2014. Craig would also like to thank two men who served as the best mentors one could hope to have, Christopher L. Blakesley, Cobeaga Law Firm Professor of Law at the University of Nevada, Las Vegas, William S. Boyd School of Law; and Nicholas P. Lovrich, political science professor emeritus of Washington State University. Many years ago, Chris took a young law student at McGeorge School of Law under his wing and taught me a love for the law and the Constitution and started me on the path of research that has been so very rewarding for my entire career. Not long after I finished law school, Nick picked me out of a group of graduate students at Washington State University and undertook to teach me what it means to be a scholar. Nick taught me how to comport myself with integrity and passion as a political scientist, as a mentor to my own students, and as a person. I could never have accomplished so much without the benefit of these two wonderful mentors.

Finally, my wife, Leah Adams-Curtis, and my two children, Anna and Galen, put up with me talking incessantly about the book, about the law, and about the results of our research and writing for well over a year. Their patience and love is critical to my mental health and my joy in doing the research that makes me happy.

In the end, while we could not have written the book without the assistance of a large number of people, and are grateful for their help and support, responsibility for any errors remains entirely with us.

The Fourth Amendment
in Flux

PART I

1. Explaining the Roberts Court's Fourth Amendment Jurisprudence

David Leon Riley was stopped by a San Diego police officer for having an expired vehicle registration in August 2009. When the officer learned that Riley also had a suspended driver's license, he placed Riley under arrest. Riley was searched and handcuffed. His car was impounded, and an inventory search of the car was conducted, revealing loaded guns under the hood. These weapons were later matched by ballistics testing to guns used in a shooting that took place three weeks prior to Riley's arrest. During the initial search of Riley when he was arrested, the police officer seized his smartphone and scrolled through the stored messages on it. At the station, a more thorough search of the digital content on the phone revealed evidence of gang affiliation and gang activity in Riley's text messages, pictures, and videos. These digital files were seized and used as evidence at Riley's trial. His attorney objected to the use of the digital files, but the judge allowed the jury to see them. Riley was convicted of attempted murder, assault with a semiautomatic handgun, and shooting at a vehicle. Because the jury believed that he was a member of the Bloods street gang and that the shooting was part of gang activity, Riley was given an enhanced sentence of 15 years to life.

David Riley's attorneys appealed his conviction through the California courts, but lost at every stage. Their last step was to appeal to the United States Supreme Court, asking the Court to grant a writ of certiorari and hear the case. Throughout the appellate process, Riley's attorneys maintained that the search of his cell phone was a violation of his Fourth Amendment right to be free from unreasonable searches and seizures. The search of his phone was done without a warrant, and there was no emergency to justify a warrantless search. The Supreme Court granted certiorari in January 2014, held oral argument in April, and then, in late June 2014, issued a decision in favor of Riley and another defendant from Massachusetts named Brima Wurie. The case, called *Riley v. California*, was unanimous in its outcome. All nine justices ruled in favor of the defendants, with just one brief concurring opinion. In a decision that has been viewed as a sweeping victory for digital privacy rights, Chief Justice Roberts' majority opinion ruled that prior to searching a cell phone, police must first obtain a warrant. The Court held that, unlike a wallet or other things commonly found on a person, a cell phone was different, containing a vast amount of information in which the individual had a strong privacy interest. The police can seize an arrested person's cell phone, but must then convince a neutral judge that there is probable cause to believe that the phone contains evidence of crime before they can search the digital files on the phone. Riley would get a new trial, and data stored on cell phones acquired a new and protected status under the Fourth Amendment. The decision came two years after the Court ruled unanimously in *United States v. Jones* (2012) that law enforcement also had to obtain a warrant before placing a Global Positioning System (GPS) tracking device on a vehicle. The FBI had monitored the location of Antoine Jones' vehicle for a month, and used the evidence to build a drug distribution case against him. Both decisions seemed to mark a significant departure from the normal way the Supreme Court decided search and seizure issues.

Contrast the ruling in *Riley* with the narrow 5–4 decision the year before in *Maryland v. King* (2013). Alonzo King was arrested in 2009 for assault after threatening a group of people with a shotgun. At the jail where he was booked, a sample of his DNA was taken with a cheek swab pursuant to state law. Maryland, like many states, had begun the process of routinely collecting DNA to build a forensic database to assist in the solving of crimes.[1] King's DNA sample was analyzed and added to a database of DNA from known criminals and arrestees. As a matter of routine practice, the results were compared to DNA evidence from unsolved crimes. Four months after his arrest, the DNA test revealed a match with a DNA sample from a rape that occurred in 2003. King was charged and convicted of that rape. At his trial, his attorney unsuccessfully argued that the evidence obtained from the DNA swab in 2009 was an unreasonable search and violated his Fourth Amendment rights. The conviction was overturned on appeal, and the state petitioned the Supreme Court to decide the case.

The Supreme Court granted certiorari and ruled for the state in an opinion written by Justice Kennedy. The DNA swab was a noninvasive procedure that did not violate King's privacy rights under the Fourth Amendment. Kennedy treated the DNA swab as comparable to fingerprinting or photographing a distinctive tattoo. The majority opinion disregarded the disconnect between the stated administrative purpose of the test, to collect identifying information about the person being booked, and the true purpose of the program, which is to collect information about a broad group of persons to be used in the detection and clearance of crimes. The information about an individual contained in his or her DNA is, for many, at least as important and as private as the pictures and record of texts and phone calls held on a cell phone, and the four dissenting justices objected vigorously.

The experiences of David Riley and Alonzo King illustrate some of the issues that are at stake in Fourth Amendment cases. Each year, more than 60 million people come into contact with the police.[2] Traffic stops make up more than 40 percent of these encounters, followed by requests for assistance after an accident and stops of people walking on the street. Police officers have enormous discretion to search, issue citations, arrest, or use physical force during these encounters. The law that governs what the police can legally do in these encounters is the Fourth Amendment, which protects against unreasonable searches and seizures. The Supreme Court determines what this law means in practice. Unlike many other parts of the Constitution, the Fourth Amendment is put into practice by police officers thousands of times each and every day. While many of the search and seizure cases that the Court decides are not as high profile as cases judging the constitutionality of the Affordable Care Act or the Voting Rights Act, the Court's Fourth Amendment jurisprudence plays a large role in shaping the relationship between citizens and the police. It is also an area of constitutional law that the Court hears cases on every year, having decided more than 300 search and seizure cases since the start of the Warren Court in 1953.

In many ways, these two cases illustrate a central tension that exists not only in the constitutional law of criminal procedure, but the criminal justice system as a whole. Herbert Packer first articulated this in his book *The Limits of the Criminal Sanction* (1968).[3] Packer argued that criminal law can be thought of as being torn between two different sets of goals, what he labeled due process and crime control. The Bill of Rights focuses on the rights that the state has to provide the accused before depriving them of life, liberty, or property. Due process includes those steps that are needed to ensure fundamental fairness. When followed faithfully, the demands of due process slow down the criminal process, creating an obstacle course of sorts for police and prosecutors, who must take steps to ensure that the individual's rights are not denied. This creates tension with the goal of crime control. In a criminal justice system where there are new crimes being committed on a daily basis, there are huge pressures on police, prosecutors, and judges to process cases quickly, and for police to maximize their efficiencies in combating crime. If due process is focused on, then crime control is frustrated. If, on the other hand, crime control is given primacy and police are given extensive discretion and tools to energetically fight crime, then individual rights are diminished.

The tension between due process and crime control is ubiquitous in a democracy such as ours, but for most of the past half-century, the Supreme Court's approach to the Fourth Amendment has been shaped by the broader politics of crime control that has dominated American politics. Rising crime rates beginning in the 1960s led to a "get tough on crime" approach to public policy characterized by a war on drugs, long sentences, and an end to the leniency that described the American approach to crime and punishment for much of the first half of the twentieth century. Beginning with the presidency of Richard Nixon, justices were appointed to the Supreme Court who shared the desire to mold the law in ways that made it easier to apprehend and prosecute criminals. The Supreme Court pulled away from legal precedents that favored the rights of the accused in the 1970s and 1980s, and replaced them with doctrines that expanded police power, limited application of the exclusionary rule, and carved out numerous exceptions to the Fourth Amendment's warrant requirements. The transformation that occurred resulted in defendants losing in three out of every four Fourth Amendment cases they brought to the Court from 1981 through 2010.

The ruling in *Maryland v. King*, allowing DNA evidence to be used in nonrelated cases, was quite consistent with the Court's general approach to Fourth Amendment issues. By contrast, *Riley v. California* not only went against the general trend of decisions; it established a broad claim to an individual right in the area of digital privacy. This was different from most of the cases that resulted in outcomes favorable to the defendant in the prior 25 years. Most of those decisions served only to curb some of the excesses of law enforcement activities that sought to expand their power and discretion beyond what even the Court was willing to grant. *Riley* did more than restore balance; it asserted an individual right with potentially broad consequences for other cases.

Riley v. California and *Maryland v. King* are both indicative of a tension that exists in the Roberts Court's Fourth Amendment jurisprudence. Some of this is due to uncertainty about how to apply the Fourth Amendment to new technological innovations, including both those tools used by the police to combat crime and technological devices that citizens rely on in their daily lives. There is evidence that the justices are not particularly adept in the use of all the digital technologies that are a part of modern life,[4] but we argue that there is more at play than just an inability of the justices to relate to the digital technology of the twenty-first century. For more than a generation, the vast majority of Fourth Amendment cases decided by the Supreme Court have expanded police power in the name of public safety and the need to control crime. *Maryland v. King* very much reflected that approach. It showed little concern for the privacy implications of government having a record of an individual's genetic makeup. By contrast, the decision in *Riley* emphasized the need to protect privacy rights. The Court's approach to the Fourth Amendment has appeared to be in a state of uncertainty since 2010, as almost half of its search and seizure decisions have favored the defendant, after more than a quarter-century where 75 percent of cases have favored the state. Yet, there is no clear evidence of a new pattern favoring the individual.

Even though law enforcement interests prevail in the vast majority of Fourth Amendment cases, those times when defendants win can generate a sense of dissonance in the law, and certainly send mixed messages to police. You can collect DNA evidence, but you cannot search a cell phone. For every time the Court insists on a warrant before a search, there are two or three cases where it carves out exceptions. The Court has long insisted that searches of a house require a warrant, but will now permit warrantless entry when there are exigent or emergency circumstances, even where the actions of the police themselves create the exigency. Inventory searches of impounded vehicles are allowed to protect against claims of liability, and evidence inadvertently found from the inventory is admissible in court, but the Court ignores the fact that police often impound a vehicle just as a way to conduct a search when they lack probable cause to search otherwise. The Court excludes evidence when police misconduct is the reason for the constitutional violation, but will not do the same when a violation results from judicial error. Individualized suspicion based on probable cause is required for searches, but suspicion-less K9 sniffs for narcotics in automobiles are not even considered to be searches.

There have always been contradictory Fourth Amendment decisions, but from 1981 until 2010, defendants prevailed in a relatively small number of cases. A full 75 percent of all search and seizure decisions since 1981 have favored the police over individual privacy claims. This held true for the last six terms of the Burger Court and the entire Rehnquist Court. The Roberts Court, however, has taken a less certain path. The Supreme Court has decided 36 Fourth Amendment cases in the decade since John Roberts was appointed as chief justice. Roberts' appointment, closely followed by that of Samuel Alito, marked the first change in the composition of the Supreme Court in 11 years. Chief Justice Rehnquist's death and the retirement of Justice O'Connor did not mark a significant change in the Court's makeup. Roberts and Alito shared the same ideological predispositions of their predecessors. It is not surprising, then, that many early Roberts Court search and seizure decisions were entirely consistent with the Rehnquist Court's decisions. In its first five terms, 73 percent of the 15 search and seizure decisions favored law enforcement interests. But since the appointments of Sonia Sotomayor and Elena Kagan in 2009 and 2010, there has been a marked change in Fourth Amendment cases. Defendants have won in 47 percent of the 21 search and seizure cases decided since 2010. In total, the Roberts Court has ruled for law enforcement interests in only 61 percent of cases.

The Roberts Court's Fourth Amendment jurisprudence appears to be in a state of flux, something that has not been seen since the early years of the Burger Court in the 1970s. Evidence of this can be seen in the mixed signals that the Roberts Court has sent about its interpretation of some areas of the law. For example, in *Georgia v. Randolph* (2006), the Court limited consent searches where one of two cotenants objects to the consent provided by the other, but the decision in *Fernandez v. California* (2014) allows consent searches over a cotenant's objection when that tenant is not physically present in the home. In *Fernandez*, the Court was unconcerned that the cotenant had refused consent just an hour before the search and was not physically present only because he had been arrested and removed from the scene by the very same police who wanted to search his apartment in the first place. While the Court's decision in *Virginia v. Moore* (2008) continues to permit police to arrest individuals for nonjailable, citation-only offenses, the Court was willing to place a fairly significant limit on vehicle searches after arrest in *Arizona v. Gant* (2009). The Court's decision in *Rodriguez v. United States* (2015) placed limits on the ability of police to extend the length of a traffic stop in order to conduct a narcotics dog sniff, but the same Court, just one year earlier, held that reasonable suspicion for an investigative traffic stop was justified by nothing more than an anonymous 911 call.[5]

Fourth Amendment cases involving the application of technology are responsible for some of the tension within the Roberts Court. The Court has long struggled with how to apply the Constitution to new technologies. In the 1920s, the Court had to determine how wiretapping fit into the Fourth

Amendment's proscription against unreasonable searches and seizures. The pace of technological innovations today is much faster than it was in the past. Not only will police continue to utilize new technologies in their zeal to combat crime, but they will also be tasked to try to combat crime committed by individuals who make use of a wide range of technologies. Whether it is a smart watch, virtual eyeglasses, or more powerful phones and tablets, new technologies are always being introduced into modern life. These devices grow smaller in size, but provide access to incredible amounts of information.

Our task is to make sense of the sometimes-conflicting decisions of the Roberts Court in Fourth Amendment cases, to try to explain why some cases are unanimous, while others are close decisions with a slim majority. We argue that it is possible to understand how some Roberts Court decisions seem to be departures from prior precedents, while others are very much consistent with the crime control approach of the Burger and Rehnquist Courts. To accomplish this, it is first necessary to explore the context of the politics of crime control that has shaped American politics since the 1970s.

THE POLITICS OF CRIME CONTROL

We believe that it is impossible to explain the Fourth Amendment decisions of the Roberts Court without understanding how the law evolved during the Courts that preceded it. The more than 200 search and seizure decisions by the Burger and Rehnquist Courts have framed the way the justices understand the Fourth Amendment today. Those Courts did not decide cases in a vacuum. Search and seizure cases were a part of the broader political environment focused on what we will call a politics of crime control. The law and order issues stemming from a decades-long crime wave in the 1960s helped enable a war on drugs in the 1970s and 1980s, and resulted in the naming of justices to the Court who were strong supporters of police power and seemed little inclined to consider individual due process concerns raised by criminal defendants.

The Burger and Rehnquist Courts' Fourth Amendment jurisprudence, in turn, can only be understood as a response to the decisions of the Warren Court in the 1960s, which expanded the rights of the accused, and generated controversy both among police and in the political arena. This began with the Court's decision in *Mapp v. Ohio* (1961), imposing the requirements of the exclusionary rule on state criminal proceedings. There had been an exclusionary rule in federal courts since 1914, but state criminal justice proceedings were not subject to it unless mandated by state law. *Mapp* instantly made the entire criminal justice system subject to the Court's Fourth Amendment rulings. As the 1960s progressed, the Court decided several other controversial criminal procedure cases. *Gideon v. Wainwright* (1963) applied the Sixth Amendment's right to counsel to the states, thus requiring that counsel be provided to defendants who could not afford a lawyer on their own. This created a new and costly bureaucracy in each county to provide for this right. Of course, no case had a bigger impact on the public than *Miranda v. Arizona* (1966) and its requirements that police inform suspects of their right to remain silent and the guarantee of counsel prior to being interrogated.

The Warren Court's expansion of individual rights for the accused came at the same time that the nation was experiencing one of the largest crime waves in generations. Not only was crime increasing, there was an increasing sense of social disorder and tension caused by civil rights protests and then the antiwar movement. The combination of these factors created a political backlash, magnifying criticism of the Court's decisions expanding the rights of the accused, and providing easy fodder for conservative politicians proclaiming the need for "law and order" to argue that the Supreme Court was oblivious to what was going on in the streets. Republican candidate Barry Goldwater first tried to make the Warren Court a campaign issue in the 1964 presidential election. While Goldwater was unsuccessful, Richard Nixon was able to make law and order a much more viable campaign strategy for 1968, particularly given the nature of the antiwar protests and social upheaval at the time. Nixon orchestrated his campaign in such a way that he was running not only against Lyndon Johnson, but against the Supreme Court itself. He promised that if elected, he would appoint justices to the Court who would undo the Warren Court's decisions.

Nixon made good on his promises, having the rare opportunity to name four justices to the Supreme Court in three years, including the chief justice. His appointments of Chief Justice Warren Burger, and Associate Justices Harry Blackmun, Lewis Powell, and William Rehnquist all proved to be consistent votes for crime control and expanding police capacity to combat crime. These four justices formed the nucleus of a majority who reframed the Fourth Amendment into what we call a jurisprudence of crime control. The Court's decisions provided police with a constitutional toolbox of legal doctrines that both enabled the war on drugs and supported the broader politics of crime control.

A fundamental shift in how the Fourth Amendment was interpreted occurred during the 17 years of the Burger Court. The Court imposed significant limitations on the exclusionary rule, lowered the threshold for establishing probable cause, carved out numerous warrant exceptions, and minimized the types of issues where it would acknowledge reasonable expectations of privacy. This did not come quickly, and it took more than a decade. By the early 1980s, the Burger Court had reframed the Fourth Amendment into one that could best be understood through the lens of a jurisprudence of crime control.

Our argument draws on the work of Mark Richards and Bert Kritzer, who explained how major shifts in legal doctrine could be characterized as a change of "jurisprudential regime."[6] Richards and Kritzer defined a jurisprudential regime as a "key precedent, or a set of related precedents, that structures the way in which the Supreme Court justices evaluate key elements of cases in arriving at decisions in a particular legal area."[7] Search and seizure law is one of their primary examples, and they argued that six cases decided in 1983 and 1984 served as the demarcation of a new regime in search and seizure jurisprudence.[8] Before the regime shift, the Court utilized more rigorous standards for evaluating Fourth Amendment claims; afterward, it provided more accommodations to police, and lowered the standard to determine reasonableness. In effect, the regime shift marks the establishment of a jurisprudence of crime control—one that has shaped the Court's approach to the Fourth Amendment ever since. We agree that 1983 and 1984 represented a tipping point for this jurisprudential regime shift, but place it in a longer-term context, and view the regime change as one that built up over more than a decade, in a case-by-case approach, dating back to the very beginning of the Burger Court. The jurisprudence of crime control redefined the Fourth Amendment, weakened its protections, and set the foundation for all future Fourth Amendment analysis.

In many ways the Rehnquist Court illustrates the triumph of the Burger Court's regime shift. William Rehnquist was one of the primary architects of the jurisprudence of crime control, and it flourished during his tenure as chief justice. Rehnquist Court decisions significantly aided law enforcement efforts to wage a war on drugs. The Court significantly expanded the tools police could use to conduct vehicle searches, building upon the Burger Court precedent of *New York v. Belton* (1981). The Rehnquist Court's decisions provided constitutional support for pretextual traffic stops where the traffic code was used as a pretense for a criminal investigation. Police could arrest an individual for even the most minor offense, and they could then search the driver and the passenger compartment of the vehicle. The police could use K9 units for narcotics sniffs without any individualized suspicion, and they could search a vehicle even when the arrest did not occur in the vehicle, but when the arrestee was its recent occupant. The Rehnquist Court reinforced the good faith exception to the exclusionary rule, and its decisions in many areas made it clear that reasonableness, and not the existence of a warrant, was the true measure by which the Fourth Amendment was to be judged. This is the Fourth Amendment jurisprudence that the Roberts Court inherited when John Roberts and Samuel Alito joined the Court in 2005.

UNDERSTANDING THE ROBERTS COURT AND THE FOURTH AMENDMENT

We began this book by suggesting that the Roberts Court appears to be sending mixed messages in its Fourth Amendment case law, sometimes seeming to depart significantly from Rehnquist Court precedents, but in other cases in the same term ruling in a way that is completely consistent with the jurisprudence of crime control. Our explanation of the Fourth Amendment under the Roberts Court provides a way to interpret how the Court is changing, the ways in which it is in sync with the jurisprudence of crime control that came before it, and how it is likely to progress in future years. While the primacy of the jurisprudence of crime control is not in jeopardy, there are due process challenges emerging in how the Court interprets the Fourth Amendment.

Our argument is in four parts. First, we believe that the Roberts Court's Fourth Amendment case law has been fundamentally shaped by the jurisprudence of crime control. The development of the law during the Burger and Rehnquist Courts has framed how the justices on the Roberts Court approach Fourth Amendment issues. The narrative by which conservative politicians, citizens, and justices themselves see the criminal justice system is one in which overreach by the Warren Court created a need for judges to be firm in prosecuting criminals, who, if left unchecked, would overwhelm our society. In most ways, decisions of the Roberts Court have continued the jurisprudence of crime control.

One of the ways to visualize this is to evaluate search and seizure cases using an ideological measure developed by political scientists. The Supreme Court Database includes detailed information on every case decided since 1946.[9] The database includes a "decision direction" variable that creates a simple typology for Fourth Amendment cases.[10] The outcome of each case is coded as either liberal or conservative. It similarly classifies the votes of the justices in each case. A liberal criminal procedure decision is one that is favorable to the defendant: either the search is suppressed or the ruling advances individual rights. A conservative decision is one in which the state's position prevails, and where either police discretion or authority is enhanced, or Fourth Amendment limits are not imposed. While there are other ways to evaluate cases, and not every liberal decision necessarily means that the defendant has the evidence suppressed or the conviction overturned, in general the typology provides a useful, if simplistic, tool to look at the general trend of Fourth Amendment cases over time.

Using the Warren Court as a baseline, the decision direction variable shows that from 1953 through 1968, 67 percent of search and seizure cases had liberal or prodefendant outcomes. The breakdown is not consistent through the Warren Court's entire tenure, however. Before 1960, 56 percent, or 12 of the 23 search and seizure cases, had liberal outcomes, but that percentage increased to 72.5 percent, or 40 of the 55 cases, during the terms from 1960 to 1968. That almost three-quarters of search and seizure cases in the 1960s were decided in favor of the defendant, coupled with a rise in actual crime and increase in the political salience of crime during the same time period, helps explain some of the political backlash against the Court that came later in that decade. More than 70 percent of search and seizure cases favored defendants at a time when crime was increasing dramatically.

The addition of the four Nixon justices in the early 1970s had an almost immediate impact on search and seizure law, as the percentage of prodefendant outcomes was cut in half. During the first decade of the Burger Court, defendants won in only 36 percent of cases. From 1980 to 1986, that percentage dropped to 20 percent. This is also consistent with the jurisprudential regime shift. Over the 1982 and 1983 terms, the Court decided 23 search and seizure cases, 19 of which, or 82.6 percent, resulted in conservative outcomes. The regime shift moved the Court definitively away from the defendant-friendly decisions of the Warren Court, and established a new jurisprudence of crime control.

Starting in the early 1980s, through the end of the Rehnquist Court, approximately 75 percent of cases resulted in outcomes favorable to the state. This trend continued through the first five terms of the Roberts Court. The jurisprudence of crime control is alive and well on the Supreme Court. It helps explain such Roberts Court cases as *Herring v. United States* (2009), which reinforced the good faith exception to the exclusionary rule, as well as *Brigham City v. Stuart* (2006) and *Kentucky v. King* (2011), cases that broaden the exigent circumstances exception to permit warrantless entry into homes. Most of the changes in the Roberts Court Fourth Amendment jurisprudence have occurred since 2011.

Explaining Prodefendant Decisions: Corrective Measures

The second part of our argument is that many of the prodefendant decisions that the Court issues can best be understood as minor corrections within the dominant paradigm of crime control. If we use Richard and Kritzer's designation of 1983 as the beginning of the regime shift in Fourth Amendment cases, an examination of decision direction shows that through 2015, 71 percent of all search and seizure cases have favored the state, a 180-degree shift from the last six years of the Warren Court, when 72 percent of case outcomes favored defendants. Put another way, in a jurisprudence of crime control the state wins almost three out of every four cases. Defendants win cases, but only about one-quarter of the time. Some of those cases, such as *Arizona v. Gant*, are high-profile decisions that prompted significant negative response from the law enforcement community, but upon further analysis appear to be decisions that only make small changes to Fourth Amendment law.

It is important for our argument to explain the prodefendant decisions. Most of those decisions from the late Burger Court through today do not carve out broad new rules or limits on the police, but instead serve as a corrective measure to curb some of the excesses of the system. The jurisprudence of crime control has resulted in a growing body of law that expands police power. As police are given more authority and Fourth Amendment protections are diminished, they tend to use that power to aggressively combat crime. When this increase in discretionary authority is combined with a "get tough on crime" political environment and a war on drugs, the police tend to push the boundaries of the Fourth Amendment. Sometimes the Court grants the desired accommodations, but occasionally, when it seems like the system is being pushed too far, the Court responds with decisions that provide a check on the system. But in doing so, it does not fundamentally challenge the underlying tenets of the system. Liberal decisions within the jurisprudence of crime control do not usually result in broad expansions of individual rights like *Mapp v. Ohio* or *Katz v. United States* (1967), but instead tend to be narrow and technical in scope. Three example cases from the Rehnquist Court help illustrate this.

Knowles v. Iowa (1998) invalidated an effort by the state of Iowa to expand the ability to conduct passenger compartment searches to situations where the officer issues a traffic citation rather than making an arrest. Under the *New York v. Belton* standard, police could search the passenger compartment of a vehicle whenever they arrested a driver or recent occupant of a vehicle. Iowa had passed a law that extended *Belton* searches to citation-only cases. Patrick Knowles challenged the admission of the evidence gained from just such a search. Chief Justice Rehnquist wrote the opinion for a unanimous Court, declaring that the Iowa law went too far. He drew on the precedent from his own decision in *United States v. Robinson* (1973), which explained the rationale for search incident to arrest. Search incident to citation was not contemplated by that rationale and thus, to Rehnquist, was impermissible. The opinion he wrote in *Knowles* was focused solely on the application of the rationale in his earlier opinion and never once discussed the individual privacy rights of the defendant.

The Court's decision on the knock and announce doctrine in *Wilson v. Arkansas* (1995) is another good example. Police entered a home where the screen door was open to make an arrest without announcing themselves first. A unanimous Court held that the long-standing common law practice of police announcing their entry before entering a home had to be respected. But Justice Thomas' opinion also encouraged police to seek case-by-case exceptions for no-knock entries. While the decision was prodefendant, the Court went out of its way to encourage states to carve out individual exceptions permitting no-knock entry.

Our last example is *Florida v. Wells* (1990), which stemmed from an inventory search that was invalidated because police did not have a standard set of procedures and criteria specifying when and under what circumstances warrantless inventory searches would be conducted. The Court was not opposed to inventory searches, but limited them to situations where the police were following standard operating procedure. This prodefendant decision fully condoned warrantless inventory searches, and only limited the state by forcing it to develop standard policies to follow when implementing them.

Many of the prodefendant decisions of the Rehnquist and Roberts Courts have served as a corrective measure to restore balance within the framework of the jurisprudence of crime control. We can think of the Court providing a check and balance on its own crime control regime, and in the process enhancing the legitimacy of the underlying regime by creating the appearance of judicial neutrality. The Court permits police wide latitude in conducting criminal investigations, but there are still outer limits. Most of these liberal decisions have not fundamentally challenged the prevailing jurisprudence of crime control.

From the beginning of the Roberts Court in 2005 through the end of its fifth term in the spring of 2010, the Court decided 15 search and seizure cases (about par for the Rehnquist Court of the prior decade). Of those cases, 11 were decided for the state. The Roberts Court's decisions were entirely consistent with the Rehnquist Court decisions that preceded it. The few prodefendant cases also seemed to fit the model of being corrective measures. *Georgia v. Randolph* placed limits on cotenant consent searches, so that if one tenant objects over the consent for a search given by the other tenant, it invalidates the consent. *Safford United School District v. Redding* (2009) ruled that a student strip search exceeded the school administration's authority under the Fourth Amendment, but the Court used the doctrine of qualified immunity to protect the administrators responsible for the search in question from liability, claiming that they were acting in what they thought was good faith reliance on the law at the time. The Court set an outer boundary, and ruled that student strip searches were impermissible, but made it so it was only prospectively applicable to future cases.

Perhaps the best Roberts Court example of a prodefendant case that serves as a corrective measure to curb the excesses of a jurisprudence of crime control is *Arizona v. Gant*. That case modified the 28-year-old precedent from *New York v. Belton* allowing the police to search a car's passenger compartment whenever they arrested a person who had been driving. *Belton*'s bright line rule permitted a vehicle search after any arrest. In words taken from the testimony of the arresting officer at Gant's trial, the reason for the search was "because I can." There was no attempt to even pretend that there was a threat to officer safety or a need to preserve evidence, which were the original justifications for search incident to arrest. Gant was handcuffed in the back of the police cruiser at the time of the search, and the arrest was for driving with a suspended license. The Court's ruling effectively eliminated *Belton*'s bright line rule, and replaced it with a standard that permitted a vehicle search incident to arrest only if it was reasonable to believe further evidence from the crime of arrest would be found. The decision served as a corrective measure, bringing vehicle searches incident to arrest back in sync with their original rationale.

Corrective measure decisions swing in a liberal direction, but not too far, and serve to strengthen the legitimacy of the Court itself. Recent surveys on public perceptions of the Court indicate that its legitimacy is weakened when the justices are perceived as behaving in an overtly political manner.[11] The justices are certainly aware of this fact, although some are more concerned than others about the status of the Court as an institution. Harvard law professor William Stuntz understood that the Court must not be seen as too ideologically extreme lest it risk losing some of its luster.[12] Political scientist Charles Sheldon perceived the Court as forever in flux as it seeks a balance between judicial independence from the elected branches and accountability to the larger political system.[13] When all of the decisions of the Court go in a single direction, it is hard to maintain that balance. Thus, the error correction function serves to remind the general public that the police do not always win and that the law protects the rights of citizens from excessive behavior by the agents of the executive and legislative branches. It preserves balance and, in doing so, preserves the Court's legitimacy.

Do the Justices Matter?

The third component of our argument is that one must pay attention to the small-group dynamics of the Court to understand its decisional output. There were only four prodefendant cases in the first five terms of the Roberts Court, but things began to change after the appointment of Justices Sotomayor and Kagan. In its second five years, defendants won 47 percent of cases, or 10 of 21. Many of these cases were certainly corrective measures, but it is hard to discount the shift that has occurred. The Roberts Court ruled for the state 73 percent of the time in its first five years, and only 53 percent of the time in its second. A large part of this can be explained by the changing composition of the Court, and by a surprising change in judicial decision making by Justice Scalia, who had been one of the Court's leading conservatives on Fourth Amendment issues.

The decision-making record of the justices on the Roberts Court is revealing. The Court's membership has changed fairly significantly over ten terms. When it began, the Roberts Court consisted of one Ford appointee (Stevens), two Reagan appointees (Scalia and Kennedy), two George H. W. Bush appointees (Thomas and Souter), two Clinton appointees (Ginsburg and Breyer), and two George W. Bush appointees (Roberts and Alito). Stevens retired in 2009, and Souter in 2010, and they have been replaced by two Obama appointees (Sotomayor and Kagan). The decision direction variable in the Supreme Court Database for justice votes enables us to examine the voting patterns and changes in individual justices over time. The replacement of Justices Stevens and Souter with Sotomayor and Kagan is important to understand the Court's changing decision outcomes. Justice Sotomayor is slightly more liberal than Justice Stevens, who ruled for defendants in 67 percent of cases. In her first six years, Sotomayor has been on the liberal side in 71 percent of cases.

The more significant change in personnel on the Court was the replacement of Justice Souter by Justice Kagan. Compared with the other Reagan and Bush justices, David Souter was quite moderate, ruling for the state in only 56 percent of search and seizure cases. Justice Kagan, to the contrary, has voted for the defendant's position in 71 percent of cases in five years. The end result is that one fairly liberal justice (Stevens) was replaced with a justice (Sotomayor) who is even more liberal; and a moderate justice (Souter) who could be counted to join the conservative side only slightly more than half of the time was replaced by a justice (Kagan) who is considerably more liberal. We can only speculate about how Justices Sotomayor and Kagan have affected the small-group dynamics of the Court, but their voting record alone suggests they are more liberal and more open to Fourth Amendment privacy claims than their predecessors.

Not only do new justices matter, but changes in the approach of sitting justices can also be equally important. There has been no greater surprise on the Roberts Court than the shifting voting record of Justice Scalia on Fourth Amendment issues. A consistent, reliable conservative during the Rehnquist Court, Scalia ruled for the state in 79 percent of search and seizure cases. He is widely considered as one of the most conservative members of the Court, but during the Roberts Court, his voting record has changed dramatically in Fourth Amendment cases, ruling for the state in only 61 percent of cases since 2005. The change in Scalia's voting pattern has been clearer since 2010, as he has voted for the conservative outcome in only 50 percent of cases. And when he has been in dissent in cases where the state has won, Scalia has issued stinging rebukes of the Court's crime control mentality and logic. Yet, when he votes with the conservatives, he fails to see the inconsistencies between his own opinions. He is both unpredictable and idiosyncratic. Scalia has provided a key fifth vote in several cases, and has pushed an originalist approach to the Fourth Amendment, in which he has tried to limit his rulings to be compatible with the original understanding of the Fourth Amendment at the time it was ratified.

Originalism is an approach to constitutional interpretation based on the idea that the Constitution should mean now what it meant when it was written. Proponents of originalism often look to the text of the document itself, and then to documents written at the time the language was drafted. Scalia has argued that deciding cases is easy: "I don't agonize at all. I look at the text, I look at the history of the text. That's the answer. It's not my call."[14] Originalists are very contemptuous of what they call legislating from the bench.[15] Critics of originalism, who include both Justices Brennan and Rehnquist, have suggested that it is a smoke screen for justices to simply achieve the policy outcome they want, since the original intent of the Framers is not written in stone. But originalism has gained considerable support among judges and some conservative lawyers.[16]

Scalia's unique version of originalism is relatively new in his Fourth Amendment decisions, and is best illustrated by his majority opinions in *United States v. Jones* (2012) and *Florida v. Jardines* (2013). In these cases, Scalia argued that the original understanding of the Fourth Amendment was based on a common law concept of trespass, and as such, the Constitution was violated when there was a physical intrusion into a constitutionally protected place, for example, one's person, home, papers, or effects. Scalia resurrected the old trespass doctrine that had been rejected by the Court in *Katz v. United States* and replaced with a reasonable expectation of privacy standard. Scalia's trespass doctrine resulted in defendant-friendly outcomes in these two cases, but did so through a narrow understanding of the purpose of the Fourth Amendment. Scalia also garnered the support of the Court's other originalist, Justice Thomas, in both cases.[17] Scalia's shifting approach to the Fourth Amendment is most certainly an important factor in the changing landscape of the Roberts Court, as he has voted for the defendant's position in 9 of the 10 prodefendant cases decided since 2011.

What about the other justices? Chief Justice Roberts and Associate Justices Kennedy, Thomas, and Alito represent the conservative wing of the Court. All four are solid conservative votes. Justice Kennedy had a solid 75 percent voting record for the state on the Rehnquist Court, and has only varied slightly during the Roberts Court, with a 72 percent record for the state. Justice Thomas has become more conservative over time, voting for the state in 77 percent of Rehnquist Court cases and 81 percent of Roberts Court cases. The chief justice and Justice Alito are practically identical. Roberts votes for the conservative position in 75 percent of cases, Alito in 79 percent.

Justice Breyer remains the least reliable liberal on the Court and the one most likely to join the conservative bloc. During the Rehnquist Court, he voted for the liberal outcome only 35.9 percent of the time. While appointed by Democratic President Bill Clinton, Breyer was a judge who began his judicial experience on the United States Court of Appeals for the First Circuit in 1980, at the same time that the Supreme Court's jurisprudence of crime control was building to a culmination. He has become slightly more liberal on the Roberts Court, joining the liberal position in 43 percent of search and seizure cases, although he has voted for the defendant exactly 50 percent of the time in the Roberts Court's second five years. He is truly a swing vote on Fourth Amendment issues and, like Souter and Stevens before him, a moderate. The other Clinton appointee, Ruth Bader Ginsburg, had a 57.5 percent liberal record on search and seizure cases during her tenure on the Rehnquist Court. She was the liberal counterpart to Justice Souter. On the Roberts Court, that percentage has risen to 63 percent. Since 2010, 76 percent of her votes have favored the liberal outcome in search and seizure cases.

What this suggests is that the makeup of the Court matters, and the voting behavior of Justice Scalia is pivotal to understanding the Roberts Court's Fourth Amendment jurisprudence. The changes that have occurred on the Court are the strengthening of the liberal bloc and the weakening bond of Justice Scalia to conservative outcomes, but not total abandonment of it. Justices Ginsburg, Sotomayor, and Kagan are three solid liberal votes. Justice Breyer provides a fourth vote about half of the time, and in recent years, Justice Kennedy has provided a fourth vote about 40 percent of the time. This often leaves Justice Scalia to provide the fifth vote. He sometimes is able to persuade Justice Thomas to vote with him. The individual behavior of the justices is a factor that helps explain some of the decisions on the Roberts Court, but there are a couple of key cases in which all of the justices have voted against the state.

Do Technology Issues Matter?

The fourth component of our argument is that cases in which digital privacy rights are at stake are handled by the Court differently than other types of

Fourth Amendment cases. Not all prodefendant decisions can be dismissed as merely corrective measures meant to serve as a check and balance on the jurisprudence of crime control. While corrective measures explain a lot of prodefendant rulings, they do not explain them all. This chapter began with a discussion of the *Riley v. California* cell phone search case. The language in that case suggests that more is at stake than just curbing the excesses of overzealous police. We argue that cases involving privacy and information technology generate public attention in such a way that the Court is attuned to the fact that its decision will have wide ramifications, and the justices are increasingly cognizant of the unique nature of the privacy interests raised by these facts. *United States v. Jones* and *Riley v. California* were two of the most closely watched decisions in recent years. *Jones* dealt with whether law enforcement could conduct warrantless GPS surveillance of suspects. *Riley* questioned whether police could search the content of cell phones incident to arrest. It is one thing for a police officer to conduct physical surveillance by following a suspect's vehicle when it is on the public thoroughfares; it is altogether another thing to use a GPS and have 24/7 real-time locational data on the suspect available from a computer. Likewise, searching a person's wallet incident to arrest might be permissible, but searching all the personal files commonly stored or accessible on a smartphone is altogether different.

While other prodefendant decisions like *Arizona v. Gant* and *Florida v. Jardines* were based on narrow 5–4 majorities, *Jones* and *Riley* were unanimous decisions. *Jones* was divided into three sets of justices in their rationale for why the warrant was required, but all nine justices agreed that the warrantless surveillance of Antoine Jones with a GPS tracking device was unconstitutional. These cases were quite salient, much more so than the run-of-the-mill search and seizure case. Both cases resulted in major newspaper editorials, before and after the Court's decisions.[18] Fourth Amendment issues intersecting privacy and technology might very well represent issues where the Court is forced to revisit the broader privacy concerns that have been largely ignored in the past 30 years. They may represent a wedge issue that is causing a small crack in the jurisprudence of crime control and forcing the Court to reconsider such things as permitting warrantless searches of phone and bank records. Yet, it is not simple. We cannot just infer that the Court will always rule differently in technology cases than in other Fourth Amendment cases. Take, for example, *Maryland v. King*, where the Court ruled that the Fourth Amendment permits jail authorities to collect DNA evidence from arrestees and use it to create a database for use in other criminal investigations. If people have a protected privacy interest in the contents of their cell phones, one might think they also have a protected privacy interest in their genetic makeup. It is clear that there are unanswered questions that the Court will need to address, but we are confident that the intersection of technology and privacy represent one issue where the Court is approaching the Fourth Amendment differently.

CONCLUSION

Our argument has four parts. First, the jurisprudence of crime control is alive and well. The Court's baseline for understanding the Fourth Amendment is defined by the jurisprudential regime created by the Burger Court and strengthened by the Rehnquist Court. The Court's conservative majority still exists and has continued to remain strong on many issues, although the size of its majority is smaller. The exclusionary rule retains but a shadow of its original purpose. The Court is willing to carve out and extend warrant exceptions. The expansion of the exigent circumstances exception during the Roberts Court in four separate cases is a perfect example. The Court continues to expand police power in many areas, and diminish the Court's historical heightened protection of the home against warrantless intrusions. The jurisprudence of crime control sets the foundation for Fourth Amendment analysis in the Roberts Court.

Second, the 30 years that have elapsed since the jurisprudential regime shift of the early 1980s have resulted in the need for occasional corrective measures, to either restore some balance to the Fourth Amendment or at least curb excessively aggressive behavior by the police. Several prodefendant Roberts Court cases serve as corrective measures, as was true with many prodefendant decisions from the Rehnquist Court. While the justices support the regime they have created, they recognize that its legitimacy requires that there be limits and that the Court enforce those limits in a way that creates the appearance of political and ideological neutrality.

Third, the changing approach of Justice Scalia in Fourth Amendment cases has created a situation where the Court's three most reliable liberals (Justices Ginsburg, Sotomayor, and Kagan) may be able to secure a vote from Justice Scalia, depending on how he sees the interaction between the facts of the case and his version of originalism. When they are able to attract a fifth vote (often from Kennedy or Breyer), there is enough to make a majority. The changing composition of the Court and the increasingly idiosyncratic decision making of Justice Scalia help explain some of the change in the Roberts Court. Justice Scalia's evolving views, 30 years after joining the Court, have resulted in a once solid conservative justice becoming something of a wild card.

Finally, a broader societal push for privacy in technological issues may be playing a role in the Court in that such cases generate a public interest that is often not present in criminal cases. Perhaps the long decline in crime over the past 15 years and increased criticism of the war on drugs are weakening the foundations of the politics of crime control. The justices are not immune from the political environment. The tension that exists between the jurisprudence of crime control and the societal focus on privacy in technology, along with increasing criticism of police tactics (in some instances), suggests a different approach in some cases. This is certainly the most speculative element of the argument. But there are many issues outstanding with which the Court may be forced to grapple. When it rules with broad endorsements of digital privacy, this reveals inconsistencies with the dominant jurisprudential regime.

This book is in two parts. Part 1 provides the historical foundation for the Roberts Court. Chapter 2 sketches the early history of the Fourth Amendment, explains the major decisions of the Warren Court, and provides context for the political backlash that it unleashed. Chapter 3 describes the Burger Court's transformation, demonstrating how the Court redefined Fourth Amendment analysis, placed limits on the exclusionary rule, stunted the development of the reasonable expectation of privacy jurisprudence, and resulted in a regime shift that established a jurisprudence of crime control. Chapter 4 focuses on how the Rehnquist Court refined the crime control philosophy, paying particular attention to how Court decisions served to enable the politics of crime control, as it matured in the 1980s and 1990s into an all-out war on drugs.

Part 2 offers an in-depth examination of the evolution of the Fourth Amendment on the Roberts Court. Chapter 5 provides a broad overview of the Roberts Court, and illustrates how the Fourth Amendment is in flux. We return to the technology cases in greater detail, and explore the changing role of Justice Scalia. Chapter 6 considers how the jurisprudence of crime control is alive and well on the Roberts Court. We consider the exigent circumstances exception, as well as the Court's further limiting of the exclusionary rule, and illustrate how the Court relies on the jurisprudence of crime control in many of its cases. Chapter 7 uses *Arizona v. Gant* as the centerpiece of an examination of how the Roberts Court has treated some of the excesses of crime control, and considers how the Roberts Court has decided cases that have provided a check and balance on the criminal justice system, while still remaining faithful to the primary jurisprudence of crime control. The book concludes in chapter 8 by summarizing the argument and suggesting some of the hard issues that the Court is likely to face in future years. We make the case for unshackling the Fourth Amendment from the jurisprudence of crime control. We will argue that while the jurisprudence of crime control explains how the Fourth Amendment has evolved, it does not have to dictate its future. Technology cases are creating a tension on the Court that could potentially result in a reevaluation of the meaning of Fourth Amendment privacy and new protections for the digital privacy rights of Americans.

2. Setting the Stage

The Fourth Amendment played a minor role in the criminal justice system before the 1960s because it was only applicable to actions by federal agents, and federal criminal cases were relatively rare. The exclusionary rule prohibiting the admission of evidence obtained by unreasonable searches and seizures did apply when federal agents violated the Fourth Amendment, but, until well into the twentieth century, almost all criminal prosecutions were brought in state courts. With few exceptions, state criminal justice systems were free to follow their own state constitutions in terms of how to provide due process and fundamental fairness. The Court did not even hold that the Fourth Amendment applied to the states until 1949, and it wasn't until 1961 that the exclusionary rule was imposed on the states. In this chapter, we lay the groundwork for our argument about how the jurisprudence of crime control evolved by sketching important Fourth Amendment issues prior to the Warren Court and explaining how the Warren Court's decisions from 1960 to 1969 served to expand the rights of the accused and, at the same time, sparked a political backlash.

The Fourth Amendment was ratified as part of the original Bill of Rights in 1789, but was not interpreted by the Supreme Court for almost 100 years. This is not surprising really. The behavior by the crown that had prompted the inclusion of the Fourth Amendment in the Bill of Rights consisted mostly of the enforcement of smuggling laws. Widespread efforts to control the types of criminal behavior that often prompt legal battles over the admission of evidence, searches for guns, alcohol, and drugs in the process of attempting to control local criminals, did not become common until much later in American history. And since the Bill of Rights was widely understood as applying solely to actions of the federal government, there was not much law enforcement activity that was even subject to it.

The Supreme Court first considered a Fourth Amendment issue in 1886, in *Boyd v. United States*. The firm of E. A. Boyd and Sons was believed to have failed to pay the import duties on 35 panes of glass. Under a federal statute in force at the time, the federal government moved to force the owners of the glass to produce the invoices under which it was imported or forfeit the goods. The importers argued that the law under which the government proceeded itself was a violation of the Fourth Amendment because it would force them to disclose potentially incriminating evidence. The Court did hold for the importers but what is interesting is that they relied heavily on an eighteenth-century English case as the basis for their analysis because there were no precedents in American law for them to follow.[1]

EARLY DEVELOPMENT

The Fourth Amendment's command against unreasonable searches and seizures does not explicitly provide for a remedy in terms of what happens when an individual is subjected to an unreasonable search or seizure. The very idea of a constitutional right implies that if the Fourth Amendment is violated, then there has to be a consequence. The Court first dealt with this problem in a case called *Weeks v. United States* (1914). Fremont Weeks had been accused of using the US mail to illegally transport lottery tickets in St. Joseph, Missouri. Police had entered his home without a warrant, and seized papers that they turned over to the US marshal. A subsequent search by federal officials seized envelopes from his desk. These were used as evidence to convict him.

Weeks petitioned the Court to return his property, which the district court had partially agreed to, but it had refused to return papers used as evidence. The case was ultimately decided by the Supreme Court, and in a unanimous decision, Justice Day ruled that the warrantless search of Weeks' home and the seizure of his papers represented a violation of the Fourth Amendment. Day viewed the warrantless entry and search of Weeks' home and the seizure of his property as an invasion of his constitutional rights, relying on the common law notion that "every man's house is his castle" and the requirement that government agents must have a warrant issued by a neutral magistrate before they enter a home. He drew on *Boyd v. United States* to reiterate that the offense done by the government is more than just rummaging through his drawers. The essence of the violation is the "invasion of his indefeasible right of personal security, personal liberty, and private property."[2] The Fourth Amendment serves to protect this "sacred right," and places limits on federal officials to make sure they secure the people, as well as their persons, houses, papers, and effects, against unreasonable searches and seizures. Day argued that when those limits are violated, evidence seized must be returned, and thus excluded from criminal proceedings.

Weeks established an exclusionary rule, but it applied solely to the actions of federal officials. The Court had not yet held the Fourth Amendment applicable to the states, and was unwilling to apply the exclusionary rule to state actors, going so far as to create a strange loophole known as the silver platter doctrine, which permitted illegally obtained evidence to be used in federal court if the illegal search had been conducted by state and not federal agents. What this meant was that a state law enforcement agency could violate the Fourth Amendment rights of a suspect and then turn over the evidence to federal law enforcement agencies, where it could be used on the theory that the violation was committed by the state, not by the federal government.

The Trespass Doctrine

Implicit in both *Boyd* and *Weeks* was the understanding that the Fourth Amendment only implicated searches that involved a physical intrusion on a constitutionally protected area, defined in the text of the Fourth Amendment as one's "person, houses, papers, or effects." The property-centric understanding of the Fourth Amendment limited unreasonable searches to those instances where government agents trespassed on protected areas. *Olmstead v. United States* (1928) raised the question of whether the Fourth Amendment was implicated when the search consisted of a wiretapping of a phone line. Federal authorities suspected Roy Olmstead of running a large bootlegging operation and hired a contractor to place wiretaps on the phone lines used by those involved in the operation. At trial, agents were allowed to testify about what they had overheard and to use the transcripts of more than 775 pages of information obtained from the wiretaps to refresh their memories. Olmstead was convicted and sentenced to four years in prison.

In a close 5–4 vote, the Court defined a search as requiring a physical trespass on a constitutionally protected area—one's person, houses, papers, or effects. The Court ruled that because no physical trespass to the property of any of the defendants had occurred, there was no Fourth Amendment violation. The trespass doctrine was important because it significantly limited the scope of what would be considered a search or seizure. Writing in dissent, Justice Brandeis challenged these limits and illustrated how technology and science could dramatically expand the government's ability to conduct surveillance. Brandeis saw the Fourth Amendment as focused on individual privacy against unwanted governmental interference, and he accurately predicted how science would increase the ability of the government to engage in surveillance of its own citizens:

> The progress of science in furnishing the government with means of espionage is not likely to stop with wire-tapping. Ways may some day [sic] be developed by which the government, without removing papers from secret drawers, can reproduce them in court, and by which it will be enabled to expose to a jury the most intimate occurrences of the home. Advances in the psychic and related sciences may bring means of exploring unexpressed beliefs, thoughts and emotions.[3]

Brandeis questioned how it could be possible that the Constitution would not protect against such invasions of personal security. He believed that the Constitution provided such protections, and pointed to language in *Boyd* that drew on the reasoning in the eighteenth-century English case of *Entick v. Carrington* (1765). Brandeis argued that the Fourth Amendment applies to "all invasions on the part of the government and its employees of the sanctities of a man's home and the privacies of life. It is not the breaking of his doors, and the rummaging of his drawers, that constitutes the essence of the offense."[4]

The Fourth Amendment's focus was less about property than it was about privacy, or what he called "the right to be let alone." Brandeis used some of the most eloquent language in constitutional law to make his point. The Framers of the Constitution "recognized the significance of man's spiritual nature" and knew that "only a part of the pain, the pleasure and satisfactions of life are to be found in material things. They sought to protect Americans in their beliefs, their thoughts, their emotions and their sensations. They conferred, as against the government, the right to be let alone—the most comprehensive of rights and the right most valued by civilized men." In this broad privacy-based conception of the Fourth Amendment, it was not merely an intrusion on protected areas that violated the Constitution; it was any "unjustifiable . . . intrusion on the privacy of the individual."[5]

Brandeis ended his opinion with a warning about what was at stake. He argued that liberty demanded that the government be "subjected to the same rules of conduct that are commands to the citizen." If the government does not follow the laws, then its very existence is called into question. In eloquent language, Brandeis continued: "Our Government is the potent, the omnipresent teacher. For good or for ill, it teaches the whole people by its example. Crime is contagious. If the Government becomes a lawbreaker, it breeds contempt for law; it invites every man to become a law unto himself; it invites anarchy."[6] The philosophy of the Fourth Amendment that Brandeis articulated would remain in dissent on the Court for 40 years, and it would not be until 1967 when the Court would abandon the trespass doctrine. Even then, we will see, competing pressures of crime control and the imperative to get tough on crime will force considerations of privacy in a pure sense to take second place behind the practical desire to gain control over America's cities and streets. But Brandeis' dissent is important in articulating the underlying privacy concerns that are in constant tension with the pressure to convict the guilty in Fourth Amendment cases.

Applying the Fourth Amendment to the States

When the Bill of Rights was added to the Constitution, its provisions applied only to the federal government. The Fourteenth Amendment purported to extend the Fifth Amendment's due process clause to the states, which quickly gave rise to the question of whether all of the rights contained in the first 10 amendments to the Constitution now applied to the states. Some justices argued that the liberty that states could not deny without due process included the entire Bill of Rights. Known as total incorporation, this view of the Fourteenth Amendment has never commanded a majority on the Court. Over the next half-century, the Court selectively began to incorporate specific provisions of the Bill of Rights into the Fourteenth Amendment, thus making them applicable to the states. While the First Amendment guarantee of freedom of speech was incorporated in 1926, it wasn't until the Court decided *Wolf v. Colorado* in 1949 that the mandates of the Fourth Amendment were extended to the states, although when the Court acted, it still provided for flexibility in the administration of criminal justice from state to state.

Wolf involved a charge of conspiracy to perform a criminal abortion and the defendant's effort to suppress evidence illegally obtained when agents of the Denver District Attorney's Office raided his medical practice, seized his practice records, and arrested him and his fellow physician, Montgomery, without a warrant. In a 6–3 decision, Justice Frankfurter refused to impose the exclusionary rule, and held that states were free to find other methods to discourage unreasonable searches and seizures. This reflected the approach Frankfurter took to most issues, providing discretion to majoritarian processes. Thus, even after the decision in *Wolf*, the incorporation of the Fourth

Amendment to state criminal justice proceedings was incomplete. The states had to guard against unreasonable searches and seizures, but they were not bound to use the same methods that the Court had imposed on actions of the federal government.

During the time between the decision in *Weeks* and the start of the Warren Court in 1953, the Court had also begun to carve out exceptions to the warrant requirement. The enforcement of the Eighteenth Amendment's prohibition of the use and sale of alcohol created a number of cases that sought to provide exceptions to the warrant in the name of illegal alcohol interdiction.[7] Two good examples are *Hester v. United States* (1924) and *Carroll v. United States* (1925). In *Hester* the Court held that the police were allowed to stand in an open field to observe the behavior of bootleggers. The more important warrant exception came the next year in *Carroll*, when the Court established what has today become known as the automobile exception to the warrant requirement. Police suspected that a particular vehicle was being used to illegally transport alcohol and unsuccessfully attempted to find it on the highway in Michigan. Several months later, they saw the vehicle on the road and stopped the car. Police arrested the driver and then searched the car without first securing a warrant. The Court upheld the search and seizure based on the rationale that, had they waited to get a warrant from a judge, the vehicle—and the evidence within it—could simply be driven away. The Court established a warrant exception that permitted police to search a vehicle when officers had probable cause to believe that the vehicle contained contraband. The decision also illustrates the low threshold for establishing probable cause. The officers making the arrest had nothing other than a four-month-old tip that the vehicle was being used for bootlegging alcohol, but the Court seemed perfectly willing to accept the arrest without question.

THE WARREN COURT AND THE DUE PROCESS REVOLUTION

When President Eisenhower selected Earl Warren as chief justice, few had any inkling of just how significant his appointment would become. Warren was considered a safe choice. He had been a prosecuting attorney, the governor of California, and a Republican candidate for vice president of the United States. His confirmation was swift and without significant controversy. By the time of his retirement in 1969, the Warren Court had made sweeping changes in civil rights, voting rights, and criminal procedure. Warren presided over a Court that dramatically expanded the rights of the accused, and established what many called the "due process revolution."[8]

The Fourth Amendment that Earl Warren inherited was ripe for development, and rife with contradictions. The exclusionary rule applied to the federal government but not the states. There were exceptions to the warrant requirement that allowed for significant abuse of discretion by the police. There was no provision for applying the Fourth Amendment to rapidly developing communication technologies. Still, the early Warren Court's Fourth Amendment jurisprudence was quite consistent with what came before it. Perhaps no case better illustrates this than the Court's decision in *Draper v. United States*, a case from 1959 that provided a definition for probable cause. A paid confidential informant named Hereford had provided information to a federal narcotics agent that James Draper was going to transport heroin on a train from Chicago to Denver. Hereford provided the agent with a precise description of the suspect, describing him as a "Negro of light brown complexion, 27 years of age, 5 feet 8 inches tall, weighed about 160 pounds, and he was wearing a light colored raincoat, brown slacks and black shoes."[9] The informant said he would be carrying a "tan zippered bag" and that he walked "real fast." The federal agent, accompanied by local police, went to Denver's Union Station looking for someone to match the description. On the second day of surveillance, they found someone coming off a Chicago train that matched the description perfectly. They stopped him, arrested him, and proceeded to search his person, where they found two envelopes with heroin in his pocket. Two days later the informant died, and was thus unable to testify in the trial. Since Hereford had died, the only evidence about the justification for the arrest came from hearsay evidence that originated with the informant and the federal agent's testimony that the information he had provided had been reliable in the past.

The Court, in an opinion by Justice Whittaker, argued that the standards for determining whether probable cause existed to make an arrest are much less stringent than those used to determine guilt at trial. As long as a reasonable person would believe that it was probable that the suspect was violating the narcotics laws, the arrest would be justified and the evidence would not be excluded. The Court saw no problem with the use of hearsay evidence to establish probable cause, even though hearsay evidence would be inadmissible for purposes of establishing guilt or innocence.

Justice Douglas' dissent illustrated the limited protection offered by the Court's ruling, and explained why the Court isn't naturally inclined toward greater protection. He wrote, "Wherever a culprit is caught red-handed, as in leading Fourth Amendment cases, it is difficult to adopt and enforce a rule that would turn him loose. A rule protective of law-abiding citizens is not apt to flourish where its advocates are usually criminals. Yet the rule we fashion is for the innocent and guilty alike."[10] Douglas was quite insightful when he acknowledged that the facts of the case resembled what many would consider good police work. He then pointed out how the entertainment media shape how the public views policing:

> The education we receive from mystery stories and television shows teaches that what happened in this case is efficient police-work. The police are tipped off that a man carrying narcotics will step off the morning train. A man meeting the precise description does alight from the train. . . . He is arrested and narcotics are found in his pocket and a syringe in the bag he carried. This is the familiar pattern of crime detection dinned into the public consciousness as the correct and efficient one.[11]

Justice Douglas then explained how this story is actually a distortion of the constitutional system under which we live. No warrant for Draper was issued because no warrant could be issued. There was no probable cause, no suspicion whatsoever, except what the informant provided. The police had no evidence to support the accusation beyond the word of the accuser. Douglas points out quite accurately that there was only evidence after the arrest was made and the search complete. "But a search is not made legal by what it turns up." Douglas' words are powerful and, to the modern reader, could have easily been written today, as they accurately describe the Court's crime control jurisprudence and the public's willingness to accept arguments of effective law enforcement. *Draper*, like *Carroll* before it, shows the long history of developing a rather low standard for establishing probable cause and foreshadows the development of a crime control jurisprudence that is very lenient in its scrutiny of the behavior of law enforcement.

Mapp v. Ohio *and the Exclusionary Rule*

Had the Warren Court continued to interpret the Fourth Amendment like it did in *Draper*, there probably wouldn't be a story to tell about the evolution of the Fourth Amendment. But just two years later, the Court began a fundamental shift that would redefine how the Warren Court would approach the Fourth Amendment and criminal procedure in general. The Court's extension of the exclusionary rule to the states in *Mapp v. Ohio* (1961) marks the beginning of this shift, and represents the beginning of what can be thought of as the Warren Court's due process revolution. It took an extreme fact pattern of oppressive police behavior to force the Court to impose the exclusionary rule against illegal state action, and *Mapp v. Ohio* provided just that set of facts.

Believing that Dollree Mapp was hiding fugitives from a bombing, officers of the Cleveland Police Department came to her house and asked for entry. She refused to allow them in without a search warrant. The police came back in a larger force three hours later and forced their way into the house. When Mapp demanded to see the search warrant, an officer held up a piece of paper that was snatched by Mapp and thrust into her bosom. The officers then wrestled her to the ground and handcuffed her. The paper was not a search warrant. The police then proceeded to thoroughly search the house. They did not find any evidence of the bombing, or any betting equipment that they also suspected she had. They did find printed material in a footlocker in the basement, which, at the time, was in violation of Ohio pornography statutes. She was arrested and convicted for possession of pornography. The Ohio state courts upheld her conviction.

In describing the behavior of the police in the *Mapp* case, Justice Clark's majority opinion used terms including "high-handed" and "roughshod." Clark condemned the officers' behavior and used it to justify extending the exclusionary rule to the states. Clark overruled the part of *Wolf v. Colorado* that separated the exclusionary rule from the Fourth Amendment. He made three arguments to justify the extension of the exclusionary rule to the states. First, he accepted Brandeis' view of the Fourth Amendment protecting a right to privacy, and argued that since the Fourth Amendment is enforceable against the states, it is essential that the same sanction of exclusion utilized in federal cases is used when the right is violated by the states; otherwise the amendment is "a form of words, valueless and undeserving of mention in a perpetual charter of inestimable human liberties."[12] Clark viewed the Fourth Amendment as a fundamental constitutional right. Second, he argued that there is a principle of judicial integrity that compels the use of the exclusionary rule when the Fourth Amendment is violated. He challenged the famous quip from Justice Cardozo that "the constable blunders and the criminal goes free" by arguing that "the criminal goes free, if he must, but it is the law that sets him free." Clark drew on Brandeis' dissent from *Olmstead*, pointing out how the government teaches by example, and how, when the government violates the law, it breeds anarchy and encourages everyone to become a "law unto himself." Finally, Clark argued that the exclusionary rule is necessary to deter police from committing illegal behavior. Over time, deterrence would become the sole rationale for the rule, but in *Mapp* it was just one of three arguments, and perhaps the least important.

The decision in *Mapp* was not unanimous. Justice Black concurred in the outcome but challenged the idea of whether exclusion was a constitutional right or was instead just a judicial remedy. Justice Harlan's dissent was highly critical of the Court's action: "In overruling the *Wolf* case, the Court, in my opinion, has forgotten the sense of judicial restraint which, with due regard for *stare decisis*, is one element that should enter into deciding whether a past decision of this Court should be overruled."[13] Justice Harlan questioned the logic of why exclusion necessarily was demanded by *Wolf*'s incorporation of the Fourth Amendment against the states.

The Warren Court's Expansion of Rights

Mapp v. Ohio quickly became the focus of critics of the Warren Court's expansion of the rights of the accused. *Mapp* completed the incorporation of the Fourth Amendment promised by *Wolf*, and made the entire criminal justice system subject to Fourth Amendment scrutiny. *Mapp* also represented a turning point for the Warren Court in terms of the expansion of individual rights. A mere five years after the decision in *Draper*, the Warren Court shifted its standard for determining the existence of probable cause. *Aguilar v. Texas* (1964) involved two Houston police officers' reliance on an informant for the information that Nick Alford Aguilar was dealing heroin from his house. The information provided to the trial court at the time that the warrant was requested was that there was an informant and that the police trusted him. The Court held that this was not sufficient. The Fourth Amendment required that the police provide not only information about the informant to the judge but also the basis for the informant's belief that a crime has been committed. *Aguilar* imposed a reliability test that judges had to use. There had to be evidence that an informant's testimony was reliable.

Five years later, at the very end of the Warren Court, *Spinelli v. United States* (1969) added a veracity component to the *Aguilar* standard to determine whether hearsay evidence from an informant was sufficient to justify a search warrant. The FBI suspected William Spinelli of running an illegal gambling operation in Missouri. As in *Aguilar*, the information provided to the magistrate was based on information from an informant who did not appear in court. It was not enough for police to assert to a court that they believed the informant was providing them with accurate information. *Aguilar* and *Spinelli* together required that the police inform the judge why they think the information is reliable and let the judge decide whether he or she believes that this is so. Similarly, with regard to the inferences drawn by the informant, the judge must be the one who determines whether the facts known to the informant justify drawing the inference that a crime is being committed. This two-prong test was substantially more protective of individual rights than the totality of the circumstances approach used in *Draper*.

Brandeis Is Vindicated: Katz *and the Reasonable Expectation of Privacy*

One of the most enduring decisions of the Warren Court was *Katz v. United States* (1967). *Katz* forced the Court to reexamine the trespass doctrine and resulted in the vindication of Justice Brandeis' famous dissent from *Olmstead*. *Katz* considered the question of what constitutes a search, and what action by the government triggers Fourth Amendment protection. *Katz* served to fundamentally change the basic approach the Court used to define searches, and separated the legal concept of Fourth Amendment privacy from common law property rights.

Charles Katz was part of a multicity gambling operation. Federal agents became aware that he was using a phone booth in Los Angeles to make calls related to the gambling business and placed a listening device on the top of the booth. They did not seek judicial authority to place the device on the phone booth. They were able to hear his side of the conversations and used that information to convict him of gambling charges. Katz argued that the use of the recording device to listen to his phone conversations was an unreasonable search. The government justified the action by arguing that the recording device was placed on the outside of the telephone booth, and thus there was no physical intrusion on a constitutionally protected place. There was no trespass and, thus, no search.

The Court overruled the Ninth Circuit and established an entirely new standard for determining the meaning of privacy within the context of the Fourth Amendment. Justice Stewart distinguished between what a person knowingly exposes to public view, which is not subject to Fourth Amendment protection, and "what he seeks to preserve as private, even in an area exposed to the public, [which] may be constitutionally protected."[14] Stewart challenged the government's argument that the place where Katz made the phone call—the telephone booth—was made of glass and partially observable, asserting, "But what he sought to exclude when he entered the booth was not the intruding eye, it was the uninvited ear." Stewart rejected the government's reliance on the trespass doctrine, calling it no longer good law, and "once this much is acknowledged, and once it is recognized that the Fourth Amendment protects people—and not simply 'areas'—against unreasonable searches and seizures, it becomes clear that the reach of that Amendment cannot turn upon the presence or absence of a physical intrusion into any given enclosure."[15]

Stewart's reasoning in *Katz* was important, but the two-part standard that emerged for judging Fourth Amendment privacy claims came from Justice Harlan's concurrence: "My understanding of the rule that has emerged from prior decisions is that there is a twofold requirement, first that a person have exhibited an actual (subjective) expectation of privacy and, second, that the expectation be one that society is prepared to recognize as 'reasonable.'"[16] Harlan argued that if a person exhibits a subjective expectation of privacy, it is up to the Court to determine whether that claim is reasonable. While the Court viewed the societal judgment of a privacy claim's reasonableness as an objective standard, the reality is that the Court's test is quite subjective itself, since the only measure of what society views as legitimate is what a majority of the Court believes. That said, the reasonable expectation of privacy standard has been used in numerous cases. In the Burger Court alone, it was utilized at least 40 times.

While there were many Warren Court decisions that expanded the rights of the accused, the Court did not rule for the defendant all the time. The single most cited Fourth Amendment decision by the Warren Court is *Terry v. Ohio* (1968), a case that dramatically expanded police power at the expense of the probable cause and warrant requirement. *Terry* involved the question of whether the Fourth Amendment permitted a brief on-the-street detention of an individual for questioning, and whether an officer could conduct a frisk or pat-down of the individual's outer garments for weapons. The case involved a quick pat-down search of two suspects whom the police believed were casing a retail establishment with an eye toward committing a robbery. The officers found guns. The search was without a warrant and without probable cause, but the behavior in question was hardly extreme. In fact, it is a pretty easy argument to make that this is simply good police practice since an armed robbery was likely thwarted. But good police work and the protections of the Fourth Amendment may be in conflict in some cases. In *Terry* the officer had neither probable cause nor a warrant to conduct the stop (seizure) or the frisk (search).

The Court held that a limited stop for a limited purpose could be conducted if the police had a reasonable, articulable suspicion that wrongdoing was afoot. If they had reasonable suspicion that the person intended to commit a crime, they could briefly detain the person to determine whether their suspicions were justified. The officer was allowed to conduct a limited search, a pat-down, for officer safety. This came to be commonly known as a stop and frisk or a *Terry* stop. Two aspects of the ruling were significant for the future. First, the ruling was based on pragmatic concerns. The Court clearly thought that the police practice in question made sense and could be highly effective in thwarting a crime before it ever happened. This focus on practical matters is important for future cases only because it allows the justices to make arguments based on very appealing pragmatic arguments, regardless of the larger legal principles. Second, the rationale can so easily be expanded to a wide range of situations without worrying about the restrictions of warrants or probable cause. The *Terry* stop has become an almost universally used tool by police everywhere in the nation and is especially useful when dealing with suspected gang members who often have guns on their persons and who also may have an outstanding warrant or may be convicted felons not legally allowed to possess firearms.

As he did a decade earlier in *Draper*, Justice Douglas dissented from the Court's abandonment of the probable cause standard for the new standard of reasonable articulable suspicion to conduct a stop and frisk. Douglas defined a reasonable search and seizure by the issuance of a warrant based on probable cause: "Only that line draws a meaningful distinction between an officer's mere inkling and the presence of facts within the officer's personal knowledge which would convince a reasonable man that the person seized has committed, is committing, or is about to commit a particular crime." Permitting the police officer to make the decision as to whether a search or seizure is reasonable gives the police officer "greater power than the magistrate," and to do so is "to take a long step down the totalitarian path. Perhaps such a step is desirable to cope with modern forms of lawlessness. But if it is taken, it should be the deliberate choice of the people through a constitutional amendment."[17]

Once again, Douglas put the issue into greater context, fully cognizant of the rising tide of a push for crime control in the late 1960s, writing that "there have been powerful hydraulic pressures throughout our history" that serve to diminish constitutional rights and "give the police the upper hand." He argued that "hydraulic pressure has probably never been greater than it is today. Yet if the individual is no longer to be sovereign, if the police can pick him up whenever they do not like the cut of his jib, if they can 'seize' and 'search' him in their discretion, we enter a new regime. The decision to enter it should be made only after a full debate by the people of this country."[18] While it is an eloquent defense of individual liberty in many ways, Justice Douglas' concerns fell on deaf ears, as the rising tide of crime and the increasing perception of disorder made arguments for restraint of police discretion unpopular. His point of view remains a minority position even to this day.

THE BACKLASH TO THE WARREN COURT'S CRIMINAL PROCEDURE REVOLUTION

The Fourth Amendment evolved during Earl Warren's 17-year tenure, and the Court's decisions shifted dramatically in terms of outcomes that favored defendants and individual due process after 1960. Fourth Amendment cases contributed to a broader shift in how the rights of the accused were viewed, but they were not the only cases and, in some ways, were not the ones that most resonated with the public. *Mapp* was shortly followed by the landmark decision in *Gideon v. Wainwright* (1963) establishing the defendant's right to counsel, and mandating that, if the defendant is indigent, the state must provide an attorney. The next year, in *Escobedo v. Illinois* (1964), the Court held that the guarantee against self-incrimination applied to state criminal justice proceedings, and not just federal ones. Finally, the Court's decision in *Miranda v. Arizona* (1966) brought together both the right to counsel and the guarantee against self-incrimination, by mandating that police have to read suspects their rights prior to custodial interrogation. These four cases represented to the public a fundamental shift in constitutional law that seemed to place the rights of the accused over concerns of public safety. Together, the Warren Court's criminal procedure decisions resulted in a significant political backlash, driven by both police discontent and public perceptions that the Court was frustrating the ability to swiftly apprehend and prosecute criminals. In many ways, the Warren Court's prodefendant decisions helped spark a politics of crime control and "get tough" policies that have been a part of the national and local political landscape for almost 50 years.

While decisions such as *Mapp*, *Gideon*, or *Miranda* would be controversial regardless of external events, the Warren Court's focus on the rights of the accused had the unfortunate timing of occurring as the nation was experiencing one of its largest crime waves in history. The homicide rate in cities such as Chicago and New York was increasing rapidly to levels not seen in the modern era.[19] The antiwar movement and counterculture were generating disorder in the streets, and the once nonviolent civil rights movement of the early 1960s was resulting in increasingly violent responses as the movement's focus shifted from eliminating legal segregation to fighting de facto segregation in America's cities. As these separate factors converged in the second half of the 1960s, it appeared as if the Supreme Court was oblivious to concerns of law and order, and instead was tying the hands of police with increasingly strict procedural requirements that impeded their ability to fight the rising tide of crime.[20] The Court appeared to be advocating for the rights of the accused while oblivious to what was happening in American cities, including rising crime, civil unrest, and social upheaval.[21]

Criticism of the Court began as early as the 1964 presidential campaign, which itself was shaped by the assassination of President John F. Kennedy the year before. Republican Barry Goldwater tried to make law and order one of his key issues. Goldwater's focus on law and order was somewhat disingenuous, however, since his focus on crime was largely a smoke screen for a covertly racist campaign, as he tried to equate street crime with African Americans and the civil rights movement. Yet Goldwater's campaign specifically targeted Supreme Court decisions, including *Mapp*, *Gideon*, and *Escobedo*. He tried to blend together issues that were independent of one another, and his efforts were generally unsuccessful. Lyndon Johnson was able to brand him as an extremist and win reelection by a landslide.

Several things changed over the next four years to make law and order a much more viable campaign strategy for 1968. First, the Warren Court continued to expand the due process revolution with more cases, none of which was more important than *Miranda v. Arizona*, which seemed to epitomize the length to which the Warren Court would go to protect the rights of the accused, excluding evidence from confessions that did not follow *Miranda*'s script. Today the *Miranda* decision is much more popular than it was in the 1960s, but at the time, police loudly voiced their concerns that the decision would eliminate confessions, and would make it much harder for them to apprehend and convict criminals.

The backlash against the Court's criminal procedure decisions made it an easy target for a skilled politician such as Richard Nixon to manipulate. He used *Mapp* and *Miranda* as lightning rods for criticism of the Supreme Court, and crafted his campaign as if he were running not only against Lyndon Johnson, but against Earl Warren, too. This had the double advantage of appealing to southern antagonism to the Court over its civil rights decisions dating back to *Brown v. Board of Education* (1954). By focusing his attack on the Court on law and order issues, he avoided making it appear as if his criticism was aimed at civil rights, and instead made it seem that his criticism was limited to the Court's coddling of criminals. Nixon promised that if elected president, he would turn back the clock on the Warren Court's criminal procedure decisions by appointing justices who were "strict constructionists" and who would interpret the Constitution narrowly. Kevin McMahon documented how Nixon made use of landmark criminal procedure decisions to illustrate how guilty defendants were set free, based on nothing more than legal technicalities. Nixon continually warned about the rise in crime: "In the last seven years while the population of this country was rising some ten percent, crime in the United States rose a staggering 88 percent. If the present rate of new crime continues, the number of rapes and robberies and assaults and thefts in the United States today will double—by the end of 1972. That is a prospect America cannot accept."[22]

Writing about the 1968 campaign, Fred Graham noted, "Presidents had feuded with the Supreme Court before, but never had a candidate won the office on a specific promise to use his appointive power to change the Court's direction on a particular issue."[23] Nixon was able to fulfill his campaign promises, having the rare opportunity to replace four justices from the Warren Court in the next three years, including Chief Justice Warren himself. Earl Warren had announced his retirement before the election, but President Johnson's nomination of Associate Justice Abe Fortas as chief disintegrated after it was revealed that there were conflicts of interest in some of his earlier decisions. The failed Fortas nomination provided the new president with not only the appointment of a chief justice in early 1969, but also a second vacancy, after Fortas resigned his seat amid the controversy. The Burger Court would begin not with just a new chief justice, but the promise of more change to come.

Perhaps more importantly, Nixon had created a narrative about liberal judges and crime that would come to dominate the thinking of conservatives across the country for decades. In this narrative, the Warren Court had overreached, gone beyond its proper role in the system of checks and balances envisioned by the founders. In the process, the rights of the guilty had become more important than the rights of the victims. Crime was out of control. The way to address this was to appoint federal judges who understood the need for the judicial branch to support executive branch actions to control crime and who would overturn the Warren Court's unacceptable decisions. Over time, the Burger Court would transform what had been a campaign promise into a jurisprudence of crime control, remaking the Fourth Amendment and providing support for the get tough on crime policies that would follow.

3. The Burger Court and the Rise of a Jurisprudence of Crime Control

From its very beginning, the Burger Court was positioned to make changes to the Warren Court's approach to the Fourth Amendment. The new Court began with two vacancies, after the retirement of Chief Justice Warren and resignation of Justice Fortas. President Nixon had promised to name a law and order jurist as chief, and federal court of appeals Judge Warren E. Burger actively campaigned for the post with the new Nixon administration. The president nominated Burger in early May 1969. Burger had long been critical of the Warren Court's criminal procedure jurisprudence, especially the imposition of the exclusionary rule on the states.

It took another year to fill Fortas' seat, and, after two failed nominations,[1] Nixon ultimately settled on Burger's childhood friend Judge Harry A. Blackmun. The retirements of Justices Hugo Black and John Marshall Harlan in the summer of 1971 gave Nixon two final appointments, which he filled with former president of the American Bar Association Lewis F. Powell and Assistant Attorney General William H. Rehnquist. These four justices would all prove to be consistent votes for expanding the police's ability to combat crime. Powell and Rehnquist, in particular, would play a significant role in the development of a jurisprudence of crime control.

The four new justices had an immediate impact on the Court. Each was committed to pulling back from major Warren Court holdings. The Burger Court's reshaping of criminal procedure law did not come by overruling the exclusionary rule or eliminating *Miranda* warnings for the accused. Instead, change occurred through shifting the terms of the discussion about criminal procedure and the frame through which Fourth Amendment claims were evaluated. The Court did this slowly, starting in the early 1970s and building to a tipping point in 1983 and 1984. Our analysis explains how the Burger Court changed the terms of the debate and altered the landscape of the Fourth Amendment.

Changes to legal doctrines often occur incrementally, and the Burger Court did not abandon the Warren Court's precedents overnight. When we look at the evolution of the Fourth Amendment over the 17 years of the Burger Court, there is a clear trajectory in the development of legal policy. Precedents were modified, case by case, and by the mid-1980s, challenges based on the Fourth Amendment were evaluated in very different ways compared to the early 1970s. The Court abandoned the idea that the exclusionary rule was part of the Fourth Amendment or of constitutional status. It was instead seen as a judicial remedy that existed only for the purpose of deterring police misconduct. The Burger Court expanded warrant exceptions and reframed the Fourth Amendment so that reasonableness, and not the existence of a warrant, became the touchstone of constitutional analysis. Finally, the Burger Court made it clear through its decisions that it was reluctant to rule that many privacy concerns amounted to a reasonable expectation of privacy. Instead, the Burger Court expanded police discretion and relegated philosophical discussion of individual rights to dissenting opinions by Justices Brennan, Marshall, and Stevens.

RESHAPING THE EXCLUSIONARY RULE

Frustration over the use of the exclusionary rule played an important role in the Burger Court's movement toward a jurisprudence of crime control. Several justices believed that the Warren Court had been too willing to let obviously guilty criminal defendants go free on legal technicalities. Justice Cardozo's oft-quoted line about allowing criminals "to go free because the constable has blundered"[2] resonated both with the general public and with the newly appointed members of the Court. When a highly publicized case involving the brutal murder of a child resulted in a ruling in favor of the defendant, the dissenting justices in *Coolidge v. New Hampshire* (1971) were incensed. This case prompted efforts by these members of the Court to work toward the abolition, or at least limitation, of the exclusionary rule.

On January 14, 1964, 14-year-old Pamela Mason went missing after leaving home in response to an offer of a babysitting job. Her body was found seven days later, shot in the head with her throat slashed. Police focused their attention on Edward Coolidge, to whom police officers had provided assistance the night Mason had disappeared, near the location where they eventually found Mason's body. Evidence linking Coolidge was uncovered, including a shotgun that was tied to the crime. The police presented the evidence to the New Hampshire attorney general, who was authorized under state law to issue warrants. A justice of the peace employed by the attorney general's office issued a search warrant for Coolidge's car. The defendant challenged the validity of this warrant in a pretrial motion to suppress evidence, but was denied after a hearing on the matter. Vacuum sweepings from the car were introduced at trial. Coolidge was convicted and, on appeal, challenged the validity of the search warrant as not coming from a neutral magistrate. The New Hampshire Supreme Court upheld the conviction, and the Supreme Court granted certiorari.

After oral argument, five justices voted to reverse the lower court and exclude the evidence from the vehicle search. Justice Stewart was assigned the majority opinion, and held that a warrant issued by the attorney general's office was invalid, because a neutral and detached magistrate did not issue it. Stewart argued that searches conducted outside of the judicial process, with no prior approval by a judge or magistrate, are per se unconstitutional. Stewart rejected claims that the search was incident to arrest, that it fell under the automobile exception, or that it was in plain view.

The use of the exclusionary rule in this case generated a harsh response from several justices, including Justice Harlan, who had concurred with the result. Harlan argued that the time might be right to overhaul the Fourth Amendment by reexamining *Mapp v. Ohio*. The chief justice echoed this request by pointing to the argument he made in a case decided that same day. In *Bivens v. Six Unknown Federal Narcotics Agents* (1971), Burger went so far as to call for the elimination of the exclusionary rule, and provided possible language for Congress to use to craft a legislative remedy for when unreasonable searches and seizures occur. Burger believed that the exclusionary rule should be overruled, but not until Congress passed legislation that provided some consequence for when the police violate the law. His dissent would be frequently cited by opponents of the exclusionary rule, and suggested that *Mapp*'s demise was simply a matter of time.[3]

Justice Black also argued against the exclusionary rule, claiming, "The Fourth Amendment prohibits unreasonable searches and seizures. The Amendment says nothing about consequences."[4] Black believed that the only exclusionary rule mandated by the Constitution was the Fifth Amendment's command against self-incrimination, and went so far as to argue that the evidence excluded in *Mapp* was by the Fifth Amendment and not the Fourth. Justice Blackmun added a brief statement to Black's opinion, saying he agreed that the "Fourth Amendment supports no such exclusionary rule," but did not elaborate on it.

Justice White did not take a position on overruling *Mapp* in *Coolidge*, but his actions a mere four days before the case was slated to be handed down made it clear that not only was he willing to reconsider it, but he thought the time to do so was ripe. White wrote a memorandum to the eight other justices to suggest that *Coolidge* should be held over for reargument.

> With publication of *Coolidge* and *Bivens*, four justices (Burger, Harlan, Black, and Blackmun) will have stated for the record their dissatisfaction with *Mapp v. Ohio* insofar as the exclusionary rule is based on the Fourth Amendment. For myself, our struggles this term suggest at least a reexamination of the premise that gave rise to them. My present view is that the exclusionary rule should at least be narrowed. Thus I suggest we consider whether we should call for reargument in *Coolidge*, limited to the single question whether *Mapp* should be overruled.[5]

Encouraged by White's memo, Burger tried to convince the Court to go along with White's suggestion, and he proposed a two-part question for reargument. There is no official record of the discussion that followed, but Woodward and Armstrong report that in the Friday conference, Justice Harlan had the decisive vote, and he did not think *Coolidge* was a good case to modify the exclusionary rule. As a result, *Coolidge* was handed down the following Monday.[6] This brief exchange illustrates an important point that we make in this chapter. From the earliest days of the Burger Court, there was a desire among several justices to limit the application of the exclusionary rule. By June 1971, only two of President Nixon's four justices were on the Court. Justices Powell and Rehnquist would not join the Court until January 1972.

Justice Powell had well-formed views on the exclusionary rule. One year into his tenure on the Court, Powell wrote a long memorandum for his own files devoted to his views of the exclusionary rule.[7] He thought that the exclusionary rule neither was rooted in the Constitution, nor actually accomplished its intended goals. Powell would become a voice on the Court to either eliminate the exclusionary rule or redefine its purpose and limit its application. Powell's opposition to the exclusionary rule is perhaps somewhat surprising, in that he had never actually practiced criminal law. Powell was also concerned that if the Court were to consider overruling the exclusionary rule, that it have the right case to do it.

Justice Rehnquist's hostility toward the exclusionary rule predated his time on the Court, and continued through the end of his tenure as chief justice.[8]

There is perhaps no better example of his disdain for the exclusionary rule than the comments Rehnquist made to Chief Justice Burger in the student search case *New Jersey v. T.L.O.* (1985). Rehnquist wrote: "I now vote to reverse this case. Whatever may be the arguments for and against this particular limitation on the exclusionary rule, my disagreement with *Mapp v. Ohio* remains so fundamental that I will seize any opportunity to limit the damage done by that case."[9] Rehnquist did not care what the issues were in the case; he was driven by the goal of limiting the exclusionary rule.

The appointment of the four Nixon justices resulted in a strong coalition against the exclusionary rule, but given Burger's unwillingness to overrule it outright, and White's support to simply narrow it, there was no majority to overrule *Mapp*. The appointment of Justice Stevens in 1975 did not change the balance. But if the Court could not overrule *Mapp*, it could narrow its application and redefine its underlying rationale. Justice Powell played a large role in the development of a revisionist interpretation of the meaning and purpose of the exclusionary rule. As we recall from chapter 2, Justice Clark's opinion in *Mapp v. Ohio* justified the exclusionary rule as protecting the constitutional rights of the defendant, deterring police misconduct, and promoting judicial integrity by not permitting judges to allow illegal behavior to go unchecked. Clark acknowledged the social costs of excluding evidence, as a criminal might go free, but viewed this as necessary to protect constitutional rights. Powell challenged that in his concurring opinion in *Schneckloth v. Bustamonte* (1973) by arguing that this was too high a price to pay. In Powell's mind, the exclusionary rule was solely driven by deterrence, and he thought that the courts should use it only when the police engaged in a flagrant violation of the law.

Powell's first majority opinion in a search and seizure case came in *United States v. Calandra* (1974), where he held that the exclusionary rule does not apply to grand juries, in situations where a witness brought to testify before a grand jury refuses to testify because the questions are based on evidence illegally obtained. Powell focused on the centrality of deterrence in justifying the exclusionary rule: "The rule's prime purpose is to deter future unlawful police conduct and thereby effectuate the guarantee of the Fourth Amendment against unreasonable searches and seizures."[10] The rule exists to deter behavior and "to compel respect for the constitutional guaranty in the only effectively available way—by removing the incentive to disregard it." Powell ignored *Mapp*'s judicial integrity and constitutional rights arguments. He also articulated the second element of the conservatives' reinterpretation of the rule, denying that the rule is a constitutional command. Instead, "it is a judicially created remedy."[11] By separating the exclusionary rule from the claim of a constitutional right, Powell opened the door to the argument that if one set of judges creates a remedy, another set of judges can carve out a new remedy short of exclusion or eliminate it altogether.

Justice Blackmun's majority opinion in *United States v. Janis* (1976) echoed Powell's efforts to narrow the rationale for the exclusionary rule. Blackmun retreated somewhat from his initial assessment in *Coolidge* that the Fourth Amendment supports no exclusionary rule. *Janis* considered whether good faith action by the police involving a warrant that was later found to be invalid would require exclusion of evidence from a federal civil tax case stemming from the litigation. Blackmun repeated Powell's argument that the primary purpose of the rule was to deter police misconduct and that it was merely a judicial remedy. He questioned whether there was any empirical evidence supporting the exclusionary rule's actual deterrent effect since the time of *Mapp*. Blackmun claimed that exclusion imposes a "substantial cost on the societal interest in law enforcement by its proscription of what concededly is relevant evidence."[12] Blackmun did caution that much of the empirical evidence about the rule was flawed in that record keeping before *Mapp* was spotty at best, and given the constant changes in Fourth Amendment doctrines, it was difficult to make accurate assessment of the effect of the rule.

Toward a Good Faith Exception

The Court decided several cases involving limitations on the exclusionary rule in the 1970s. The private papers of Justices Blackmun, White, and Powell indicate that the Nixon justices often sought to either overrule or significantly limit the exclusionary rule. No issue garnered as much attention by the Court as the question of a good faith exception. Justice White was the primary proponent of limiting the use of the exclusionary rule in cases where there was objective good faith reliance on the part of police. This issue was highly contentious. If police were acting in good faith, having obtained a warrant, it was not their fault that the warrant they were using was invalid, and thus there was no deterrence rationale for exclusion of evidence.

The Court came close to establishing a good faith exception in *Michigan v. DeFillippo* (1979), a case that involved a misdemeanor arrest for failure to identify oneself, when the city ordinance that made it a crime to fail to do so was later invalidated as vague. Detroit police encountered a man and a woman in an alley while the woman was in the process of dropping her "slacks" in order to "relieve herself." DeFillippo gave the officer inconsistent and evasive responses as to his identity, and he was arrested. Incident to his arrest, he was searched, and drugs were found on his person. He was ultimately only charged with the drug offense, and sought to have the evidence suppressed due to the invalid identification law. Four justices were willing to support a good faith exception, but the chief justice took the advice of Justices Stewart and Powell that this was not the best set of facts to use for the creation of such a broad exception, and decided the case more narrowly. Burger held that when an officer has probable cause to arrest someone under a validly enabled criminal law, he has not violated the Fourth Amendment, even if the law itself is later invalidated.[13]

The next effort to establish a good faith exception came in *Illinois v. Gates* (1983). Police in Bloomingdale, Illinois, received an anonymous letter in the mail informing them that a couple named Sue and Lance Gates were making a living selling drugs. The letter provided detailed information about the suspects, including the fact that Sue Gates drove to Florida and bought the drugs, and then her husband flew down and drove them back while she flew home. The tip was forwarded to a detective who confirmed that the Gateses lived where the letter indicated, determined that he had purchased airfare to Florida, and had the Drug Enforcement Agency (DEA) conduct surveillance of the flight when it landed. DEA agents confirmed that Gates went to a Holiday Inn and entered a room registered to his wife. He left in a vehicle with Illinois plates on it the next morning. The anonymous tip and the corroborating information were used to secure a search warrant for Gates' car and home. When Lance Gates arrived in Bloomingdale, 36 hours after leaving Chicago, police met him, searched the car, and found 350 pounds of marijuana.

The trial judge suppressed the evidence from the search because the warrant lacked probable cause. The warrant did not satisfy the Supreme Court's standards of veracity and reliability established in *Aguilar v. Texas* (1964) and *Spinelli v. United States* (1969). The Illinois Supreme Court affirmed the ruling and the United States Supreme Court granted certiorari. The original question before the Court was whether there was probable cause for the warrant. After oral argument, the question of applying a good faith exception came up when the justices were split about the reason to reverse the Illinois Supreme Court. Justice White sought a compromise, asking the Court to call for reargument to permit the parties to address the question of a good faith exception to the exclusionary rule.[14] After a spirited debate among the justices, the push for a good faith exception prevailed, and the justices agreed to ask the parties to submit new briefs and scheduled the case for a second oral argument. It seemed as if the good faith exception was about to become a reality. But then, after the second oral argument, the justices reconsidered. There were adequate grounds to reverse on the probable cause issue, by eliminating the *Aguilar* and *Spinelli* standards, and returning determinations of probable cause to a totality of the circumstances rationale, as originally used in *Draper v. United States* (1959). Moreover, several justices, including Powell and Rehnquist, were disturbed that the good faith exception arguments were never litigated in the lower court, making *Gates* a less than ideal candidate to establish a major exception to the exclusionary rule. By this time, there was another case on the docket, *United States v. Leon* (1984), which, they thought, might provide a better vehicle for the establishment of a good faith exception.

Ultimately, *Illinois v. Gates* was decided on the probable cause issue, and ironically, the decision the Court handed down came to be a major victory for advocates of crime control. The elimination of the two-prong standard that required that the warrant applicant pass threshold tests of veracity and reliability when considering anonymous tips resulted in the expansion of judicial discretion to grant warrants. The totality of the circumstances standard that emerged in *Gates* transformed the law of probable cause, significantly enhancing the discretion of police at the expense of individual rights. To date, *Gates* remains the second most cited search and seizure decision decided since the 1950s.[15] The ruling played a large role in tipping the balance toward a jurisprudence of crime control.

United States v. Leon (1984) provided the Court with an ideal fact pattern for creating a good faith exception to the exclusionary rule. The case was similar to *Gates* in that it involved an unproven confidential informant who provided information to police that two persons, known as Armando and Patsy, were selling large amounts of drugs from their residence in Burbank, California. The residence was placed under police surveillance, which led them to several individuals, including Alberto Leon, who had been arrested on drug charges the year before. An informant provided information that Leon had been heavily involved in importing drugs into the United States. A search warrant was issued for three addresses that had been identified, and police found a substantial quantity of drugs. Leon and the others were arrested for conspiracy to distribute a controlled substance.

At trial, a motion to suppress was filed and was partially granted, concluding that the affidavit was insufficient for probable cause. The government appealed, and the Ninth Circuit affirmed, holding that there was not probable cause, as the information provided by the informant did not satisfy either the *Aguilar* or *Spinelli* tests. The solicitor general petitioned for certiorari, but explicitly chose not to ask the Court to address the issue of probable cause, but instead to decide whether the Fourth Amendment's exclusionary rule should be modified to ensure the admission of evidence seized in reasonable good faith reliance on a search warrant later held to be defective. The petition for certiorari came after reargument in *Gates* but before the decision had been handed down.

The decision to establish a good faith exception did not go unchallenged. Justices Brennan, Marshall, and Stevens argued that the case should just be remanded to the California courts in light of *Gates*. They also were bothered that the Court was establishing a good faith exception in a case where the majority did not think a Fourth Amendment violation had occurred. Thirteen years after first raising the question of reconsidering the exclusionary rule in *Coolidge v. New Hampshire*, Justice White prevailed. His decision made it clear that the exclusionary rule's sole purpose was to deter police misconduct, that the rule was a judicial remedy and not a constitutional right, and that when police were acting in objective good faith with what they had every reason to believe was a valid warrant, there was no reason to suppress evidence. When the police act in good faith with what they believe is a valid warrant, suppression provides no deterrent effect and comes with what the justices perceived to be a huge social cost. *Leon* did not abolish the exclusionary rule, but it forever changed the terms by which it would be used. In the analysis of Richards and Kritzer, *Leon* served as the second major decision that tipped the scales toward a new jurisprudential regime.[16] It was the embodiment of what we term the jurisprudence of crime control. The exclusionary rule was no longer a constitutional right, but was only a judicial remedy that should be reluctantly and sparingly applied.

THE LIMITS OF THE *KATZ* REASONABLE EXPECTATIONS OF PRIVACY TEST

Katz v. United States (1967) established a two-prong test to determine when a search occurred under the meaning of the Fourth Amendment. The reasonable expectation of privacy standard made it such that for there to be a search within the meaning of the Fourth Amendment, a person had to exhibit a subjective expectation of privacy that society viewed as legitimate. It was up to the Court to determine if a subjective expectation of privacy was reasonable. The Burger Court made regular use of the reasonable expectation of privacy standard, applying it in more than 40 cases between 1970 and 1986. As the Court's shift toward crime control strengthened, however, it became clear that there were few privacy expectations that the Court would view as legitimate.

The Court first considered an application of the reasonable expectation of privacy standard in *United States v. White* (1971). In 1966, a federal narcotics agent directed a confidential informant named Harvey Jackson to record conversations between Jackson and James White, whom the government suspected of trafficking in narcotics. Jackson was wired with a radio transmitter and conversations were recorded twice in White's home, once in a restaurant and twice in a car. They were used as evidence to support an arrest warrant and White was ultimately convicted of drug offenses and sentenced to 25 years in prison. White sought to have the evidence from the warrantless electronic eavesdropping suppressed under *Katz*. The court of appeals agreed and overturned the conviction. The Supreme Court reversed in an opinion authored by Justice White. *United States v. White* was one of the first to deal specifically with *Katz*'s holding. Justice White rejected the defendant's claim of a subjective expectation of privacy by arguing that those who contemplate "illegal activities must realize and risk that his companions may be reporting to the police."[17] Since the law permits people to turn information over to the police, there is little difference between reporting what was said, and providing an actual recording. Justice White's opinion ignored the argument that the informant was acting as a government agent. The doctrine of state action means that a recording made by a private person is not a search within the meaning of the Fourth Amendment, but such behavior by a government agent is a search. If the informant is considered a government agent, that would make the recordings in this case a warrantless search.

In rejecting James White's claim of a reasonable expectation of privacy, Justice White made it clear that his primary concern was with the impact such a privacy right would have on the police's ability to collect evidence. White warned that, were the Court to rule otherwise, it would be hampering the ability to convict the obviously guilty:

> Nor should we be too ready to erect constitutional barriers to relevant and probative evidence that is also accurate and reliable. An electronic recording will many times produce a more reliable rendition of what a defendant has said than will the unaided memory of a police agent. It may also be that with the recording in existence it is less likely that the informant will change his mind, less chance that threat or injury will suppress unfavorable evidence and less chance that cross-examination will confound the testimony.[18]

The decision provided a sense of the skepticism that proponents of the reasonable expectation of privacy standard would face.

Over the course of the 17 years of the Burger Court, the reasonable expectation of privacy standard would only be used to establish a legitimate expectation of privacy in 10 cases. Four of these involved the home. *Steagald v. United States* (1981) held that an arrest warrant did not permit DEA agents to conduct a warrantless search of a home while executing the arrest. *Payton v. New York* (1980) ruled that police could not enter a home to make a routine felony arrest without a warrant. Two cases found that there is no murder scene exception permitting warrantless entry into a home to conduct a search. *Mincey v. Arizona* (1978) struck down a murder scene exception created by the Arizona Supreme Court that arose when homicide detectives arrived on the scene of a drug raid on an apartment where an undercover officer was shot and killed and conducted a four-day warrantless search. Seven years later the Court reinforced *Mincey* in *Thompson v. Louisiana* (1984), overruling the Louisiana Supreme Court's attempt to establish a similar murder scene exception.

Two Michigan cases dealt with privacy interests related to a fire investigation. *Michigan v. Tyler* (1978) involved a fire in a furniture store. Justice Stewart held that a warrant was not needed to enter the building to fight the fire, or to initially investigate the cause of the fire; any additional inquiries to investigate the fire beyond the initial entry required at least an administrative warrant. *Michigan v. Clifford* (1980) considered a warrantless search of a home by arson investigators who arrived five hours after an early morning home fire was extinguished. They did not obtain a warrant, and proceeded to search the home looking for evidence of arson. Justice Powell held that the expectation of privacy one has in the home requires fire investigators to obtain a criminal warrant if the purpose is to gather evidence of criminal activity and, at minimum, an administrative warrant, if the purpose is to determine the cause of the fire.

The Court ruled that there were legitimate expectations of privacy in four additional cases, none of which involved entry into a home or building. *United*

States v. Chadwick (1977) and *Arkansas v. Sanders* (1979) established that individuals could claim an expectation of privacy from warrantless searches in their luggage and in a footlocker. In *Winston v. Lee* (1985), the Court ruled that the government could not force a suspect to undergo a surgical procedure to have a bullet removed as evidence in a shooting. Finally, in *Delaware v. Prouse* (1979), the Court held that suspicion-less roadside checks for driver's licenses and automobile registration, when there was no reasonable articulable suspicion to stop a vehicle, violated a reasonable expectation of privacy.

The Third Party Doctrine

Two Burger Court cases addressed the question of whether individuals had a reasonable expectation of privacy in their bank and telephone records. Justice Powell held in *United States v. Miller* (1976) that there was no expectation of privacy against government subpoenas to search one's bank records. Mitch Miller was suspected of running an illegal distillery and engaging in tax fraud. The bank records in question were obtained by subpoena from two banks where Miller had accounts. Miller was not notified that the subpoenas had been requested, issued, or followed. The grand jury received the records and indicted Miller. At trial, the defendant claimed an expectation of privacy in his bank records and sought to have them suppressed as evidence. The Fifth Circuit reversed the conviction claiming that *Boyd v. United States* (1886) prohibited the turning over of a "man's private papers to establish a criminal charge against him."[19]

In his opinion for the Court, Justice Powell ruled that Miller had no expectation of privacy in his bank records. They were not his private papers but were instead business records of financial transactions. "The checks are not confidential communications but negotiable instruments to be used in commercial transactions," which only contain "information voluntarily conveyed to the banks and exposed to their employees in the ordinary course of business." Powell rejected Miller's privacy claim that his banking records, while obviously viewed by bank officials, represented his personal papers. The bank was a third party, and information is voluntarily given to it, and the individual takes the risk that the bank employees will turn the records over to the government.[20]

Three years later, the Court extended the third party doctrine to phone records in *Smith v. Maryland* (1979). When investigating a robbery in which the suspect had been stalking his victim with phone calls, police had the telephone company install a pen register on the defendant's home phone line. A pen register makes a record of the numbers dialed by a phone but not the actual contents of any conversations. They did this without a warrant. The pen register provided evidence that Smith's phone was used to call the victim's home. A search warrant was issued for Smith's home, and evidence from the search (his phone book was opened to the listing for the victim) provided probable cause for the arrest. Smith sought to have the evidence gained from the pen register suppressed as violating a reasonable expectation of privacy in his phone records.

Justice Blackmun ruled that Smith had no reasonable expectation of privacy in the phone numbers he dialed. Blackmun distinguished the pen register from the electronic recording device used in *Katz*. The pen register does not record communication; it merely indicates that a call was made. Moreover, Blackmun rejected any privacy claim, arguing, "We doubt that people in general entertain any actual expectation of privacy in the numbers they call." As with bank records, when Smith used his phone, he was assuming "the risk that the company would reveal to police the numbers he dialed."[21]

The third party doctrine effectively eliminated privacy claims to common activities that are a part of everyday life. Together with *United States v. White*, *United States v. Miller* and *Smith v. Maryland* limited what the Court would accept as a search, and provided police with a valuable tool for crime control. They could seek bank or phone records and even wire an informant for sound without implicating Fourth Amendment concerns. They illustrate the limited application that the Burger Court was willing to give to the reasonable expectation of privacy standard. Lower courts seeking to justify the police use of cell phone location data obtained from cellular service providers have relied heavily on the third party doctrine and often cite *Smith v. Maryland*. The third party doctrine will become important for our argument when we examine how technologies like cell phone and Global Positioning Satellite (GPS) tracking are viewed by the Roberts Court.

The Diminished Expectation of Privacy in Motor Vehicles

Katz might have established the reasonable expectation of privacy, but the Court had viewed automobiles as having a diminished expectation of privacy as far back as the 1920s. *Carroll v. United States* (1925) established that because of the mobility of the automobile, police could conduct a warrantless search if they had probable cause that the vehicle possessed contraband or evidence of a crime. The Burger Court strengthened the automobile exception in *Chambers v. Maroney* (1970) by permitting police to seize a vehicle where probable cause existed that it contained contraband, and then wait to search it until it was at the police station, expanding the exception to include more than on-the-street searches. Twelve years later, the Court expanded the exception again in *United States v. Ross* (1982) by permitting police to search not just the interior of the vehicle and trunk, but also any closed containers within it. The Burger Court also held that a motor home, which resembles a residence, is also covered by the automobile exception, as is a boat.[22] In *Gooding v. United States* (1974), the Court rejected the vehicle owner's privacy claim to the 16-digit vehicle identification number (VIN) embedded in every car's dashboard.

The diminished expectation of privacy in the automobile shaped the development of the search incident to arrest doctrine in ways that have had lasting impact on American politics, by enabling the war on drugs. The automobile exception permitted police to search an automobile only when there was probable cause that the vehicle contained contraband. In many traffic stops, however, officers don't have probable cause of any crime other than the traffic offense. The search incident to arrest doctrine provides a means around this. *Chimel v. California* (1969) established that incident to an arrest, police can search the person of the arrestee and the area within his or her reaching distance or wingspan. This search was permitted for purposes of officer safety and to prevent the destruction of any evidence that might be within reach of the arrestee. In 1973, the Court applied the doctrine to vehicles in *United States v. Robinson*.

The reaching distance standard seems to be fairly easy for police to implement, but applying it in the context of an arrest of the driver or passenger of a vehicle raises important questions. Does the driver's reaching distance extend to the whole passenger compartment? Does it include open or closed containers in the vehicle? The Burger Court resolved these questions in 1981 by establishing a bright line or per se rule in *New York v. Belton* that provided police with a standing rule for vehicle searches incident to arrest. Justice Stewart argued that *Chimel*'s reaching distance rule was difficult to administer in a vehicle due to its subjectivity. People with longer arms have a larger reaching distance. Stewart simplified the doctrine of search incident to arrest by holding that when an individual was arrested in a vehicle, police could search the entire passenger compartment, including any open or closed containers, but not the locked glove compartment or trunk. This was a bright line rule in that it applied for any arrest, regardless of its purpose. Given that there was already a diminished expectation of privacy in the vehicle, the driver could not claim a subjective privacy claim, and the Court instead drew on an existing warrant exception to widen the scope of vehicle searches.

The *Belton* rule was meant to make it easier for police to know what they could and could not search after an arrest, but it served to disconnect search incident to arrest from its constitutional moorings. Searches incident to arrest are justified by concerns for officer safety and to prevent the destruction of evidence. When an individual is arrested, he or she is handcuffed, frisked for weapons, and almost always placed in the back of the patrol car. The arrestee is no longer in or near the vehicle, and has no ability to obtain weapons or destroy evidence. Likewise, searches for evidence only make sense in some arrests. If an individual is arrested for driving under a suspended license, there is no reason to conduct a search. But the Court ignored this, and permitted searches after all arrests. In doing so, the *Belton* rule provided police with an extremely valuable tool. If a vehicle is stopped, and there is an arrestable offense, the police could automatically conduct a search of the entire passenger compartment. If that resulted in finding contraband, it triggers the automobile exception and permits a warrantless search of the entire vehicle. But probable cause was not needed beyond the traffic offense for the initial passenger compartment search. The Drug Enforcement Agency quickly realized this, and began training law enforcement in how to make use of vehicle profiles in conjunction with a *Belton* search. This was known as Operation Pipeline. The DEA taught state and local police how to profile likely vehicles driven by drug couriers, and then take advantage of the flexibility of the traffic code to use the excuse of a traffic stop as the basis for an investigation.[23] The bright line rule transformed traffic stops into an essential tool in the war on drugs.[24]

Technology, Surveillance, and Katz

The *Katz* reasonable expectation of privacy standard arose out of the government listening to a phone conversation with a recording device. Surveillance using technology has always been an important tool in the arsenal of police in combatting crime. One of the areas of surveillance that the Burger Court dealt with definitively was the question of using radio transmitters (commonly referred to as beepers) to track the location of vehicles. The Burger Court handed down *United States v. Knotts* and *United States v. Karo* in 1983 and 1984. In both cases, data provided by radio beepers were the basis for the probable cause for a search warrant that led to an arrest for drug manufacture.

Knotts involved surveillance of individuals suspected of manufacturing amphetamine. Police attached a radio beeper inside a canister of chloroform, a chemical used in the making of the drug, which they then tracked once it was picked up by the suspect. The canister was traced to a property surrounding a remote cabin. The location was placed under physical surveillance, and a search warrant was obtained for the cabin and the surrounding property. In executing the warrant the police discovered a drug laboratory. Knotts sought to have the evidence collected from the cabin suppressed, claiming that the search warrant was defective due to the warrantless use of the transmitter. The motion was denied at trial, but the Eighth Circuit reversed and held that Knotts had a reasonable expectation of privacy and a warrant was needed before police could use a beeper to determine the location of noncontraband materials.

The Supreme Court reversed the Eighth Circuit and rejected Knotts' contention that he had a reasonable expectation of privacy. In Justice Rehnquist's view, the case was about beeper surveillance of automobiles on public streets and highways, and his opinion relied heavily on the historically diminished expectation of privacy in a vehicle. He drew on a case from 1974, *Cardwell v. Lewis*, to argue, "One has a lesser expectation of privacy in a motor vehicle because its function is transportation and it seldom serves as one's residence or the repository of personal effects. A car has little capacity for escaping public scrutiny. It travels public thorough fares [sic] where both its occupants and its contents are in plain view."[25] Rehnquist accepted that Knotts had a traditional expectation of privacy at his cabin, but this did not extend to protection against visual police surveillance identifying the vehicle in which the chloroform had been transported. It did not matter that the police only found the cabin because of a helicopter overflight. Instead, he argued that nothing in the Fourth Amendment prevents "police from augmenting the sensory faculties bestowed upon them at birth with such enhancement as science and technology afforded them in this case."[26]

In its next term, the Court addressed the questions left unanswered by *Knotts*, whether the installation of the beeper itself violated the Fourth Amendment, and whether monitoring of a beeper infringes on the Fourth Amendment when it reveals information that could not be obtained through visual surveillance. In *United States v. Karo* (1984), Drug Enforcement Agency agents installed a beeper in a can of ether that they suspected was going to be used by the suspect to extract cocaine impregnated in clothing imported into the United States. DEA agents observed the suspect pick up the vehicle with the can of ether in question, and followed him to his home. Over several days they followed the movement of the can to several locations, eventually ending up at a commercial storage facility. They tracked the chloroform for five months, until it ended up at a home in Taos, New Mexico. A search warrant was issued, police found a cocaine laboratory, and Karo was arrested.

In the lower courts, Karo won his suppression motion that the initial warrant for the installation of the beeper was invalid, but was reversed in the Supreme Court in a 6–3 decision by Justice White that rejected Karo's claim of an expectation of privacy. White wrote that the can of chloroform in which the beeper was placed belonged to the DEA, and "by no stretch of the imagination could it be said that respondents then had any legitimate expectation of privacy in it."[27] The ether belonged to the informant who provided consent to include the beeper. Moreover, the beeper contained no information that Karo wanted to keep private, because it conveyed no information at all.

Justice White then addressed the question of whether presence of the beeper inside the house in Taos implicated the Fourth Amendment. He found that it did. Unlike in *Knotts*, where the beeper in the chloroform did not indicate any information about the interior of the cabin, the beeper in the ether canister was in a home, and it did provide information about a home that would normally only be accessible to a person inside the home. White argued, "Private residences are places in which the individual normally expects privacy from government intrusion not authorized by a warrant."[28] Searches and seizures at a home without a warrant are presumptively unreasonable. The beeper told the government that the ether was in the house. White also found that while the information from the beeper was inadmissible for securing the search warrant for the home, there was plenty of other evidence that provided probable cause to justify the warrant.

These two cases established an important precedent that permitted police to use electronic beepers to engage in warrantless surveillance of vehicles. These decisions were not overruled by the Roberts Court's ruling in 2012 in *United States v. Jones*, which held that the installation of a GPS surveillance device required a warrant, but the latter decision seriously undermined their logic.

ESTABLISHING A JURISPRUDENCE OF CRIME CONTROL

When Richard Nixon campaigned on a law and order platform, he probably never imagined that he would have the opportunity to name four justices to the Court who would work so tirelessly to accomplish the goal of reversing the Warren Court's criminal procedure jurisprudence. The Burger Court is often considered a disappointment from the perspective of reversing other liberal decisions, but in the area of criminal procedure, it was very successful in accomplishing the goals that President Nixon had in appointing justices who would focus on law and order.

Chief Justice Burger and Associate Justices Blackmun, Powell, and Rehnquist proved to be strong advocates for expanding police power and limiting individual rights. But the four Nixon justices were not able to do this on their own. They needed the assistance of Justices White, Stewart, and O'Connor. Moreover, the Court was unwilling to simply overturn the exclusionary rule. Instead, the justices chose to reframe its purpose and narrow its application. This incremental approach to judicial decision making is not uncommon, but we believe that if we want to understand how the Burger Court shifted the focus of the Fourth Amendment toward a jurisprudence of crime control, we cannot simply say that there was a regime shift in 1983 and 1984, but instead have to recognize that the shift that occurred was a long time coming, and was the result of many cases. For example, the development of a good faith exception to the exclusionary rule was the result of at least four prior efforts. Justice White showed initial support for a good faith exception in *Coolidge v. New Hampshire*. Justice Rehnquist began arguing for a good faith exception in 1975 in his opinion in *United States v. Peltier*, but the justices wanted to find the right case. Ironically, the case they chose to use, *United States v. Leon*, probably wasn't the best case, in that they would have upheld the search regardless. But by 1984, the justices who favored the creation of a good faith exception had the numbers and were tired of waiting.

There is little doubt that Richards and Kritzer were accurate in identifying the 1982 and 1983 terms of the Court (spanning from October 1982 through June 1984) as the time when the jurisprudential regime shift came to fruition. They focused on six important cases, but in fact there were a total of 23 cases decided over those two years, and 83 percent of them favored the state. *Illinois v. Gates* and *United States v. Leon* certainly represented the tipping point toward a jurisprudence of crime control. The Court's redefinition of probable cause from the two prongs of *Aguilar* and *Spinelli* to the totality of the circumstances test represented a significant diminishment of the Fourth Amendment as a constitutional right. In some ways, the Court had gone full circle back to the decision from 1959 in *United States v. Draper*, but by 1983 the use of a totality of the circumstances standard was even more favorable to the police in that the Court had also succeeded in reframing the entire Fourth Amendment from one where violations were measured using the standard of a warrant and probable cause to one where probable cause was merely measured loosely, and the warrant requirement had become the exception rather than the rule. The Burger Court made reasonableness the touchstone of Fourth Amendment analysis and, in doing so, played right into the hands of advocates of crime control. Public safety and administrative ease for police became primary concerns. Individual privacy took a backseat and rarely was mentioned in the Court's opinions outside of the passionate dissents of Justices Brennan, Marshall, and sometimes Stevens. The Warren Court had expanded the definition of a search beyond purely property concerns in *Katz*, but in the 40 cases where the Burger Court applied the reasonable expectation of privacy standard, only 10 cases established a privacy expectation, and these were quite narrow. The Burger Court's jurisprudence of crime control reframed the entire Fourth Amendment. It dramatically expanded police power in the name of fighting crime, and ultimately provided the foundations for a war on drugs; longer, more punitive sentences; and the rise of mass incarceration.

4. The War on Drugs and the Triumph of the Rehnquist Court

Chief Justice Burger's resignation in 1986 to chair the Commission on the Bicentennial of the Constitution provided President Ronald Reagan with the ability to name a new chief. Reagan's preference for very conservative judges, especially on issues such as crime and abortion, was well known. Reagan's choice came from the remaining three Nixon justices. In elevating William Rehnquist from associate to chief justice, Reagan selected a justice who was perhaps the single strongest supporter of the jurisprudence of crime control. As an associate justice, Rehnquist voted in favor of the state in 88 percent of all Fourth Amendment cases. There was little doubt among scholars that Rehnquist would continue the Burger Court's approach.[1] With President Reagan's war on drugs in full swing, Rehnquist was in a position to push the Court further in the direction of providing police with a full range of tools to combat crime.

Reagan's choice opened up a second vacancy to fill Rehnquist's associate justice seat. His appointment of Judge Antonin Scalia served to effectively maintain the status quo, replacing one conservative justice with another. A year later, Justice Powell retired, and Reagan nominated outspoken conservative Judge Robert Bork. The Senate rejected Bork after a highly contentious confirmation battle. Ninth Circuit Judge Anthony Kennedy became the compromise appointee. While considered far more moderate than Bork on most issues, Anthony Kennedy has been, and still is, a reliable conservative vote when it comes to the Fourth Amendment, voting for the state in more than 70 percent of cases.

Two years later, when liberal Justice William Brennan retired, President George H. W. Bush appeared positioned to firmly cement in place one of the most ideologically one-sided Courts in recent history. President Bush, wary of the power of Democrats in the Senate and mindful of the scarring battle over the Bork nomination, settled on a relatively unknown judge from New Hampshire. David Souter had served on the New Hampshire Supreme Court before his very brief service on the First Circuit. At the time of his appointment, it was assumed that he would be another solid conservative vote, but Souter demonstrated his independence, and carved a moderate path on the

Court, ultimately voting for the state in just 56 percent of search and seizure cases. The retirement of liberal Justice Thurgood Marshall provided President Bush with a second nomination. President Bush was well aware that Marshall's seat would have to be filled with an African American to be acceptable. His choice was Clarence Thomas, a 43-year-old court of appeals judge who had been groomed for the Court by the Reagan administration. The battle over Thomas' confirmation was bitter, with allegations that he had engaged in serious misconduct while serving as head of the Equal Employment Opportunity Commission and a "not qualified" rating by the American Bar Association. Thomas was confirmed in the Senate by a narrow majority, garnering only 53 votes. Thomas has proved to be a very reliable vote in support of the jurisprudence of crime control. While Justice Marshall dissented in most of the major search and seizure cases during the Burger Court, Thomas quickly aligned himself with Rehnquist and the conservative bloc. Once Justice Thomas was on the Court, advocates arguing in favor of the state in search and seizure cases had a seemingly overwhelming majority of relatively safe votes for their side in Rehnquist, Scalia, Thomas, Kennedy, O'Connor, and Blackmun, with regular support from White and Souter.

The last two changes to the composition of the Rehnquist Court were in 1993 and 1994, when Justices White and Blackmun retired. This enabled President Clinton to appoint Judges Ruth Bader Ginsburg and Stephen Breyer. The addition of these two justices had only a minor impact on the Court's approach to search and seizure. Ginsburg and Breyer were both political moderates, and while Ginsburg was certainly more liberal than Justice White, her nomination did not really change the Court's ideological makeup. The nomination of Stephen Breyer added a justice who was certainly less conservative than Harry Blackmun, but far from liberal in criminal cases. Breyer would align more closely with Justice Souter than with Ginsburg. After 1994, the Rehnquist Court would experience an 11-year period of stability with the same nine justices until Rehnquist's death in 2005.

THE WAR ON DRUGS AND THE JURISPRUDENCE OF CRIME CONTROL

The war on drugs had begun long before the beginning of the Rehnquist Court, but the Court's decisions served to expand the tools the police could use and to institutionalize them. The ideological predisposition of the Rehnquist Court's members made it highly unlikely that the Court would change course from the trajectory begun by the Burger Court. Concern with crime remained highly salient throughout most of the Rehnquist Court years and the "get tough on crime" politics showed no signs of abating.[2] At the time of Rehnquist's elevation to chief justice, the nation was in the midst of an extraordinary concern with crack cocaine, which had become extremely popular in the inner cities, particularly among the poor and minorities. Not only was this form of cocaine extremely dangerous, its distribution was tied closely to violent street gangs. The crack epidemic became the focus of President Reagan's war on drugs.[3] A new Drug Abuse Policy Office was created in the Executive Office of the President. It would later come to be called the Office of National Drug Control Policy, and its director would come to be called the "Drug Czar" by President George H. W. Bush. It was endowed with billions of dollars in federal money year after year.[4] The Supreme Court's jurisprudence of crime control went hand in hand with the war on drugs. Burger Court rulings in cases such as *Illinois v. Gates* (1983) and *New York v. Belton* (1981) had already provided police with vast discretion in conducting criminal investigations. Rehnquist Court decisions would build on them, and would ultimately provide law enforcement with a constitutional toolbox of Fourth Amendment legal doctrines that would allow them great latitude in prosecuting a war on drugs and crime.

The Automobile: Searches in a Mobile Society

The bright line rule established in *New York v. Belton* provided police with much more latitude for searches than the automobile exception to the warrant requirement upon which it was based. The *Belton* rule permitted searches incident to any arrest following a traffic stop, whereas the automobile exception permitted a search only if there was probable cause that the vehicle contained contraband. This gave police the power to use the pretext of a traffic violation as the means to conduct a criminal investigation. A traffic stop provides the officer the ability to check the driver's license, registration, and proof of insurance, check for warrants, and do a plain view search of the interior of the car. If the officer finds any reason to arrest the driver, the *Belton* rule permits a search of the vehicle's passenger compartment, with the hope of uncovering evidence of more serious crimes, usually drugs or other contraband. The *Belton* search laid the foundation of a large set of tools available to the officer, most of which were developed by the Rehnquist Court. Key to this was the use of profiling to target vehicles and drivers for investigatory stops.

The Drug Enforcement Agency (DEA) first developed the drug courier profile to target likely drug smugglers at airports. The drug courier profile is a set of general observations about a suspect that would lead the officer to believe that the person in question is transporting drugs. These profiles were later adapted to bus stations and then to vehicle stops. Airplane passengers traveling to and from common drug destination cities were singled out for further investigation if they were traveling with little luggage, were near the front or back of the line to deplane, or appeared nervous. Near the border and on major interstate highways, cars traveling on back roads, rental cars or trucks, and vehicles being driven by people of color were often singled out. The concept was widely used in training local law enforcement and amounted to a very vague set of criteria that could be used to convince a court that the police officer in question had some justification for stopping and interrogating a suspect.

The Court gave its formal approval to the use of drug courier profiles in *United States v. Sokolow* (1989). A ticket agent at the Honolulu airport flagged the suspect when he paid cash for two round trip tickets to Miami, with a 48-hour turnaround. The DEA investigated and discovered that he had also given a phone number that did not match the listing under his name in the phone book. Upon his return to Honolulu, agents were waiting for him. He was arrested without a warrant, and agents discovered that he had more than a kilogram of cocaine in his luggage. The conviction was reversed by the Ninth Circuit, which held that a set of characteristics and observations, none of which, taken individually, were clear evidence of ongoing criminal activity, was not sufficient to justify the initial seizure.

Chief Justice Rehnquist's majority opinion rejected the lower court's rationale, and used a totality of the circumstances standard to identify the factors to justify the original investigatory stop. Rehnquist thought it "out of the ordinary" to pay for two tickets with $2,100 in cash, from rolls of $20 bills: "Most business travelers, we feel confident, purchase airline tickets by credit card or check so to have a record for tax or business purposes."[5] He likewise viewed the 20-hour turnaround as suspicious: "While a trip from Honolulu to Miami, standing alone, is not cause for any sort of suspicion, here there was more: surely few residents of Honolulu travel from that city for 20 hours to spend 48 hours in Miami during the month of July."[6] Rehnquist also made reference to Sokolow's wearing "a black jump suit [sic] and gold jewelry."[7] He implied that drug smugglers exhibited not only certain behaviors but also a certain appearance. Rehnquist saw no problem with the use of a profile, as long as the government agent could articulate the factors supporting reasonable suspicion. Justice Marshall's dissent criticized Rehnquist's willingness to accept the use of profiles as good police work: "A law enforcement officer's mechanistic application of a formula of personal and behavioral traits in deciding who to apprehend can only dull the officer's ability and determination to make sensitive and fact-specific inferences 'in light of his experience.'" Marshall argued that the profile had a "chameleon[-]like way of adapting to any particular set of observations."[8]

Sokolow provided constitutional approval for the DEA's use of drug courier profiles. By the time the case arrived at the Court, the DEA had already expanded its training programs to include the use of profiles to stop possible drug couriers on the nation's highways. Its primary training program was called Operation Pipeline. Begun in 1984, this program taught law enforcement to identify possible drug smugglers, and use the pretense of a traffic stop to investigate them. Implicit in the model was the idea that the traffic code could be used as a pretext for a criminal investigation. Part of the training included considering the suspect's race as a primary factor in the profile, giving rise to what is known as racial profiling. It was not until 1996 that the Court directly addressed the issues underlying the use of profiling in traffic stops.

Whren v. United States (1996) involved a traffic stop made by two vice squad officers who were driving in an unmarked vehicle while patrolling in a "high drug" area in Washington, DC. The officers spotted a Nissan Pathfinder with temporary plates with two young African American occupants at a stop sign. The driver was looking down, and was stopped for about 20 seconds, which seemed excessive. The police did a quick U-turn and approached the vehicle, which suddenly made a sharp turn right without signaling and took off at "an unreasonable" speed. Once it stopped, the officer approached the vehicle, and as he looked in the front seat, he saw two bags of what he assumed was cocaine. The driver, James Brown, and the passenger, James Whren, were placed under arrest. Whren sought to have the evidence suppressed, claiming that the traffic stop was unreasonable under the Fourth Amendment. There was neither probable cause nor even reasonable suspicion to believe they were engaged in drug trafficking, and the officer's claimed motive of stopping the vehicle to issue a warning about traffic violations was pretextual. Whren argued that vice officers do not make routine traffic stops, and were using the traffic stop as a pretense or pretext to conduct a criminal investigation for which they otherwise lacked reasonable suspicion.

The conviction was affirmed in the lower courts, and when the case came to the Supreme Court, a unanimous court upheld it. Justice Scalia's majority opinion ruled that the underlying motivation of the officer did not matter. If the officer has objective probable cause under the traffic code to stop a vehicle, it is sufficient for the stop. The officer's underlying motivation when a traffic stop is made is not relevant to Fourth Amendment inquiry. Nor did it matter that the officers were specifically assigned to the vice division. Traffic enforcement was not a regular part of their duties, but any law enforcement officer is legally empowered to make a traffic stop. The Court chose to ignore the claim that Whren and Brown were stopped because they were Black. Justice Scalia dismissed the claim of racial profiling by arguing that a question of racial discrimination should have been raised as an equal protection and not a Fourth Amendment issue. Yet, given the Court's holding that the motivation of the officer does not matter, it is highly unlikely that the Court would have been sympathetic to the racial profiling argument. To this date, the Court has never addressed the constitutionality of racial profiling, but by not ruling on it, the Court has implicitly permitted it. While the Court ignored the racial profiling issue, litigation in state courts and public pressure have led several state legislatures to pass laws to collect information on profiling.[9]

Whren was essential in expanding the constitutional toolbox of legal doctrines for the war on drugs. Police could stop any vehicle as long as they had objective probable cause under the traffic code. This included more than speeding. There is a wide range of extremely minor traffic offenses that provide probable cause for a traffic stop, including weaving in traffic, a broken license plate light, or even mud on a license plate. The reality is that an officer can find a reason to justify a traffic stop for any vehicle.[10] Once it is stopped, the officer can escalate the encounter into a full-blown drug investigation. If the officer suspects the driver is involved in criminal behavior, an arrest for a traffic offense then permits a *Belton* search of the passenger compartment. There does not need to be even reasonable suspicion for this search. A mere hunch that the driver is hiding something could trigger the decision to place the driver under arrest for the traffic offense and conduct the search. If the search did not yield contraband, the officer could easily opt to give the driver a ticket instead of bringing him or her in to be booked.[11]

Whren left one element unanswered. Were there limits on the types of traffic offenses for which an officer could make an arrest? The Court addressed just this issue in *Atwater v. City of Lago Vista* (2001). A police officer pulled over a woman for driving without a seat belt. In Texas, a seat-belt violation is a misdemeanor fine-offense, punishable by no more than a $50 fine. The officer placed Gail Atwater under arrest, and she was booked in the jail, appeared before a magistrate, pleaded no contest, paid the fine, and was released within an hour. She sued the city, challenging the custodial arrest, and in a 5-4 decision by Justice Souter, the Supreme Court ruled that police can arrest a person for any offense, regardless of the possible penalty. *Atwater* provided the final piece of the puzzle for police tactics in the war on drugs. Police can stop a vehicle on the pretext of a traffic violation, place the individual under arrest for the most minor of offenses, and then conduct a *Belton* search of the passenger compartment incident to arrest.

At the end of the Rehnquist Court, the decisions in *Thornton v. United States* (2004) and *Illinois v. Caballes* (2005) provided even more discretion to police. *Thornton* extended the ability to conduct a *Belton* search to those instances where the arrest occurred away from the vehicle, but where the arrestee was a recent occupant of the vehicle. Chief Justice Rehnquist's opinion did not even pretend to base the ruling on the twin rationales of search incident to arrest, which would permit a search for officer safety or to prevent the destruction of evidence. Writing in concurrence, Justice O'Connor viewed the ruling as troublesome, as she acknowledged how police had come to view *Belton* searches as "a police entitlement."[12] Justice Stevens dissented, criticizing the Court's development of vehicle search case law, anticipating his later decision in the Roberts Court case of *Arizona v. Gant* in 2009.

Illinois v. Caballes provided police with yet another tool to combat the war on drugs. Police began using trained canines to conduct drug sniffs in the 1970s. The Burger Court first addressed the question of the dog sniffs in *United States v. Place* (1983), in which a suspected drug courier's luggage was detained for 90 minutes at an airport and transported to another airport to be sniffed by a dog. The Court ruled that while the seizure was too long under *Terry v. Ohio* (1968), a shorter detention to conduct a dog sniff would not violate the Fourth Amendment. The Court based its argument on the rationale that a trained narcotics dog is unique in that it only detects contraband.[13] Because the dog does not detect other materials in which an individual might have a protected privacy interest, there is no Fourth Amendment search.

Caballes involved a traffic stop of a driver on an interstate by Illinois State Police. Roy Caballes was stopped for driving 71 MPH in a 65 MPH speed limit zone. When the stop was called in on the radio, a Drug Interdiction Team that was nearby traveled to the scene and walked the dog around the vehicle. The dog alerted on the trunk, and marijuana was found when the vehicle was searched. While the facts of the case do not provide evidence that the initial stop of the vehicle was pretextual, the government offered no reason for the drug dog to be there other than that it happened to be in the area. The Illinois Supreme Court suppressed the marijuana, claiming that a routine traffic stop had unjustifiably been transformed into a drug investigation. The state sought certiorari, and in a 5–4 decision, the Supreme Court reversed. Justice Stevens' majority opinion argued that the use of a narcotics dog that was trained to only detect illegal contraband was not a search within the meaning of the Fourth Amendment, because no one has a legitimate expectation of privacy in possessing contraband. Thus, the dog sniff did not raise any Fourth Amendment issues as long as the sniff did not unreasonably extend the length of the traffic stop. Police could use a K9 unit to conduct a drug sniff for any reason. If there was probable cause for the traffic stop, the officer was free to use his or her discretion to conduct a drug sniff. If the dog alerted to the presence of contraband, then the automobile exception's requirement of probable cause was satisfied, and a full vehicle search was permissible. Justice Souter dissented, arguing that the decision rested on a "legal fiction" of the "infallible" dog.[14] The question of a dog's reliability would be reexamined in the decision in *Florida v. Harris* (2013).

In many ways, *Caballes* and *Thornton* represented the triumph of the Rehnquist Court in terms of providing police officers with a wide range of discretion in fighting the war on drugs. If an officer had any excuse based on a violation of the traffic code, with which total compliance is almost impossible, the officer could stop a vehicle, regardless of his or her motivation. Once the car is stopped, the officer can do a plain view search of the interior of the passenger compartment. The driver can be checked for outstanding warrants and compliance with license, vehicle registration, and proof of insurance laws. A K9 unit can be brought in to conduct a drug sniff without any suspicion. The officer can talk with the driver and passengers, and if they appear nervous, as most people do when confronted by a police officer, further investigation is justified. Officers can seek consent to conduct a search. The officer can arrest an individual for any offense and then conduct a search of the passenger compartment.

This toolbox of legal doctrines for vehicle searches was institutionalized into standard procedure by many state and local police departments, with the active encouragement and participation of the federal government. Police were taught to use the discretion created by these cases to stop and detain hundreds of thousands of motorists, often based on little real information and sometimes based on little more than racial profiles. Not only did the DEA train more than 25,000 state and local law enforcement officers in these tactics, but *Police Chief* magazine, the leading professional journal for law enforcement, openly encouraged police to make wide use of what had been called investigatory stops. The magazine even began giving out an annual award to officers who made major arrests out of traffic stops. Leading training manuals fully described how to conduct investigatory stops. As was argued in a recent empirical study of racial profiling, investigatory stops were approved at the highest levels and institutionalized into a major part of the way police engage in the war on drugs.[15] Perhaps even more importantly, these tactics openly encouraged officers to act on little more than their curiosity, knowing that the traffic code provided probable cause where their hunches and suspicions did not even rise to the level of reasonable articulable suspicion. It did not matter that the hit rates of these programs were low and many more innocent persons were detained than drug dealers caught.[16] There is no evidence that these efforts caused any significant reduction in the supply of illegal drugs, but there is compelling evidence that innocent people were detained and that racial profiling occurred as young African American and Latino males were targeted at a much higher rate than Caucasians.[17] The Fourth Amendment seemed to provide little protection to anyone in a vehicle when an officer had little more than a hunch. The Supreme Court created a regime in which there are virtually no restrictions on police discretion to search and seize.[18]

Routine Highway Checkpoints

The Rehnquist Court ruled in 1990 that police could set up highway sobriety checkpoints in which every car would be stopped and the driver forced to interact with the police. The Court viewed the intrusion on individual liberty as minimal, while the state's interest in preventing drunk driving is substantial.

Michigan v. Sitz (1990) allowed the police considerable leeway to escalate these encounters should they detect evidence of any other crime. Later cases, such as *Illinois v. Lidster* (2004), were generous in allowing the officers to conduct the checkpoints and to react to driver behavior with few limits. This discretion for officers to search cars was most obvious at the border. The Court upheld the use of a series of motion sensors on back roads near the Mexican border to justify the seizure of a car in *United States v. Arvizu* (2002). While the decision was unanimous, it is significant that the investigation of the vehicle was initiated solely based on the triggering of remote sensors on dirt roads by the suspect's vehicle, something that would be much harder to justify in the interior of the country.

The Rehnquist Court also decided three cases involving suspicion-less investigations at bus stops. In *Florida v. Bostick* (1991), the Court upheld a procedure whereby police officers boarded buses stopped in bus stops in Broward County, Florida, as a matter of routine and asked passengers for permission to search their luggage. The Florida Supreme Court had ruled that Bostick was effectively seized because of the crowded nature of the situation—the police were blocking the suspect's exit and the bus was stopped for only a short time before resuming its route, virtually removing the option of exiting the bus while the police were there. The Court ruled that the suspect was not seized and that his consent was willingly given. A similar program was upheld in *United States v. Drayton* (2002). Taken together with Chief Justice Rehnquist's holding in *Ohio v. Robinette* (1996) that a suspect need not be told that he or she is free to go for consent to search to be willingly given, the bus stop investigation cases created an environment in which the police could take any encounter with a suspect and escalate it into a full investigatory stop. Police could stop to investigate almost anyone that came to their attention, and escalate that encounter into a full investigation taking hours, during which time the police could bully the suspect into giving consent to search their cars and luggage. This adds to discretionary tools available to police in the context of vehicle searches, which could easily be abused by overly zealous officers.

Drug Testing

The war on drugs extended beyond the highways to the workplace. The Reagan administration sought to stop drug use in all contexts. When policies were put in place to randomly test for drug use among employees in both public and private sector workplaces, as well as students in schools, the response of the Rehnquist Court became an important part of providing constitutional justification for policies that valued drug interdiction over personal privacy. Just as in the case of stopping the sale and use of street drugs via the criminal sanction, public sector employers were given wide latitude to drug test their employees and public schools were given power to drug test many students.[19]

The concept of state action means that private sector employers can drug test their employees as long as doing so does not contravene any state law or local ordinance and as long as doing so is not prohibited by a collective bargaining agreement. In the public sector, the concept of state action means that a mandatory drug test is potentially regulated as a search within the meaning of the Fourth Amendment. If so, then such a search would have to be tested against the legal standards applicable to administrative searches, which are less stringent than those used to evaluate Fourth Amendment claims.

The balancing test for these types of cases was established in Justice O'Connor's plurality opinion in *O'Connor v. Ortega* (1987). The test involves balancing the nature of the intrusion against the interests of the state. The issue of the permissibility of drug tests of public sector employees arose in two Rehnquist Court decisions in 1989, *Skinner v. Railway Labor Executives' Association* and *National Treasury Employees Union v. Von Raab*. While the Court in *Skinner* held that drug testing is a search within the meaning of the Fourth Amendment, it also held that there are many situations wherein drug testing of employees is allowed. Applying the *Ortega* balancing test, the Rehnquist Court ruled in *Von Raab* that employees for which there was individualized suspicion, such as a past record of drug use, can be drug tested at any time. Employees who carry guns in the course of their duties, who are involved in law enforcement activities, or who operate dangerous equipment can be drug tested at random. Others may not be tested randomly, but may be tested if there is any suspicion of drug use. Coupled with the ability of private sector employers to drug test at will, this meant that a huge percentage of public and private employees can be drug tested at the whim of their employer.

After the decisions in *Skinner* and *Von Raab*, officials in many school districts across the nation began to impose drug-testing policies on students. The standards for assessing the Fourth Amendment rights of minors in the public schools were initially established by the Burger Court in the case of *New Jersey v. T.L.O.* (1985). A decade later, the Rehnquist Court approved a drug-testing program for high school student athletes in *Veronia School District No. 47J v.*

Acton (1995). The Court was convinced that the school administration's perception that a drug problem existed was sufficient to justify the drug-testing program in question. Seven years later, in *Board of Education of Independent School District No. 92 of Pottawatomie County v. Earls* (2002), the Court expanded the scope of K-12 drug testing to include the testing of all middle school students involved in extracurricular activities, regardless of the nature of the activity. Ironically, this would mean that students involved in a student group devoted to prevention of drug abuse by students at that school would have to be drug tested to participate in that activity. The Court has not gone so far as to approve of a random drug-testing policy for all students, but the Rehnquist Court was highly receptive to efforts by public employers and schools to gather information about the drug habits of students and employees, as long as the information is to be used as part of a drug prevention program.

THE PROBLEM OF UNPROVOKED FLIGHT

Terry v. Ohio's stop and frisk doctrine mandated that all police encounters in which a person is seized, however briefly, had to be justified by reasonable articulable suspicion that wrongdoing is afoot. This was intended to allow the police to stop crimes before they happened, based on their observations of suspect behavior and their law enforcement experience, but not to allow them free rein to detain anyone they wanted. Reasonable suspicion is a considerably lower threshold than probable cause, and while the Warren Court may have intended the doctrine to place limits on the scope of police seizures, the reality was that both the Burger and Rehnquist Courts used it to expand police power to conduct investigatory stops. Two Rehnquist Court decisions involving questions of whether unprovoked flight from the police satisfies the requirement of reasonable articulable suspicion provide a nice illustration of how *Terry* was interpreted under the rationale of a jurisprudence of crime control.

Two police officers in Oakland, California, were on patrol in unmarked cars in a high-crime part of the city in August 1988. The only thing that identified them as police officers were vests with the word "POLICE" on them. They turned a corner, and saw a group of five African American youths huddled around a red car. When the youths saw the officers' car, they scattered. The officers thought that behavior was suspicious and gave chase. One suspect, a juvenile named "Hodari D.," ran down an alley. One officer got out of the patrol car and, as he came around a corner, saw Hodari emerge from an alley and drop what appeared to be a small rock. The suspect did not see the officer until he was almost upon him, when he was tackled to the ground. Hodari was handcuffed, and was found to be carrying a pager and $130 in cash. The officer recovered the rock that he discarded and identified it as crack cocaine. The defendant moved to have the evidence suppressed as the fruits of an unreasonable search. While the motion to suppress was denied, the lower appellate courts reversed and held that Hodari was unreasonably seized when he saw the officer running toward him. The California Supreme Court denied the application for appeal, and the state sought certiorari.

California v. Hodari D. (1991) hinged on the question of the exact moment at which the youth had been seized within the meaning of the Fourth Amendment. California had conceded that there was no reasonable suspicion to stop him. Justice Scalia's opinion for a 6–3 Court went to great ends to avoid suppressing the cocaine. Scalia argued that even though there was no articulable reason to stop Hodari, "that it would be unreasonable to stop for brief inquiry, young men who scatter upon mere sighting of the police is not self-evident, and contradicts proverbial common sense."[20] Scalia then drew on the Old Testament proverb "the wicked flee when no man pursueth."[21]

Scalia challenged Hodari's claim that he had been seized when the officer pursued him, by making a show of authority. If he had been seized, then the drugs were the fruit of that seizure. If they weren't, then Hodari had abandoned them, and the officer could have lawfully recovered them. The argument spins on the exact point at which Hodari was seized and the precise definition of the term "seizure" within the meaning of the Fourth Amendment. To Scalia, a seizure involves "taking possession," and Hodari was not seized until he was tackled to the ground after disobeying a show of authority to halt. The cocaine was thus abandoned prior to the seizure.

The decision is confusing and based on a legal technicality. In Justice Scalia's desire to limit when a seizure occurs, he created a large loophole for police. The lesson to be learned is that even if you do not have reasonable suspicion to stop someone, make a show of authority and hope they do not comply, and thus there will automatically be reasonable suspicion for failure to comply with a police officer's order. Justice Stevens' dissent points out the problem, arguing that according to the Court, a seizure occurs "not with egregious police conduct, but rather, with submission by the citizen."[22] This narrows the range of encounters that "come under the heading of a seizure," and means that "innocent citizens may remain secure in their persons ... against unreasonable searches and seizures" only at the discretion of the police.[23]

The Court took the argument even further in *Illinois v. Wardlow* (2000). A four-car caravan of Chicago Police was driving down a road in a high-crime area on the west side of the city. As one of the officers in the caravan passed 4035 West Van Buren, he noticed the defendant, Wardlow, standing on the corner, holding an "opaque" bag. Wardlow looked in the direction of the officers and then fled. The police turned their car around, watched Wardlow run through an alley, and then cornered him. The officer did an immediate pat-down on the rationale that "it was common for there to be weapons in the near vicinity of narcotics transactions."[24] The officer found a loaded handgun and arrested Wardlow.

Wardlow sought to have the handgun suppressed on the grounds that there was no reasonable suspicion to stop or to frisk him. The motion to suppress was denied at trial, but reversed by the Illinois Appellate Court, which held that there was no reasonable suspicion for the stop. The Illinois Supreme Court affirmed, holding that sudden flight in a high-crime area does not trigger reasonable suspicion. The Supreme Court granted certiorari, and in a 5–4 decision reversed. Justice Scalia had only grudgingly accepted the California court's concession that there was no reasonable suspicion for the stop in *California v. Hodari D.* Chief Justice Rehnquist took an entirely different position in *Wardlow*. He argued that the combination of Wardlow's presence in a high-crime area and his sudden unprovoked flight upon sight of the police was highly relevant: "Our cases have ... recognized that nervous, evasive behavior is a factor in determining reasonable suspicion. Headlong flight—wherever it occurs—is the consummate act of evasion; it is not necessarily indicative of wrong-doing, but it is certainly suggestive of such."[25] Rehnquist argued that, had Wardlow just gone about his business, there would have been no basis for reasonable suspicion. He could have ignored the police, and would not even have to cooperate by answering their questions. But he didn't. Upon sight of the police, he fled: "Unprovoked flight is simply not a mere refusal to cooperate. Flight, by its very nature, is not 'going about one's business'; in fact, it is just the opposite."[26] While Rehnquist does not go so far as to hold that unprovoked flight by itself satisfies reasonable suspicion, the additional fact that Wardlow was in a high-crime area when he fled was enough to satisfy the requirement of reasonable suspicion.

The precedent in *Wardlow* is problematic in that it does not provide any objective means to establish that the location is a high-crime area. It is a subjective determination, and the Court failed to acknowledge that there may be many valid reasons to flee from the police. Justice Stevens' dissent criticized the majority for failing to acknowledge that people may not want to interact with the police. They may not want to become a witness or to have their names affiliated with criminal events. For some minorities who reside in high-crime areas, an officer's sudden appearance might indicate that there is nearby criminal activity. They may view being near the police as dangerous, or believe that interaction with the police itself could be dangerous. Such concerns are perhaps more relevant today than they were when the Rehnquist Court decided *Wardlow* in 2000. The high-profile deaths of Michael Brown in Ferguson, Missouri, and Eric Garner in New York City, both at the hands of police officers in 2014, only served to reinforce the feeling among minority youths that the police are dangerous to them.

CORRECTIVE MEASURES

It is important to remember that not every Rehnquist Court decision expanded police power at the expense of individual rights. Twenty-five percent of the Rehnquist Court's search and seizure decisions resulted in outcomes that favored the defendant. Many of these decisions can be considered corrective measures, or cases that seek to provide a counterbalance to extreme behavior by the police. The Court's jurisprudence of crime control provides significant discretion, but it is not unlimited. There are times when the police go too far, seeking to expand police power beyond the scope of what the Court is willing to provide. In chapter 1 we described three Rehnquist Court cases that illustrated corrective measures: *Knowles v. Iowa* (1998), *Florida v. Wells* (1990), and *Wilson v. Arkansas* (1995). Each provided examples where law enforcement sought to expand police power even further than the jurisprudence of crime control permitted. The Rehnquist Court issued another 16 decisions that resulted in defendant-friendly outcomes. Many of them fit nicely under the heading of corrective measures. The error correction function was in evidence when the Court, in an opinion also written by Chief Justice Rehnquist, struck down a warrantless search of soft-sided luggage in the overhead bin of a bus in *Bond v. United States* (2000). While checking the immigration status of passengers on a bus in Texas, an officer "squeezed" a canvas bag, and determined it contained contraband. Chief Justice Rehnquist held that the physical manipulation of the passenger's bag violated his reasonable expectation of privacy in his possessions. The search exceeded the scope of the seizure, which was to identify the presence of illegal aliens. Another example is *City of Indianapolis v. Edmond* (2000), which struck down a drug roadblock as an unreasonable seizure. While *Michigan v. Sitz* permitted roadside sobriety checks, the Court would not go so far as to permit general searches for criminal activity.

Sometimes, even when the Court rules in favor of the defendant, it makes it clear that it would have preferred to rule otherwise and provides clues to law enforcement what they must do in order to survive legal challenges in future cases. A good example of this is *Florida v. J. L.* (2000), which placed limits on the application of the *Terry* doctrine by ruling that an anonymous tip by itself is not sufficient to justify a stop, but the opinion left room for the lower courts to justify the stop in its final paragraphs on the issue of what constitutes sufficient indicia of reliability for an anonymous tip. The basic doctrine is left intact, and even strengthened, by the exercise of the Court's power to limit the reach of the doctrine in certain cases. This doctrine would be used in 2014 to justify a stop based on an anonymous tip in *Navarette v. California*.

Some error correction cases can be explained by the nature of the privacy interest itself. In *Ferguson v. City of Charleston* (2001), the Court struck down a policy that mandated the drug testing of pregnant mothers at a public hospital. The personal integrity of a person's body is a key privacy right that even stringent law and order conservatives are wary of violating. The fact that the data were to be used to prosecute the mothers for child abuse of their unborn children was a key fact in the Court's analysis. In essence, the general idea that drug testing is useful and effective is retained, but the use of that power to coerce pregnant mothers to provide evidence to be used in their own prosecution goes too far. Once again, a potential abuse of power is prevented and the basic doctrine strengthened by the creation of the exception.

In *Minnesota v. Olson* (1990), the Court relied on the sanctity of the home to strike down a warrantless arrest that took place in a home where the suspect was a guest. As a guest, the defendant was entitled to vicariously enjoy the same level of protection as the homeowner. Perhaps one of the most interesting corrective measures cases decided by the Rehnquist Court was *Kyllo v.*

United States (2001). Suspecting that Danny Kyllo was growing and manufacturing marijuana, federal agents drove to his neighborhood, and used a thermal imaging device to measure the level of heat of the exterior of the home. The police suspected that the occupants of the home were using grow lamps to cultivate marijuana. The temperature data collected were used to establish probable cause for a search of the home where the police found grow lamps and marijuana plants. In *Kyllo*, the Court ruled that the use of a thermal imaging device was not within the officer's plain view, and held for the defendant. In a decision by Justice Scalia, the Court ruled that because the device was not commonly available to the general public and had the potential to reveal intimate details of the interior of the home, its use without a warrant violated the Fourth Amendment. Scalia was persuaded both by the historical significance of the home in Fourth Amendment analysis and by a refusal to let police use any technological enhancement of the senses to claim the evidence was in plain view. *Kyllo* served to place an outer limit on the expansion of the plain view doctrine, at least in the context of the home.

LIMITING THE REACH OF THE FOURTH AMENDMENT

This chapter has shown how the Rehnquist Court has interpreted the Fourth Amendment in order to expand police power to combat crime and to limit individual privacy claims under the Fourth Amendment. The jurisprudence of crime control thrived under the Rehnquist Court, and the disdain for the exclusionary rule continued. The Rehnquist Court expanded the good faith exception to include errors by court clerks in *Arizona v. Evans* (1995). The Rehnquist Court's decisions expanded police power and provided police with a powerful toolbox by which they could wage the war on drugs. The Court ignored concerns about racial profiling. With the Court under the leadership of William Rehnquist, its Fourth Amendment decisions resulted in outcomes favoring the state in more than 75 percent of cases. Rehnquist himself authored majority opinions in one-third of all of the Fourth Amendment cases decided during his time as chief justice. The foundation for crime control was laid by the Burger Court, and the Rehnquist Court's decisions served to flesh out the extent to which the Court was willing to go to empower police in their fight against drugs and crime.

The Rehnquist Court's success in solidifying the jurisprudence of crime control was not surprising. Rehnquist led a Court whose members largely shared his views on crime control. Crime was a highly salient public issue, especially in the 1980s and early 1990s. The politics of crime control shifted to a focus on crack cocaine and gang violence. Presidents Reagan and Bush both made the war on drugs a central part of their domestic policy agenda. Combating crime remained a top priority for President Bill Clinton; he sought to put 100,000 police officers on the street through his crime bill in 1994. Despite the declines in actual crime during most of the tenure of Chief Justice Rehnquist, the prospects for a continuation of the jurisprudence of crime control seemed in place when the Roberts Court began in 2005.

PART II

5. The Roberts Court in Flux

We argued in chapter 1 that to understand how the Roberts Court approaches the Fourth Amendment, it is important to first begin with the changes in the Court's composition and the evolution of the decision-making process of Justice Scalia in search and seizure cases. Scalia's voting pattern shifted dramatically. But we also argued that any assessment of the Roberts Court has to be put into the context of the jurisprudence of crime control that has shaped the meaning of the Fourth Amendment since the 1980s and was developed early in the Burger Court. Crime control still sets the foundation of the Roberts Court decision making, not only affecting those cases where the state is likely to prevail, but limiting the application of cases where defendants win as well. It sets the starting point for evaluating Fourth Amendment issues. It also helps explain many of the prodefendant outcomes that the Court has handed down. Many of these decisions do not establish broad new individual rights, but instead seek to curb the excesses of the crime control model. While the Court has provided police with substantial discretion in their decisions, law enforcement sometimes seeks to go even further, pushing the system out of balance. Corrective measure cases serve to rein in the system, and ultimately provide accountability by not letting the police go too far. Finally, we argued that a small set of highly salient issues involving information technology is creating further tensions on the Court, and forcing the justices to reevaluate issues that long seemed settled.

After a decade of Roberts Court cases on search and seizure, it is fair to say that the early expectations of an uneventful continuation of the jurisprudence of crime control have not panned out quite as anticipated. In what follows, we provide an overview of the Roberts Court's Fourth Amendment case law, consider how Justice Scalia's decision making shifted and look in particular at two key cases, *United States v. Jones* (2012) and *Riley v. California* (2014). These cases illustrate how technology is forcing the Court to take a fresh look at the Fourth Amendment. We address in chapter 6 the hold that the jurisprudence of crime control still has on many Fourth Amendment issues, and consider in chapter 7 how corrective measures help explain many prodefendant decisions. Finally, in chapter 8 we will look toward the future and examine some of the issues that are likely to come to the Court in the next decade.

THE COMPOSITION OF THE COURT

The membership of the Rehnquist Court had remained constant for 11 years after Stephen Breyer was appointed in 1994. That long period of continuity came to an end in the summer of 2005. Chief Justice Rehnquist had been diagnosed with thyroid cancer in 2004, and missed oral argument in 44 cases during the 2004 term. It was widely expected that he would retire after the end of the term. In a surprise move, however, it was Justice Sandra Day O'Connor who announced her retirement to care for her ailing husband. Rehnquist was silent on his plans. While O'Connor's retirement was not completely unexpected, it was assumed that only one of the two justices would retire. O'Connor's announcement provided President George W. Bush with his first appointment, and he chose Judge John Roberts, a former clerk of Chief Justice Rehnquist, and a Reagan-era counsel in the Department of Justice who had been appointed to the United States Court of Appeals for the DC Circuit two years earlier. Before the Senate could conduct its confirmation hearings, there was more change. Chief Justice Rehnquist passed away. Bush almost immediately decided to withdraw Roberts' nomination as associate justice, and renominated him as chief justice. While there was some opposition to Roberts on ideological grounds, Democrats were unable to muster significant votes to oppose the amiable and well-qualified jurist. The Roberts Court had begun.

President Bush waited until after Roberts was confirmed before naming his choice for the O'Connor seat. His first choice, White House counsel and close personal friend Harriet Miers, was met with bipartisan disapproval in the Senate, primarily over questions about her legal credentials and fitness for the position of an associate justice. Many conservative interest groups, who saw her as insufficiently conservative, also opposed Miers' confirmation.[1] Miers withdrew her nomination, and three days later the president named Third Circuit judge Samuel Alito as his nominee. Alito had served as assistant solicitor general in the Reagan administration for four years before being appointed to the court of appeals in 1990. Like Roberts, Alito's legal credentials were impeccable, and he was very much acceptable to the conservative groups who so closely monitor judicial appointments. His nomination was met with criticism from Democrats who viewed Alito as a hard-line conservative in the mold of Judge Robert Bork, but the Senate narrowly confirmed him in January 2006.

Early Expectations

There was little expectation from legal scholars that the Roberts Court would differ significantly from the Rehnquist Court, at least as it approached criminal procedure issues. The two new justices appointed by President Bush both had stellar conservative credentials, and their appointments generally resulted in maintaining the status quo, with conservative judges filling the seats of conservative judges. Indeed, the results from the first five years of the Roberts Court were very much a continuation of the crime control jurisprudence that had dominated the Burger and Rehnquist Courts.

Prior to the appointments of Justices Sotomayor and Kagan, the Roberts Court's decisions were a virtual mirror reflection of the Rehnquist Court's Fourth Amendment decisions. The state won in 73 percent of cases from 2005 through 2010, losing in just four cases. While the early Roberts Court decided some important prodefendant cases, such as *Arizona v. Gant* (2009), *Georgia v. Randolph* (2006), and *Safford Unified School District v. Redding* (2009), those cases were the outliers. The Court expanded the good faith exception to the exclusionary rule and they decided two cases strengthening the exigent circumstance exception for entry to a home, and, while Rehnquist and O'Connor were gone, it made little difference in terms of case outcomes. The jurisprudence of crime control was still in ascendance.

New Faces and Unexpected Change

More change came to the Roberts Court in the spring of 2009, when Justice David Souter unexpectedly announced his resignation. Souter had carved out a place for himself as a moderate on the Rehnquist Court. An intensely shy person, Souter never liked being in Washington, DC, and wanted to return home to New Hampshire. His retirement provided the new Democratic president, Barack Obama, with his first nominee. President Obama's choice was only the third woman to serve on the Court and the first justice of Hispanic origin. Sonia Sotomayor had served as a judge on the United States District Court for six years before being appointed to the United States Court of Appeals for the Second Circuit in 1997. A year later, Justice John Paul Stevens, the longest-serving member of the Court, announced his retirement. This time, President Obama selected his solicitor general, Elena Kagan, the former dean of Harvard Law School. Both Sotomayor and Kagan were confirmed despite earning only a handful of Republican votes, creating a Court with three women on it for the first time.

The appointments of Justices Sotomayor and Kagan, as well as the shifting views of Justice Scalia, have resulted in a very different Roberts Court in its second five years. Since the 2010 term, the state has won in only 53 percent of search and seizure cases, with defendants winning 47 percent of the time. Defendants have had favorable rulings in 10 of 21 decisions. The Court has handed down sweeping endorsements of digital privacy. Three cases have placed limits on the use of K9 narcotic sniffs. The Court has banned the use of warrantless surveillance techniques using GPS technology, and held that the placement of a "satellite-based monitoring" device on a sex offender who has served his sentence is a search. It has ruled that the inevitable dissipation of blood alcohol evidence of a possible DUI suspect is not an exigent circumstance that would justify a forced blood draw. Yet, the Court has also ruled that arrestees' DNA can be collected without a warrant, it has expanded the exigent circumstances doctrine for warrantless entry into a home, it narrowed third-party consent objections, and it held that reasonable suspicion is satisfied by little more than an anonymous 911 call. For the first time since the 1970s, the Fourth Amendment appears to be in a state of flux and uncertainty.

AN OVERVIEW OF THE ROBERTS COURT'S FOURTH AMENDMENT JURISPRUDENCE

The Roberts Court decided 15 Fourth Amendment cases in its first five years, 11 of which favored the state. *Brigham City v. Stuart* (2006) reinforced the emergency assistance exception for exigent circumstances to permit warrantless entry into the home. *United States v. Grubbs* (2006) upheld the use of anticipatory warrants, in which the particularity of when the warrant could be executed was based on the presence of a "triggering condition" that determined whether there was likely to be probable cause of evidence being present. The knock and announce rule to enter a home was weakened in *Hudson v. Michigan* (2006). In this case, police announced their presence, but waited only three to five seconds before entering. Justice Scalia argued that while this was technically a violation of the Fourth Amendment, it did not rise to the level that justified use of the exclusionary rule.

Scott v. Harris (2007) involved a high-speed chase case where the defendant was paralyzed after being run off the road by police. The Court rejected the claim of excessive force due to the fact that Timothy Scott initiated the chase by not complying with the police request to pull over. A civil case arising over the execution of a search warrant where the targets of the warrant had moved out three months earlier resulted in a per curiam decision in *Los Angeles County v. Rettele* (2007). The Court held that the resulting search was reasonable even though the new residents were dragged out of their bed naked. It did not matter that the two individuals were of a different race than the African American individuals the search warrant was aimed at, as the Court opined that the police did not know if the subjects of the search were elsewhere in the house. In *Virginia v. Moore* (2008), the Court considered the legality of a search incident to arrest after police arrested the defendant for a traffic offense for which state law only permitted a citation. The Court held that, as in *Atwater v. City of Lago Vista* (2001), probable cause of a traffic violation is all that is needed to make an arrest.

Perhaps the strongest statement reinforcing the jurisprudence of crime control came in *Herring v. United States* (2009), which considered whether the good faith exception to the exclusionary rule applied to data entry errors created by civilian law enforcement personnel. The Sheriff's Office staff failed to remove an expired warrant from the database, and Bennie Dean Herring was arrested on the invalid warrant and further contraband was found. As in *Arizona v. Evans* (1995), and *United States v. Leon* (1984) before it, the Court reiterated that the sole purpose of the exclusionary rule was to deter illegal police misconduct. Chief Justice Roberts went even further in *Herring*, claiming that the exclusionary rule was "the last resort." The end result was a strong statement to lower courts that the exclusionary rule was to be used sparingly.

There were four prodefendant cases in the first five years of the Roberts Court. *Georgia v. Randolph* was an early decision that saw the Court stepping away from its decision in 1990 in *Illinois v. Rodriguez*, by holding that the withholding of consent to search by a resident of a home served to override the consent of a cotenant who was willing to permit a search. The next term, the Court held in *Brendlin v. California* (2007) that a passenger in a traffic stop was seized, and thus could challenge the constitutionality of the seizure. *Safford Unified School District v. Redding* involved a student strip search done by a school administrator. The Court ruled that a warrantless search of this nature was unconstitutional, but used qualified immunity to hold the principal and school free from liability in the suit. Finally, the decision in *Arizona v. Gant* in 2009 was probably the most significant Roberts Court decision in potentially challenging one of the foundational doctrines used in the war on drugs. In contrast to the three other liberal cases decided in the first five years of the Roberts Court, *Gant* represents a significant departure from existing precedent, modifying the *New York v. Belton* (1981) bright line rule, which permitted searches of vehicle passenger compartments incident to arrest.

Gant initially sent shock waves throughout law enforcement, and was the first decision to suggest some possible changes in the Court's approach to the Fourth Amendment.[2] The suggestions of major change did not come to fruition, as the Court proceeded to hand down two strong crime control decisions later in the same term. In addition to *Herring*, the Court's decision in *Arizona v. Johnson* (2009) upheld the frisk of the passenger of a vehicle that was the subject of a traffic stop. *City of Ontario v. Quon* (2010) ruled that a search by a police department of an officer's pager messages did not violate the Fourth Amendment. *Davis v. United States* (2011) held that *Arizona v. Gant* did not apply retroactively to searches that were done prior to the *Gant* decision, but that were still under appellate review. The Court decided three exigent circumstances cases in 2010 and 2011. In addition to per curiam decisions in *Michigan v. Fisher* (2010) and *Ryburn v. Huff* (2011), the Court's decision in *Kentucky v. King* (2011) expanded the exigent circumstance exception by largely ignoring the existing rule that when entering a home without a warrant due to an exigency, that exigency cannot be created by the actions of the police themselves.

The Effects of New Faces

Things began to change after Justices Sotomayor and Kagan arrived on the Court. Perhaps the biggest surprise was the decision in *United States v. Jones*, which held that police needed a warrant prior to installing a GPS tracking device to conduct surveillance of a vehicle. Not only did the Court reverse course from the two Burger Court precedents that had been widely used by lower courts to justify GPS surveillance, but the decision garnered the support of all nine justices. Equally surprising was the majority opinion by Justice Scalia, which resurrected the trespass doctrine from *Olmstead v. United States* (1928) to determine whether a Fourth Amendment violation occurred. The next term, in *Florida v. Jardines* (2013), Scalia used the trespass doctrine again, this time to invalidate the use of a K9 dog sniff at the front step of a home. In *Florida v. Harris* (2013), the Court held that the reliability of a drug-sniffing dog could be challenged. That same term saw two additional prodefendant decisions. *Missouri v. McNeely* held that a warrantless blood draw of someone suspected of DUI was not justified as an exigency even though blood alcohol evidence inevitably dissipates with the passage of time. Justice Kennedy's opinion in *Bailey a.k.a. Polo v. United States* (2013) ruled that the detention of a suspect during the execution of a search warrant does not extend beyond the immediate vicinity of the place to be searched. Yet, that same term, Kennedy also wrote for a 5–4 majority in *Maryland v. King* (2013), holding that police can collect a DNA sample of arrestees at the time of the arrest.

The 2013 term saw further challenges to the crime control approach. The most salient decision was the Court's unanimous ruling in *Riley v. California* that police needed a warrant to search the content of a smartphone seized incident to arrest. Chief Justice Roberts wrote for eight justices, with a brief concurrence by Justice Alito. The Court also decided two traditional crime control–oriented decisions the same term. *Navarette v. California* (2014) held that an anonymous tip to a 911-dispatch center was sufficient to establish reasonable suspicion to stop a vehicle. *Fernandez v. California* (2014) narrowed the holding of the 2006 decision in *Georgia v. Randolph*, by arguing that for a cotenant to object to a consent search, he or she had to be physically present at the location of the search. The Court was not persuaded by the fact that the only reason Fernandez was not present was because he had been arrested and removed from the scene by the police. The Court also split on two issues of qualified immunity in *Stanton v. Sims* (2013) and *Tolan v. Cotton* (2014).

The 2014 term had an additional six cases. *Rodriguez v. United States* (2015) considered whether the length of a traffic stop could be extended to conduct a K9 dog sniff. Justice Sotomayor wrote for a 6–3 Court that once a citation was issued, the traffic stop was over, and a K9 sniff could not extend beyond the length of the seizure. In a per curiam opinion, the Court held in *Grady v. North Carolina* (2015) that the state conducts a search when it attaches a surveillance device to a person's body (an ankle monitor) without their consent to track their movement if they are no longer under correctional supervision. *Heien v. North Carolina* (2015) held that even though an officer misunderstood the applicable law when he made a traffic stop, the stop was still reasonable. *City of Los Angeles v. Patel* (2015) ruled that a Los Angeles municipal ordinance that required hotel operators to turn over guest registry information to police without a warrant was facially invalid under the Fourth Amendment because it did not provide an opportunity for review by a neutral magistrate prior to the release of the information. Two qualified immunity cases upheld the protections of government actors from civil liability. In *San Francisco v. Sheehan* (2015), the Court held that police officers that enter the room of a mentally ill suspect without a warrant are shielded from liability. Likewise, in *Carroll v. Carman* (2014) the Court ruled that a lower court was in error when it held that an officer wrongfully entered a home.

What is clear from this brief overview is that the Court's Fourth Amendment decisions since 2011 look a lot different from those before it. Of the cases decided in the past five years, 47 percent have been rulings for the defendant. The two most salient cases, *United States v. Jones* and *Riley v. California*, saw all nine justices agreeing with the outcome. Justice Scalia was in the majority in all but 1 of the 10 prodefendant rulings, and was joined in each case by Justices Ginsburg, Sotomayor, and Kagan. Fifth votes came from Justice Thomas in one case, Breyer and Roberts in two cases, and Kennedy in three cases. A strong case can be made that the Court truly is in flux, with four solid votes for Fourth Amendment rights and a shifting group of justices who may or may not provide a fifth vote for a majority. Justice Alito, to the contrary, is the most consistently conservative jurist, voting for the majority in only the GPS and cell phone cases, but still writing a separate concurring opinion in both, and dissenting in all other prodefendant decisions. Justice Breyer's and Justice Kennedy's voting records have been fairly consistent throughout their careers. This was not true for Justice Scalia, who made a fairly profound shift to the Left. It is to his place in the Roberts Court that we now turn.

THE IDIOSYNCRATIC EVOLUTION OF JUSTICE SCALIA

Justice Antonin Scalia was one of the most vocal members of the Supreme Court since his appointment by Ronald Reagan in 1986. Scalia considered himself the intellectual leader of the Court's conservative bloc, and was its most provocative writer. His opinions varied from highly technical and succinct majority opinions, to dissents that were often extremely personal, mean, and caustic attacks on the Court's reasoning.[3] During his tenure on the Rehnquist Court, Scalia was a consistent, reliable conservative who voted for the state in

79 percent of search and seizure cases. Scalia authored 10 majority opinions in search and seizure cases on the Rehnquist Court, only three of which were favorable to the defendant. His major decisions included *Whren v. United States* (2006), which held that an officer's underlying motivation for a traffic stop is irrelevant to the Fourth Amendment as long as he has objective probable cause for a traffic stop. In *Wyoming v. Houghton* (1999), Scalia wrote that if officers had probable cause under the automobile exception to search a car, they could search the belongings of a passenger. In *Illinois v. Rodriguez* (1990) Scalia held that police did not have to be correct in assessing whether an individual had common authority over a property to justify a consent search; they merely had to show that it was reasonable for the officer to believe they did. His opinion in *California v. Hodari D.* (1991) held that a show of authority for someone to stop is not enough to constitute a seizure under the Fourth Amendment. It is only when the individual is physically stopped that he or she is seized. This reasoning allowed the Court to uphold the seizure of crack cocaine that had been tossed away by the defendant while being pursued by the police. *Kyllo v. United States* (2001) was probably his most important prodefendant decision, where he held that the use of a thermal visioning imager to detect heat through the walls of a home violated Kyllo's privacy rights.

Scalia's voting pattern in the first five years of the Roberts Court continued on the same trajectory, siding with the state's position in 80 percent of cases. Scalia joined the majority in three of the four cases that favored the defendant. He played a pivotal role in *Arizona v. Gant*, providing a fifth vote for the defendant in a case that modified the law of search incident to arrest, but also forcing his more liberal colleagues to agree that the search incident to arrest doctrine allows such searches when the police have reason to believe that evidence of the crime of arrest will be found. He dissented from the Court's liberal outcome in *Georgia v. Randolph*, which held that a cotenant could object to and override the consent for a search provided by another tenant. Scalia authored four majority opinions and two concurrences, including his concurrence in *Gant*.

Scalia looked like an entirely different justice in the second five years of the Roberts Court. There have been 21 search and seizure cases since the October 2010 term, and Scalia voted for the defendant in 11 of them. He went from voting for the state in 80 percent of cases from the beginning of his career until 2010 to 43 percent in the most recent five years. Scalia authored majority opinions in *United States v. Jones* and *Florida v. Jardines*, using the revived trespass doctrine to prohibit warrantless GPS surveillance and the use of K9 narcotics sniffs at the front step of a home. He joined the majority in the two other K9 cases, *Florida v. Harris* and *Rodriguez v. United States*. Scalia joined the majority in *Riley v. California*, the potentially landmark decision prohibiting warrantless searches of smartphones. He wrote stinging dissents against the conservative rulings in *Maryland v. King*, which permitted police to collect DNA samples of arrestees, and *Navarette v. California*, which held that reasonable suspicion for a traffic stop was merited by an anonymous 911 call. In the latter case, he attacked the logic of his longtime judicial ally Clarence Thomas.

How do we explain the shift of Justice Scalia? His decision in *United States v. Jones* is instructive. Scalia chose not to use the *Katz* reasonable expectation of privacy standard, and instead based his argument on the older and largely discredited trespass doctrine. Scalia had long been a proponent of originalism as a method of constitutional interpretation. For an originalist, the intentions of those who authored the text are paramount, especially when the text is unclear or admits of multiple interpretations.[4] Many of Scalia's Fourth Amendment opinions make reference to the views of the Framers of the Constitution and the historical context of the Fourth Amendment when it was first ratified. Yet, before his opinion in *Jones*, originalism only seemed to play a minor role in most of his search and seizure opinions. His opinions were normally driven by extensive reference to the precedents that the Court had developed in the prior 40 years. He might not have liked the *Katz* precedent, but he still used it. In *Jones*, however, he chose to resurrect the trespass doctrine, ignoring that it had been explicitly overruled by the Court in *Katz*. The dramatic change in approach in *Jones* may have very well marked a turning point in his approach to the Fourth Amendment.

TECHNOLOGY AND A COURT IN FLUX

New justices and a new approach to the Fourth Amendment by Justice Scalia came together in ways that contributed to the shift that occurred in the Roberts Court. Yet, it is unlikely that those changes by themselves are enough to truly unsettle the Court's approach to the Fourth Amendment. But in the past several years, the Court has been forced to consider a pair of decisions involving the application of information technology to law enforcement's efforts to fight crime. These cases resonate deeply with the American public, and have injected questions about the approach the Court has taken in Fourth Amendment cases since the 1980s. The decisions in *United States v. Jones* and *Riley v. California* illustrate not only how the Court is changing, but more importantly, raise questions for the future.

United States v. Jones *and Warrantless GPS Surveillance*

The use of technology to assist in surveillance has had a long history. We explored some of that history in chapter 2, beginning with *Olmstead v. United States*, where the Court ruled that wiretapping did not rise to the level of an unreasonable search because there was no physical intrusion into a constitutionally protected area. The Court, 40 years later, overruled the trespass doctrine in *Katz v. United States* (1967), replacing it with the reasonable expectation of privacy standard for determining whether government action constitutes a search. As we saw in chapter 3, the Burger Court used the *Katz* standard in more than 40 cases, although within the framework of a jurisprudence of crime control, it was rarely willing to acknowledge an individual's subjective expectation of privacy as meeting the requirement that it be one that society is willing to recognize as legitimate.

The Court heard two cases involving the use of radio transmitters placed on vehicles as a way of conducting surveillance in the early 1980s.[5] Radio beepers were used to track both defendants' whereabouts and provided key evidence used at trial. Justice Rehnquist's opinion in *United States v. Knotts* (1983) found no Fourth Amendment violation. The beeper simply enhanced the vision of the police, in conducting surveillance on public roads and highways: "One has a lesser expectation of privacy in a motor vehicle because its function is transportation and it seldom serves as one's residence or as the repository of personal effects. A car has little capacity for escaping public scrutiny. It travels public thoroughfares where both its occupants and its contents are in plain view."[6] There was no reasonable expectation of privacy.

The precedents in *Knotts* and *United States v. Karo* (1984) gave police a free hand in utilizing radio transmitters to conduct warrantless surveillance of vehicles. Over time, the same logic was extended to newer, more powerful technology. The military had installed "Global Positioning Satellites" in orbit beginning in 1973, which provided the military with pinpoint navigation information. In the late 1990s, the military opened up the system to law enforcement and later to civilian use. Today, GPS technology is widely used. It is embedded in all cellular phones, people use the technology in their cars, athletes use them in watches to plot distance and speeds, hikers use them in place of maps, and location-aware search engines customize search results with them. GPS technology is ubiquitous. But while civilian usage of GPS usually is for navigation, the technology can be utilized to log location, and police have found it an extremely effective tool for conducting surveillance. Unlike with a radio transmitter, which requires an officer to remain in radio contact with the beeper, with GPS, detectives have 24/7 data on the location of the suspect, limited only by the battery life of the device.

The first federal court to address the constitutionality of warrantless GPS surveillance came in 1999, and drew on the precedent from *Knotts* to uphold GPS surveillance.[7] In the next decade, another 24 federal and state courts upheld GPS surveillance. Most of these courts seemed to accept wholesale the limited expectation of privacy in the automobile, ignoring personal privacy concerns. There were exceptions. In 2003, the Washington Supreme Court ruled that the use of a GPS device to track a suspect's vehicle was not merely a way to augment the senses of officers as they follow a vehicle on the public streets, and held that the state constitution requires a search warrant before employing a GPS to conduct surveillance.[8] In 2009, the New York Court of Appeals decided *People v. Weaver*, ruling that GPS surveillance violated a state constitution–based privacy interest.[9] The next year, the United States Court of Appeals for the DC Circuit handed down *United States v. Maynard*,[10] and was the first federal appellate court to hold that warrantless GPS surveillance violated the Fourth Amendment. This case would come to the Supreme Court under the name of *United States v. Jones*.

The *Jones* case began seven years earlier, when a joint task force of the Drug Enforcement Agency and Washington, DC, Metropolitan Police began investigating nightclub owner Antoine Jones, who was suspected of trafficking in cocaine. Agents used a fixed camera near his nightclub, obtained pen register data of his cell phone, and engaged in visual surveillance. They sought and received a warrant to install a GPS tracking device on his vehicle. For unspecified reasons, the warrant was not executed until after it had expired, and the device was installed while the vehicle was not in the District of Columbia, but in Maryland. As a result, the courts treated the case as if the installation of the device was warrantless. Jones' vehicle was tracked to a house in Maryland, where they believed he was going to receive a large shipment of cocaine. A search warrant was issued for the house, and agents recovered 97 kilograms of cocaine, $70,000, as well as a variety of drug paraphernalia. Jones was arrested and sought to have the data from the GPS suppressed as the fruits of an unreasonable, warrantless search. The district court denied the motion. Jones appealed his conviction to the DC Circuit, which, for the first time, ruled that the use of GPS was a search and, in distinguishing the case from *Knotts*, held that Jones had a reasonable expectation of privacy in the movements of his vehicle over the course of a month, because he had not exposed the totality of those movements to the public.

United States v. Jones garnered national attention, even before the court of appeals decision, with the *New York Times* writing an editorial on the privacy issues it raised in 2009 and a second editorial after the court of appeals panel ruled.[11] A third editorial urged the Supreme Court to recognize the privacy interest prior to oral argument.[12] The case gained even more attention when *Gizmodo*, a popular technology blog, ran a story about a man in California who discovered an FBI tracking device on the underside of his car when he brought it in for repairs.[13] Compared with most criminal justice cases, the GPS case was highly salient. Even though the use of GPS was to combat crime and fight the war on drugs, something about the issue resonated with people.

The Supreme Court decided *United States v. Jones* in January 2012, in a ruling in which all nine justices agreed that the use of GPS required a warrant. While unanimous in the outcome, the Court was splintered into three camps. Justice Scalia wrote the opinion of the Court, joined by Justice Kennedy, Justice Thomas, and Chief Justice Roberts. Scalia held that the placement of the GPS device on the vehicle itself was a trespass against Jones' property. As such, it was an unreasonable search within the meaning of the Fourth Amendment. Justice Alito, joined by Justices Kagan, Ginsburg, and Breyer, concurred in the outcome but argued that it was unconstitutional under *Katz*'s reasonable expectation of privacy standard. Justice Sotomayor provided a fifth vote for Scalia's majority opinion, writing a concurrence in which she agreed with Scalia that the placement of the GPS device on the vehicle was a violation of the Fourth Amendment, but made an argument that was more in line with Justice Alito's concurrence.

Justice Scalia had long been critical of the reasonable expectation of privacy standard from *Katz*, because he thought that the argument was circular and highly dependent on whether there were five justices who believed that there was an expectation of privacy in any particular case. Yet, he relied on *Katz* in his prodefendant ruling in *Kyllo v. United States*, which held that the use of a thermal visioning imager violated the Fourth Amendment. In *Jones*, however, Scalia managed to convince a majority to go along with a different, much older approach to the Fourth Amendment. Scalia argued that the Fourth Amendment protects persons, houses, papers, and effects. A vehicle is an effect within the meaning of the Fourth Amendment. When the government put a tracking device on the car, it was a physical intrusion on that effect. In Scalia's view, this action would have constituted a trespass at the time of the Founding, thus making it an illegal search. Scalia's opinion ignored the fact that Justice Stewart had explicitly overruled the trespass doctrine in *Katz*, and assumed that it had been good law since first articulated in *Olmstead*. For Scalia, *Katz* was merely a deviation "from that exclusively property-based approach" that was the traditional understanding of the Fourth Amendment. Scalia argued that Fourth Amendment rights do not rise or fall with the *Katz* formulation. When government physically intrudes on a constitutionally protected area, a search has occurred. At bottom we have to preserve the degree of protection afforded to the Fourth Amendment at the Founding: "Where, as here, the Government obtains information by physically intruding on a constitutionally protected area, such a search has undoubtedly occurred."[14]

Justice Alito's concurrence argued that *Katz* was the appropriate way to resolve the case. He focused on the shortcomings of Justice Scalia's approach and criticized him for deciding the case on principles of "18th century tort law." Alito failed to see how Scalia's approach was any different from the discredited precedent from *Olmstead*. Alito also questioned how the mere placement of GPS on the car was a search, since Scalia's opinion did not overrule the holding in *Knotts* that the use of a "surreptitiously planted electronic device to monitor a vehicle's movements on public roads did not amount to a search."[15] He voiced concern with why under the Scalia test, even short-term GPS surveillance is a problem, but long-term surveillance by automobile or airplane isn't. Alito also pointed out that the trespass doctrine would not protect privacy interests when surveillance is carried out by electronic means that do not involve a physical intrusion, such as a factory-installed theft detection system. In the end, Alito argued that there may be a privacy-convenience trade-off, where Americans sacrifice some of their privacy for the convenience offered by technology, and suggested that these issues should be resolved by the legislature and not the courts.

This left Justice Sotomayor as the swing justice. She could provide a fifth vote for the trespass doctrine, or take the more traditional reasonable expectation of privacy approach and join Alito. She chose to split the difference, providing Scalia with the fifth vote he needed for a majority, but did so in an opinion in which she is much more sympathetic to a citizen's expectations of privacy. Sotomayor agreed to join the Court's opinion because "a search within the meaning of the Fourth Amendment occurs at a minimum, where as here, the Government obtains information by physically intruding on a constitutionally protected area."[16] But she argued that the Fourth Amendment is not solely concerned with physical intrusions on property, and accepted wholeheartedly the *Katz* rationale of a reasonable expectation of privacy. Sotomayor did not join Alito, however, because she believed that he discounted the relevance of the physical intrusion. The Fourth Amendment may protect both people and places. The Scalia position creates a "constitutional minimum." When government invades personal property to gather information, a search occurs.

Sotomayor's concurrence made a strong case to go further. She shared Alito's concerns about how physical intrusion is not necessary for a lot of surveillance, which can be done by factory-installed GPS or GPS-enabled smartphones. Scalia's test is narrow, and utilizing it as the sole basis for a search would impinge on societal expectations of privacy. Sotomayor made a strong case for digital privacy: "I would ask whether people reasonably expect that their movements will be recorded and aggregated in a manner that enables the Government to ascertain, more or less at will, their political and religious beliefs, sexual habits, and so on."[17] She continued by arguing, "Owners of GPS-equipped cars and smartphones do not contemplate that these devices will be used to enable covert surveillance of their movements."[18] And then, she suggested that "more fundamentally, it may be necessary to reconsider the premise that an individual has no reasonable expectation of privacy in information voluntarily disclosed to third parties." Sotomayor specifically referred to *United States v. Miller* (1976) and *Smith v. Maryland* (1979), the bank and telephone records cases:

> This approach is ill suited to the digital age, in which people reveal a great deal of information about themselves to third parties in the course of carrying out mundane tasks. People disclose the phone numbers that they dial or text to their cellular providers, the URLs that they visit and the email addresses with which they correspond to their Internet service providers, and the books, groceries, and medications they purchase to online retailers.[19]

Sotomayor challenged Justice Alito's claim that people find the trade-off of privacy for convenience worthwhile, and she "doubts that people would accept without complaint the warrantless disclosure to the Government of a list of every Web site they had visited in the last week, or month, or year."[20]

In many ways, *United States v. Jones* illustrates competing visions for the Fourth Amendment. Justice Scalia became a champion of Fourth Amendment rights, but in a narrow way, defined by his unique brand of originalism. The trespass doctrine protects against some governmental actions, but may permit many other governmental invasions of privacy. Justice Alito claims to rely on *Katz*, but his commitment to privacy is suspect, as he suggests that if the GPS tracker were used for a day or two, the intrusion on privacy might be minimal. Justice Sotomayor wants the full-fledged understanding of the Fourth Amendment as protecting privacy, while accepting a minimal baseline of physical intrusions. Her criticisms open the door to the Court reconsidering the third party doctrine, something that must be done in order to resolve the inevitable cases questioning the use of data from cell phone service providers to track the location of suspects.

Justice Scalia's trespass doctrine has been used twice since the decision in *Jones*. In *Florida v. Jardines*, Scalia wrote for a 5–4 majority that a K9 sniff couldn't be done on the front step of a home. The use of the dog is a physical intrusion into the curtilage of the home, a constitutionally protected area. In 2015, the Court handed down *Grady v. North Carolina*, a per curiam opinion, likely written by Scalia, where the Court held that the use of an ankle bracelet to track the location of a sex offender was a search, due to the fact that it was a physical intrusion on a constitutionally protected area—the person of the defendant. But the Court remanded the case back to the lower court to determine if it was a reasonable search. Yet, ironically, the trespass doctrine was not mentioned once, neither in the opinion of the Court, nor in two hours of oral argument, in the single most salient case the Roberts Court has decided on search and seizure, the *Riley v. California* ruling requiring a warrant to search a cell phone incident to arrest.

Riley v. California: *A Sweeping Endorsement of Digital Privacy*

We began this book with a description of the facts of *Riley v. California*, contrasting the decision with the Court's ruling in *Maryland v. King*. Riley held that police needed a warrant to search a cell phone incident to arrest, whereas in *Maryland v. King*, there is no privacy interest preventing police from collecting DNA samples from arrestees to create a database to be used in other cases. The two decisions illustrated the tension implicit in Fourth Amendment analysis today. In many ways, *Riley* was a far bigger test for the future of Fourth Amendment privacy analysis than *Jones*. Cell phones, and smartphones in particular, are an essential part of everyday life in the twenty-first century. Police searches of phones are not limited to just identifying a list of numbers called, and can potentially include the content of text messages, photographs, emails, videos, Internet search histories, and more. Perhaps most importantly, while the police place GPS devices only on the vehicles of people they have reason to believe are engaged in criminal behavior, criminals and law-abiding citizens alike carry cell phones. Therefore, protecting the rights of the criminal defendants with regard to their cell phones serves the interest of protecting the privacy of millions of innocent citizens in ways that few other types of cases can.

The search incident to arrest doctrine permits a search of the arrestee's person and the area within their immediate control. In recent years, police had made it common practice in conducting such searches to scroll through the content of cell phones that were on the persons of arrestees, particularly in drug cases. The combined cases of *Riley v. California* and *United States v. Wurie* involved just that scenario. David Riley was stopped for a minor traffic violation. He was arrested for driving under a suspended license. His car was impounded, and an inventory search uncovered guns. A search of his person incident to arrest included his Samsung smartphone, which uncovered evidence of gang activity in his text messages, pictures, and videos. Brima Wurie was arrested after police observed him engaged in a drug deal. Police searched his cell phone, a more traditional "flip phone," and scrolled through his call log, and saw numerous calls to "my house." The officer identified the number, traced it to Wurie's apartment, and obtained a search warrant for the apartment, where drugs were found. Both cases raised the question of whether a search of the cell phone incident to arrest was a violation of the Fourth Amendment. Riley's motion to suppress was denied, and his conviction was affirmed on appeal. Wurie's motion to suppress was also denied, but unlike Riley's, his appeal to the court of appeals was successful.

In many ways, the decision to hear the two cell phone cases sent a signal that the Court was willing to take the next step and flesh out some of the unanswered questions raised by *Jones*. The direction the Court would take, however, remained uncertain. There were several possible outcomes. The Court could follow Justice Scalia's lead from *Jones* and apply the trespass doctrine. One could argue that the cell phone is a personal effect, and that a government search of it would be a physical intrusion of it. Or the Court could take the approach of Justices Sotomayor and Alito, arguing that the search violated a reasonable expectation of privacy. A third option was that the Court could rely on the most recent search incident to arrest decision, *Arizona v. Gant*, and extend Justice Scalia's "further evidence of the crime of arrest" standard to cell phones. This would condition cell phone searches on the basis of the crime of arrest. In fact, Scalia suggested this last option during oral argument. But the oral arguments also revealed that the justices were very leery of the way a pro–crime control decision would be viewed, and several justices went out of their way to try to show their familiarity with smartphones and the use of "cloud" storage for personal information.

In the end, the Court handed down a decision in which all nine justices agreed that a warrantless search of a cell phone was not permitted incident to arrest. The phone could be seized, but not searched without a warrant. Unlike in *Jones*, however, there were just two opinions. Chief Justice Roberts wrote the opinion of the Court and was joined by all of the justices except Justice Alito, who wrote a brief concurrence. The chief justice's opinion did not rely on the trespass doctrine, the *Katz* reasonable expectation of privacy standard, or *Arizona v. Gant*. Instead, Roberts wrote an opinion that can only be described as a sweeping endorsement of digital privacy.

The chief justice considered, and rejected, each of the government's arguments that the search of a cell phone was akin to a search of a wallet. He acknowledged that the phone might contain evidence of the crime of arrest, but he rejected the idea that cell phones can be searched on that basis due to the fact that a search of the phone would reveal far more about the person than evidence of a crime. Roberts focused on the immense storage capacity of smartphones, made even larger through the advent of cloud technology, where data are stored not on the phone, but on remote servers, yet easily accessible through applications on the phone. Roberts went so far as to suggest, "A cell phone search would typically expose to the government far more than the most exhaustive search of a house."[21]

Roberts' opinion sought to make his knowledge of contemporary technology clear, even going so far as to referencing the Apple iPhone user manual. He described cell phones as being "such a pervasive and insistent part of daily life that the proverbial visitor from Mars might conclude they were an important feature of human anatomy. A smartphone of the sort taken from Riley was unheard of ten years ago; a significant majority of American adults now own such phones." Moreover, he made it clear that cell phones differ in both a qualitative and a quantitative sense from other objects that might be kept on the arrestee's person. "The term 'cell phone' is itself misleading shorthand; many of these devices are in fact minicomputers that also happen to have the capacity to be used as a telephone. They could just as easily be called cameras, video players, rolodexes, calendars, tape recorders, libraries, diaries, albums, televisions, maps, or newspapers."[22]

Roberts focused on the implications for personal privacy raised by the storage capacity of cell phones. Not only does a cell phone collect "in one place many distinct types of information—an address, a note, a prescription, a bank statement, a video," it reveals much more "in combination than any isolated record." The storage capacity of a cell phone enables "the sum of an individual's private life" to be "reconstructed through a thousand photographs labeled with dates, locations, and descriptions." The data on a cell phone can date back years in time: "A person might carry in his pocket a slip of paper reminding him to call Mr. Jones; he would not carry a record of all his communications with Mr. Jones for the past several months, as would routinely be kept on a phone."[23]

In the end, it was the pervasiveness of cell phones and how they have transformed daily life that seemed to persuade Roberts: "Prior to the digital age, people did not typically carry a cache of sensitive personal information with them as they went about their day. Now it is the person who is not carrying a cell phone, with all that it contains, who is the exception." He cited a poll that suggested that almost three-quarters of smartphone users kept their phones within 5 feet of them at all times, and 12 percent of respondents admitted they use their phones in the shower.[24]

The chief justice rejected the government's arguments that there were officer safety concerns, and largely swept aside fears about the ability of a co-conspirator to remotely wipe a phone, by suggesting that police could seize the phone and put it in a Faraday bag (an aluminum baggie designed to prevent the transmission of digital signals), turn off the phone, or remove the battery. He viewed these scenarios as anecdotal and highly unlikely to occur. His opinion did not overrule the third party doctrine, however, as he distinguished a cell phone search from that of a pen register, which merely collects a list of numbers called and received. Yet, the broad opinion in *Riley* leaves the door open for Sotomayor's criticism of the third party doctrine to be revisited.

The Court's opinion also never once acknowledges the reasonable expectation of privacy standard that has been the primary focus of Court decisions involving privacy issues since *Katz* was decided in 1967. It is clearly implied that there is an expectation of privacy in the contents of one's cell phone that society is willing to recognize as legitimate, but the fact that the Court never mentions the standard is telling. It suggests efforts to distance itself from *Katz*, something Scalia pushed for years. Of course, the Court also ignores Justice Scalia's trespass doctrine. Instead, the Fourth Amendment right is defined solely within the framework of personal privacy.

Justice Alito's brief concurrence questioned why it should be the Court's job to regulate these issues, and suggested that Congress should be the entity to regulate police and cell phones, just as it passed legislation dealing with wiretapping after the *Katz* decision. He also challenged the majority's reliance on search incident to arrest being based on only officer safety and the preservation of evidence.

The fact that the justices all voted in favor of Riley is significant. Many of the decisions made by the Court in Fourth Amendment cases split the justices along ideological lines, but not in this case and not in *United States v. Jones*. It is not technically accurate to say that a 9–0 vote on an issue creates a more compelling precedent than a 5–4 vote, but a unanimous vote sends a symbolic message about the strength of feeling on the Court about the issue and makes overruling it less likely to occur over the next few years. The lone justice who did not sign the majority opinion, Justice Alito, usually a consistent vote for the state in Fourth Amendment cases, chose to write separately, but did not question the Court's ruling that a warrantless search of the phone violated the Fourth Amendment. It is unclear where the Court will go with the privacy focus that was laid out in *Riley*, but the case, along with *United States v. Jones*, has opened the door to a variety of technology-related implications for the Fourth Amendment. Several cases related to *Riley* and *Jones* are being considered by lower courts. We will consider these in chapter 8. It is to a more detailed discussion of how the crime control model has fared in the first decade of the Roberts Court that we now turn.

6. The Jurisprudence of Crime Control on the Roberts Court

The California Highway Patrol dispatch team for Mendocino County received a call from a 911 operator from adjacent Humboldt County on an afternoon in early August 2008. The dispatcher had received an anonymous tip that a silver pickup had run another vehicle off the road. The tip provided the license plate for the vehicle, and the information was forwarded to a highway patrol officer in the vicinity as a possible drunk driver. The officer located the vehicle 12 minutes later, and followed it for 5 minutes. Despite observing no traffic violations to corroborate the suspicion that the driver was impaired, the officer decided to stop the truck to see if the driver was intoxicated. As the officer approached the vehicle, he smelled marijuana. Lorenzo and Jose Prado Navarette, the driver and passenger in the pickup, were arrested, and 30 pounds of marijuana were found. Prior to trial, they moved to suppress the marijuana on the grounds that there was no reasonable suspicion to stop them in the first place.

The law that applies to the use of anonymous tips by the police mandates that the tip be confirmed by police observations to verify the reliability of the tip.[1] Cases decided prior to *Navarette v. California* (2014) mandated that the corroborating information address the criminal behavior of the suspects, and the only information the officers had was the location, make, model, color, and license plate of their vehicle. Despite this, the Court upheld the stop of the pickup truck in a 5–4 decision. Justice Clarence Thomas wrote the majority opinion and held that in the totality of the circumstances, the 911 call and the officer's identification of the truck were sufficient to constitute reasonable suspicion for an investigatory stop. Thomas asserted that reasonable suspicion does not require that the facts justifying it come from the officer's direct observation, but that an anonymous tip can demonstrate sufficient reliability if there are confirming facts. The majority ruled that the anonymous informant provided specific information, including the license plate number and location of the vehicle and a plausible description of the alleged wrongdoing, to justify the traffic stop. Thomas' opinion illustrates how diminished the standard of reasonable suspicion has become. In reducing reasonable suspicion to just the totality of the circumstances without any indications of criminal wrongdoing, or even traffic violations, Justice Thomas showed just how malleable the legal standard had become. Rather than requiring multiple articulable facts that a crime had taken place, the Court had reduced the requirements of a *Terry* stop significantly.

Justice Scalia's dissent attacked the majority's reasoning. "The Court's opinion serves up a freedom-destroying cocktail consisting of two parts patent falsity: (1) that anonymous 911 reports of traffic violations are reliable so long as they correctly identify a car and its location, and (2) that a single instance of careless or reckless driving necessarily supports a reasonable suspicion of drunkenness." Scalia pointed out that there was only a claim of erratic driving, and no evidence of a vehicle actually run off the road. Moreover, the officers followed the car for five minutes, and the driver exhibited no signs of intoxication. He framed the issue in the context of individual liberty. Certainly drunken driving is an important matter, but "so is the loss of our freedom to come and go as we please without police interference." The risk is that "after today's opinion all of us on the road, and not just drug dealers, are at risk of having our freedom of movement curtailed on suspicion of drunkenness, based upon a phone tip, true or false, of a single instance of careless driving."[2]

Navarette v. California provides a good example of how the jurisprudence of crime control has thrived on the Roberts Court. The law provides police with maximum flexibility and discretion. The totality of the circumstances standard for probable cause no longer requires multiple facts to justify the intrusion of an investigatory stop. A *Terry* stop may be based on reasonable articulable suspicion, but the standard to determine if the suspicion is reasonable has become diminished. The decision also demonstrates something rarely seen in a crime control decision on the Rehnquist Court—a vicious dissent from Justice Scalia, chastising the Court for its "freedom-destroying cocktail" and for minimizing individual rights under the Fourth Amendment. *Navarette* provides another glimpse into the changing judicial philosophy of Justice Scalia in search and seizure cases in the Roberts Court, and the tension it is creating on the Court.

CONTINUING THE CRIME CONTROL MODEL

The majority of Roberts Court cases involving the Fourth Amendment are like *Navarette* in that they advance the jurisprudence of crime control. While the Court's search and seizure jurisprudence has become somewhat unsettled since 2011, crime control remains the dominant approach used by the justices. In this chapter, we explore how the Roberts Court has built on the foundation established by the Burger and Rehnquist Courts. We examine the key cases that the Court has handed down expanding police power and limiting the reach of the Fourth Amendment. Some of these cases were significant expansions of the power of the state. In particular, we consider the expansion of the good faith exception, the weakening of the Fourth Amendment's core protection of the home through the exigent circumstances exception, searches of parolees and probationers, preservation of a doctrine providing qualified immunity to police officers when they violate individual rights, and decisions such as *Navarette* that expand police power in the context of vehicle stops.

Vehicle Searches and Seizures

The Roberts Court decided three additional vehicle cases that reinforced the jurisprudence of crime control. The first was *Scott v. Harris* (2007), which involved a high-speed chase that was captured on film. Georgia deputy sheriff Timothy Scott was involved in a high-speed chase of Victor Harris. During the course of the chase, Scott intentionally made contact with Harris' vehicle with the intent to force it to crash. It did so, and Harris was severely injured, leaving him a quadriplegic. Harris sued the department and Scott, alleging that intentionally contacting Harris' vehicle constituted the excessive use of force, which was not justified by the circumstances of the chase. Harris' complaint was that the means used to seize him were unreasonable within the meaning of the Fourth Amendment. The Court held that the seizure did not constitute excessive force, and was reasonable under the Fourth Amendment because Harris' actions precipitated the high-speed chase. Harris "intentionally placed himself and the public in danger by unlawfully engaging in the reckless, high-speed flight that ultimately produced the choice between two evils that Scott confronted." Justice Scalia's majority opinion placed blame on Harris: "Multiple police cars, with blue lights flashing and sirens blaring, had been chasing respondent for nearly 10 miles, but he ignored their warning to stop."[3] Scalia included a link to the video footage in his opinion, and the video helped persuade at least Justice Breyer (who wrote a concurrence) that the nature of the chase made the means selected to end it reasonable. While it is likely the Court would have ruled the same way without the video, it provided visible evidence to the Court that helped it to reach the conclusion that the seizure was reasonable. Appellate courts do not normally consider direct evidence as part of their deliberations, as trial courts are supposed to be the final arbiter of facts. The majority's use of the video was surprising, although in some ways it was consistent with how some justices in a jurisprudence of crime control have attempted to base their decisions on questions of efficient or good police work, placing policy concerns ahead of the law.

Arizona v. Johnson (2009) explored the question of whether a pat-down of a passenger in a vehicle stop was permissible. The Court had previously held in *Brendlin v. California* (2007) that a passenger was seized when a vehicle was stopped and could challenge the legality of the seizure. *Johnson* was a direct application of that ruling, and in a unanimous decision Justice Ginsburg held that an officer could frisk the passenger if there is reasonable suspicion that the individual is armed and dangerous. Ginsburg drew on the per curiam opinion in *Pennsylvania v. Mimms* (1977), which permitted an officer to order all of the occupants of a stopped vehicle to exit the vehicle. There was nothing prohibiting the officer from brief inquiry of a passenger who had symbols of gang affiliation on his clothing. A pat-down based on concern for officer safety after this questioning did not violate the Fourth Amendment, even though the inquiry was unrelated to the original traffic stop. Ginsburg argued that as long as the questioning and pat-down did not extend the duration of the stop, there was nothing prohibiting them.

Virginia v. Moore (2008) was reminiscent of the Rehnquist Court decision in *Atwater v. City of Lago Vista* (2001), which held that an officer could arrest an individual for any offense, even a fine-only misdemeanor that precluded the possibility of punishment by jail time. Gail Atwater was arrested for a seatbelt violation. David Lee Moore was arrested for driving under a suspended license, even though state law did not permit a full custodial arrest for such an offense, unless the suspect refused to discontinue the violation. Justice Scalia authored the majority opinion for a unanimous Court, with only Justice Ginsburg writing a brief concurrence. Scalia made a historical argument to challenge Moore's argument that state statutes should limit the Fourth Amendment. He then went through a detailed summary of existing precedent, concluding that as long as the officer had objective probable cause that a traffic violation had occurred, he or she could arrest an individual regardless of the offense. The decision practically mirrored the result in *Atwater* and served to reinforce both *Atwater* and the earlier decision in *Whren v. United States* (1996). The case is meaningful because Scalia went to such effort to show why state laws did not limit the Fourth Amendment.

Expansion of the Good Faith Exception

The establishment of the good faith exception in *United States v. Leon* (1984) represented the triumph of the jurisprudence of crime control. Conservatives on the Burger Court had wanted such a rule for several years prior to the decision in *Leon*. Both the Rehnquist and Roberts Courts have reiterated the core principle of the good faith exception, first expanding it from errors by judges to those done by judicial clerks in *Arizona v. Evans* (1994) and then extending that rule to cover civilian police clerks in *Herring v. United States* (2009), where Chief Justice Roberts described the exclusionary rule as the absolute sanction of "last resort" to be avoided whenever possible.

On July 7, 2004, Bennie Dean Herring arrived at the Sheriff's Department vehicle impound lot in Coffee County, Alabama, to retrieve personal property from a pickup truck that the police had impounded. A police investigator, who had reason to dislike Herring because of accusations that Herring had made about his possible involvement in the killing of a local teenager, asked the sheriff's warrant clerk whether there was an outstanding warrant for Herring's arrest. There was no such warrant in Coffee County, but at the direction of the investigator, the warrant clerk called her colleague in neighboring Dale County, who reported that a warrant for Herring's arrest was outstanding. The clerk told this to the investigator, and asked the Dale County clerk to fax over a copy of the warrant. In the meantime, Herring was arrested and searched incident to that arrest. A handgun and methamphetamine were recovered. As a convicted felon, Herring was not allowed to possess a gun. While the arrest and search were being conducted, the Dale County warrant clerk discovered that the warrant had been recalled in February of that year and was no longer in effect. No warrant was faxed to Coffee County because no such warrant existed.

Herring, in effect, was arrested and searched on the word of a neighboring official that an arrest warrant existed when none actually existed. The Court's majority was not troubled by the lack of justification for the arrest and subsequent search. Chief Justice Roberts' opinion was based entirely on a cost-benefit approach to the exclusionary rule, with an underlying assumption that the only valid justification for the rule is deterrence of police misconduct. He made a subjective judgment that the exclusion of evidence in this case would not deter any future police clerks from engaging in misconduct. In his view of the case, there was an innocent clerical error, and the error had been made by an entirely different agency than the one for which the arresting officers worked. This error was negligent, but it was hardly reckless or intentional. The chief justice framed the good faith exception in terms of the relative blameworthiness of the arresting officer and his or her agency: "The extent to which the exclusionary rule is justified by these deterrence principles varies with the culpability of the law enforcement conduct."[4] Yet, in applying the reckless standard, the chief justice ignored the fact that Herring had been singled out by the investigator without any individualized suspicion.

Justice Ginsburg dissented and condemned the majority's reasoning. She accused the Court of remaking the law concerning good faith, and made a strong case for resting the exclusionary rule on a principled basis, arguing that it is an essential auxiliary to the Fourth Amendment. In her view, while the exclusionary rule serves to deter police misconduct, it also serves the goal of judicial integrity. Using it as a sanction for official misconduct sends a symbolic message to the general public that judges will not take part in official lawlessness and that the government will not benefit from such lawlessness.[5] Ginsburg was also quite cognizant that the error in this case was in the maintenance of a computer database, which today plays a central role in the work of law enforcement, and that the error made was not just a fluke. It was not lost on Justice Ginsburg and her fellow dissenters that "inaccuracies in expansive, interconnected collections of electronic information raise grave concerns for individual liberty."[6]

Herring illustrates how far the exclusionary rule has fallen from its first application to the states in *Mapp v. Ohio* (1961). The Burger Court stripped it from its constitutional moorings, and left it as merely a judicial remedy to combat police misconduct. The Rehnquist Court followed the same path, and the Roberts Court made it clear that not only was the exclusionary rule disfavored, it would be the last resort for constitutional cases and would only be considered for truly egregious conduct. The Court went even further in *Davis v. United States* (2011), arguing that when a new ruling limits the admission of evidence, the new precedent does not apply retroactively to cases already under direct appeal. *Davis* involved the Court's decision in 2009 in *Arizona v.*

Gant, which limited the ability of police to conduct vehicle searches incident to arrest. Davis' appeal was pending when *Gant* was decided, and his attorneys argued that the evidence against him should be suppressed under the new legal standard for search incident to arrest. Justice Alito's opinion held that because the police acted in good faith with the law of vehicle searches when Davis was arrested, the exclusionary rule would not apply. As a result, new precedents would not apply to criminal cases under appellate review. The law had changed, but only future defendants would benefit from it. The Court had gone back and forth on questions of the retroactivity of constitutional decisions over the years, but the *Davis* decision made a definitive ruling against retroactivity in search and seizure cases.

THE SANCTITY OF THE HOME

It is a commonly stated truism that Fourth Amendment protections are strongest in the home. The home is a person's castle; it is one's last retreat and the one place where warrantless entry by police is rarely allowed. As Justice Scalia described it in *Florida v. Jardines* (2013), "When it comes to the Fourth Amendment, the home is first among equals. At the Amendment's very core stands 'the right of a man to retreat into his own home and there be free from unreasonable governmental intrusion.'"[7] Despite this principle, the Roberts Court decided a number of cases in which an individual's privacy interest in the sanctity of the home was overridden by a desire to prosecute criminals.

Two of the first Fourth Amendment decisions of the Roberts Court involved questions about the home. *United States v. Grubbs* (2006) considered the issue of the constitutionality of an anticipatory warrant. In this case, a warrant was issued on the condition that it would not be executed by law enforcement until a parcel containing child pornography ordered by the suspect through an undercover postal agent was delivered to the home. The conditional nature of the warrant was included in a supplemental affidavit by the Court, but not in the warrant itself. When the package was delivered, Grubbs was handed the warrant, but not the supplemental information. Grubbs challenged the warrant, claiming that the actual warrant did not list the triggering condition. The Ninth Circuit agreed with Grubbs' claim, and held that the search was illegal. The Supreme Court reversed in an opinion by Justice Scalia, holding that an anticipatory warrant was no different than an ordinary warrant. The text of the Fourth Amendment only requires that the warrant specify the place to be searched and the persons or things to be seized.

That same term, the Court also decided *Hudson v. Michigan* (2006), which held that the exclusionary rule is not the appropriate remedy when the knock and announce rule for executing a warrant is violated. Police are supposed to announce their presence before executing a warrant to search a home. A court order is required to enter a home without knocking if they believe that announcing their presence will result in the destruction of evidence or danger to the officers executing the warrant. Detroit police suspected Booker T. Hudson, Jr., of being a drug dealer. They obtained a search warrant for his home and in the course of executing it knocked on the door and announced that it was the police, but only waited three to five seconds before opening the unlocked door. Hudson had not been given time to respond to the knock. All of the courts reviewing the case agreed that the knock and announce rule had been violated, but the Supreme Court held that, in spite of this, excluding evidence was too extreme of a remedy for the violation. Justice Scalia's majority opinion implied that while there was a technical violation of the rule, it was so slight of an invasion as to not merit exclusion. The underlying rationale of the opinion, seeking to minimize the extent of the Fourth Amendment violation, fits in well with a jurisprudence of crime control.

In a similar vein, the Court ruled in *Los Angeles County v. Rettele* (2007) that a search warrant executed for a residence where the suspect had moved out and sold the home was reasonable. The Los Angeles County sheriff had obtained a search warrant for a home of an African American suspect who was believed to be armed and dangerous. The sheriff's deputies did not know that the home had been sold three months prior, and was now owned by a Caucasian man, Max Rettele, who lived in the home with his girlfriend and her 17-year-old son. Deputies announced their arrival at the home early in the morning, and the teenager answered the door. He was ordered to lay face down on the floor. Deputies entered the bedroom, awaking Rettele and his girlfriend, who were ordered to get out of their bed and were held at gunpoint. They protested, as they were naked, and the sheriff would not permit the woman to cover herself. After a minute or two they were allowed to put on robes, but were forced to sit on the couch while the search proceeded. After about five minutes, the deputies verified that they were not the suspects named in the warrant and had no weapons. The deputies apologized, and left the home.

Rettele filed a civil suit, claiming that his Fourth Amendment rights were violated. The district court held that the search warrant was properly executed, but the Ninth Circuit reversed, holding that police should have known that the individuals in the home were not of the same race as the suspects identified in the warrant. In a per curiam opinion, the Supreme Court reversed, arguing that the warrant was executed in a fashion that was not clearly erroneous and that there was no basis for holding the deputies liable. The Court held that the sheriff's deputies had no way to know that the residents who were the target of the search were not elsewhere in the home. Once again, the desire to avoid use of the exclusionary rule serves to minimize Fourth Amendment violations, even in a home. The Court treats the mistaken search in the same way it does the good faith exception cases.

Expansion of the Exigent Circumstances Doctrine

The Roberts Court has decided four cases that upheld a warrantless entry into a home on the basis of exigent or emergency circumstances. The exigent circumstances exception has a long history, going back as far as the primary rationale for allowing a vehicle search without a warrant, out of concern that the vehicle (and evidence) could simply be driven away. The Court has basically argued that when an exigency arises, the constitutional requirement of a warrant can be sacrificed. Similar exceptions were created for hot pursuit, for search incident to arrest, and to prevent felons from escaping. The Roberts Court has proven quite willing to expand the exigent circumstances doctrine to permit entry into the home, beginning in its first term.

Police officers in Brigham City, Utah, were called to a loud party in a residential neighborhood at 3 A.M. When they arrived at the scene, they found a party going on, with juveniles drinking beer in the back yard. The officers observed an altercation in a kitchen through a screen door. They saw one person punch another, resulting in the person who had been punched spitting blood into the sink. The officers then entered the house and arrested the adults present for contributing to the delinquency of a minor. Writing for a unanimous court in *Brigham City v. Stuart* (2006), Chief Justice Roberts ruled that police may enter a home without a warrant when they need to do so to stop a fight and render assistance to a person who has been injured. Once inside, they can act on anything they see in plain view. Justice Stevens concurred, and described *Brigham City* as an "odd flyspeck of a case" that involved minor issues and did not create any new law, but instead just reiterated the emergency assistance exigency. He revealed that he had voted against the granting of certiorari and viewed this case as a state law issue, but because the Utah courts had done such a poor job of crafting their rulings, it left the Court with little choice but to overrule them.[8]

The Roberts Court reinforced its ruling in *Brigham City* with a per curiam decision in *Michigan v. Fisher* (2009). This case involved a disturbance complaint police received in Brownstown, Michigan. Upon arriving on the scene, officers were directed to a residence by a couple on the street who claimed a "man was going crazy." Officers found the home in complete disarray. There was a pickup truck in the driveway with its front smashed, damaged fence posts, broken windows in the home, and blood on the hood of the pickup. Through a window, they could see Fisher screaming and throwing things. A couch blocked the door, but through the window they could see blood on Fisher's hand. They asked if he needed medical assistance, but received no response. The officer attempted to gain entry into the home, but Fisher pointed a weapon at him. Ultimately, Fisher was taken into custody and charged with assault with a dangerous weapon. Fisher challenged the entry into his home, but the Court held that the officer's entry was reasonable under the emergency assistance justification for exigent entry.

Kentucky v. King (2011) considered the requirement that exigencies precipitating warrantless entry are not created or manufactured by actions of the police themselves. Lexington police officers had staged a controlled drug buy of cocaine in an effort to arrest a drug dealer. The dealer got away because the officers given the responsibility for making the arrest after the controlled buy were not in place. The officers managed to follow the dealer into an apartment building, but lost contact with him. They knew he had entered one of two apartments on either side of a hallway, but they did not know which one. Smelling what they believed to be burning marijuana behind one of the doors, they knocked and announced that they were the police. Hearing movements inside that they took to indicate the destruction of drug evidence, the police burst in to what they would later come to realize was the wrong apartment. Nevertheless, there were drugs in the apartment, and the officers proceeded to arrest Hollis King, his girlfriend, and a guest.

Justice Alito ruled in an 8–1 decision that the exigent entry was reasonable, and was not persuaded by the argument of the Kentucky courts that the exigency only existed because of the police officer's own actions. Alito went out of his way to explain the potential costs to law enforcement of following the Kentucky Supreme Court's holding that a warrantless entry was not permissible if it was reasonably foreseeable that the investigative tactics used would create the exigency. The Kentucky standard would create unpredictability in the law and force law enforcement to second-guess its actions. Alito rejected arguments that a warrant be secured in advance, as officers are under no duty to halt investigations the moment minimal probable cause is found. Throughout his opinion, Alito failed to even acknowledge that poor planning by police had created the exigency in that they were not ready to apprehend the suspect after the controlled buy, and did not have him under adequate surveillance. In the end, Alito seemed persuaded that the fact that police announced their entry into the apartment was enough to satisfy the Fourth Amendment. Nor was he bothered by the fact that the police smelled marijuana, when the controlled buy was for cocaine.

Justice Ginsburg authored the sole dissent in the case, and argued that the question faced here is "May police, who could pause to gain the approval of a neutral magistrate, dispense with the need to get a warrant by themselves creating exigent circumstances? I would answer no, as did the Kentucky Supreme Court. The urgency must exist, I would rule, when the police come on the scene, not subsequent to their arrival, prompted by their own conduct." Ginsburg went further, suggesting, "The Court today arms the police with a way to routinely dishonor the Fourth Amendment in drug cases."[9] Yet, Ginsburg stood alone in this case, not joined by any other justices. As was true in all other exigent circumstance cases, the home as castle argument failed to persuade Justice Scalia, who took such dramatically different approaches in his decisions in *Kyllo v. United States* (2001) and in *Florida v. Jardines* (2013).

The fourth exigent circumstance case came in a per curiam opinion in 2012. *Ryburn v. Huff* dealt with the question of warrantless entry into a home as a result of a police investigation of rumors that a student was planning to "shoot up" a high school. After conducting interviews at the school, police went to the home of Vincent Huff, hoping to speak to him and his parents. Mrs. Huff answered the door, and met the officers outside. She refused to let the officers in the home. When asked if there were weapons in the home, Mrs. Huff refused to answer and ran back into the house. The officers thought this was unusual, and believed that they might be in danger. They followed her into the home. After questioning her further, they decided there was no danger and left. A civil suit was filed by Huff claiming that the warrantless entry violated her Fourth Amendment rights. The Court held that the entry was reasonable, as police are not constrained by a warrant if there is a reasonable fear of imminent danger. The irony in this case is that the only evidence police had were rumors from students at a school and the decision of the homeowner to retreat into her home, ending what could be viewed as a consensual contact.

SEARCHES OUTSIDE OF CURRENT CRIMINAL INVESTIGATIONS

Not all Fourth Amendment cases involve the investigation of a crime. *Samson v. California* (2006) considered searches of parolees. In September 2002, Officer Alex Rohleder of the San Bruno, California, Police Department came into contact with Donald Curtis Samson, a person he knew to be on parole for an earlier offense. Samson was walking on a city street in the company of a woman and a child. Officer Rohleder testified at the trial that he had believed that Samson had an outstanding warrant for his arrest, so he stopped Samson to talk to him. Even though the officer determined that there was no outstanding warrant, he searched Samson anyway and found methamphetamine in a cigarette box in Samson's shirt pocket. At trial, Samson moved to suppress the evidence, but under a California statute, parolees are subject to search at any time. His motion was denied. The California appellate courts affirmed the conviction, and the Supreme Court granted certiorari.

The Court affirmed the California courts, holding that persons on parole have little expectation of privacy within the meaning of the Fourth Amendment. Justice Thomas wrote the majority opinion in a 6–3 decision that held that parolees have even fewer rights than probationers. The case came five years after the Rehnquist Court ruled in *United States v. Knights* (2001) that a warrantless search of the home of a probationer was not a violation of the Fourth Amendment. In *Knights*, however, the police at least had a suspicion that he had been involved in a further crime. In *Samson*, there was no suspicion at all. In fact, the officer in question even verified that there was no outstanding warrant. Justice Thomas went further in holding that a parolee is more akin to a prisoner with regard to his or her Fourth Amendment rights. In response to a strongly worded dissent from Justice Stevens, Justice Thomas asserted, "The concern that California's suspicion-less search system gives officers unbridled discretion to conduct searches, thereby inflicting dignitary harms that arouse strong resentment in parolees and undermine their ability to reintegrate into productive society, is belied by California's prohibition on 'arbitrary, capricious or harassing' searches."[10] As a matter of public policy, granting such broad powers over anyone currently on probation or parole significantly increases the odds that the person will go back to prison or jail on a technical violation. This has a tendency to increase the disparate impact of the criminal justice system on the poor and on minorities.[11] Advocates of crime control may certainly make a plausible argument that close supervision of convicted felons is justified, but careful analysis of just how recidivism is measured shows just how important this power is to maintaining the hold of crime control thinking in our society.[12]

DNA Collection at Booking

It has been long established that police can search an arrestee's clothing and personal effects incident to an arrest. Similarly, a person being booked into a jail or prison will have their clothes and other personal belongings seized, cataloged, and stored away and may be searched for purposes of identification. Fingerprints are taken, and any identifying marks, such as scars or tattoos, are documented. Contraband discovered during the booking process is also admissible in a criminal prosecution. In recent years, it has become a common practice in many jurisdictions that those convicted of a felony must also submit to a buccal swab for purposes of collecting a sample to be submitted for DNA analysis. A cotton swab is inserted into the mouth of a person and used to gather cells from the cheek. The procedure is quick and painless. These samples, once analyzed, are commonly submitted to state DNA databases and to the national Combined DNA Index System (CODIS), maintained by the Federal Bureau of Investigation. CODIS is frequently used by law enforcement to solve rapes and other cases that involve biological evidence. For example, once a rape kit is taken from a victim, that evidence is subjected to DNA analysis and the results submitted to CODIS and any state-maintained DNA databases. If the sample matches an existing sample already in a DNA database, it significantly increases the likelihood of a conviction.

Maryland v. King (2013) involved a challenge to a Maryland statute that mandated the collection of DNA evidence from any individuals arrested for a serious crime. Alonzo King was arrested in 2009 for assault with a shotgun, an offense covered by the state's DNA collection law. When King's DNA was analyzed and sent to the Maryland DNA database, it matched evidence from a rape kit gathered in the aftermath of a rape in 2003 that had never been solved. King was tried for that rape, convicted, and sentenced to life in prison without possibility of parole.

King's attorneys convinced the Maryland Court of Appeals to strike down that part of the state law that allowed for collection of DNA evidence from arrestees on the ground that the statute violated the Fourth Amendment. The state's justification for the statute was that it was part of the routine booking procedure necessary to positively identify the person being held in custody. The state sought certiorari, and in a 5–4 decision Justice Kennedy reversed the lower courts. He was joined by Roberts, Alito, Thomas, and Breyer. The majority focused on the relatively painless and quick nature of the buccal swab procedure, stating that the very low intrusiveness of the procedure is more than overbalanced by the state's interest in the orderly maintenance of its jails and prisons. Kennedy framed the issue of a DNA swab as being akin to a fingerprint, and tried to argue that the primary purpose of the DNA test was to identify the suspect. He failed to acknowledge that the issue was not the physical method of collecting the DNA sample, but the information that was obtained as a result of the analysis. The state was collecting the genetic makeup of individuals, and storing it in a database that was accessible by law enforcement across the country. Nor did he seem to acknowledge that this information could be used in other cases, without any level of suspicion attached to the person beforehand.

Justice Scalia led the dissenters in a cutting critique of Kennedy's argument. *Maryland v. King* fit neatly into Scalia's revived trespass doctrine. The use of the buccal swab was a physical intrusion into King's person without a warrant, and thus was an unreasonable search. Scalia also rejected Kennedy's argument that the purpose of collecting the DNA evidence was to identify the suspect as a sham: "The Court's assertion that DNA is being taken, not to solve crimes, but to *identify* those in the State's custody, taxes the credulity of the credulous." In other words, it strains the believability of those who are prone to believe virtually anything. He continued to take apart the Court's efforts to treat DNA as being akin to fingerprinting. This "can seem apt only to those who know no more than today's opinion has chosen to tell them about how those DNA searches actually work."[13] Scalia pointed out how the DNA tests were not even submitted for analysis for weeks after the arrest, and it was more than four months later, after King had already been released on bond, that the match to the rape case was identified. Scalia's dissent, as in *Navarette v. California*, illustrates how his views were shifting on Fourth Amendment issues. The justice who had been a champion of the jurisprudence of crime control had been pushed by his theory of originalism to vote against certain types of law enforcement behaviors that he regarded as abhorrent to the Framers' intentions. In this instance, general searches for evidence of crime, without any individual suspicion, were at the heart of what the Framers of the Constitution sought to prohibit with the Fourth Amendment. Yet, in what had become Scalia's typical style, he used caustic language to attack justices who are normally his closest allies.

Jail Strip Searches

The decision in 2012 in *Florence v. Board of Chosen Freeholders of the County of Burlington* considered a challenge to the practice of strip searching an arrestee when the arrest itself was not valid. In 2005, Albert Florence's vehicle was stopped in Burlington County, New Jersey, for a routine traffic offense. When the arresting officer ran a background check on Florence, an outstanding arrest warrant for failure to pay a fine associated with a conviction in 1998 was discovered. Later, the warrant was found to be in error. The fine had been paid in 2003, but Florence was held in custody for six days. During that time, he was strip searched twice.

Albert Florence filed a civil suit alleging that the strip search was a violation of his Fourth Amendment rights. The district court granted Florence's motion for summary judgment, ruling that the strip search of "non-indictable offenders without reasonable suspicion violated the Fourth Amendment."[14] The Third Circuit reversed, and Florence sought certiorari. The Court, in an opinion written by Justice Kennedy, ruled 5–4 against Florence. Justice Kennedy argued that courts should not interfere with the routine operations of jails and prisons. The indignity of such a search, which is described in rather clinical terms, was downplayed. The majority opinion did consider the implications of the ruling in *Atwater v. City of Lago Vista*, which allowed for full custodial arrest for even petty misdemeanors. Chief Justice Roberts and Justice Alito both wrote separately to emphasize that this ruling would not necessarily apply to persons who were arrested for minor infractions and not held in a general prison or jail population. Justice Breyer dissented, condemning the use of strip searches in jails. He included a description of people who had been strip searched, including a nun and pregnant or lactating women, as well as a list of cases in which minor offenses had resulted in strip searches.[15] The broad discretion given to jail officials, combined with the ability to hold persons in full custodial arrest for even minor offenses, is a very powerful tool that has enormous potential to be abused by local law enforcement.

Qualified Immunity

Under a civil rights law originally passed in the aftermath of the Civil War, persons whose rights are violated by a government actor in the conduct of their official duties may seek damages from that official. The remedies also include attorney's fees, as many such plaintiffs would not be able to afford the lawsuit otherwise. This statute was the basis for a lawsuit by Rodney King after his infamous beating by officers of the Los Angeles Police force in 1991, and is very commonly used by disgruntled citizens unhappy with their treatment by the police.[16] Over the years, the Court has often shielded officials from civil liability for actions taken as part of their official duties. The reason for this is so that officials can do their jobs without fear of their personal and family finances being under constant threat. Liability for actions taken while working for the public has been limited to situations wherein the official knew, or should have known, that his or her actions were in violation of the law. The legal test for determining whether an official is entitled to immunity from civil liability requires that the court determine whether the right in question was clearly established at the time the incident took place and whether the officer in question could have reasonably believed that his or her actions were in compliance with the law.

The Roberts Court has decided several qualified immunity cases that involve Fourth Amendment issues. The decisions in *Scott v. Harris* and *Los Angeles County v. Rettele* both provided qualified immunity to the law enforcement officers, as in both instances the Court held that there was no Fourth Amendment violation. *Safford Unified School District v. Redding* (2009), which we discuss in the next chapter, also provided qualified immunity to school administrators, even though the student strip search at issue was ruled unconstitutional. In that case, the law was unclear at the time of the alleged unreasonable search, so the Court provided immunity from damages to the school administrators, while establishing a new rule that limited searches in the future. The decision to grant qualified immunity for what was considered an illegal search illustrated the willingness of the justices to shield administrators from liability and mirrored their reasoning in good faith exception cases.

The Court decided four qualified immunity cases in the 2013 and 2014 terms. One of these, *Plumhoff v. Rickard* (2014), involved a high-speed chase similar to *Scott v. Harris*, but the decision itself did not address Fourth Amendment issues, and instead was entirely focused on the definition of when qualified immunity should be granted. Per curiam opinions were issued in three cases that addressed the substantive Fourth Amendment issues, at least in part. Two of these decisions provided immunity to the law enforcement officers being sued. *Stanton v. Sims* (2013) involved a question of a warrantless entry of a home, and injury caused to a resident by the officer. La Mesa, California, police officer Mike Stanton was in pursuit of a suspected gang member who had refused to stop when requested to do so, and who went behind the 6-foot gate of a wooden fence. Stanton crashed through the gate of a wooden fence surrounding Drendolyn Sims' house. Sims was standing just behind the gate and suffered cuts and bruises when the gate made contact with her face and shoulder. She sued Officer Stanton, who successfully moved for summary judgment in the district court, claiming that his actions were justified. Sims appealed to the Ninth Circuit, which ruled that Officer Stanton's decision to crash through her gate was "plainly incompetent." The Supreme Court overruled the Ninth Circuit, arguing that Officer Stanton's actions were based on a reasonable interpretation of the law at the time, and based on a split-second decision. Therefore, he was thus entitled to qualified immunity.

Carroll v. Carman (2014) concerned a question over whether a knock and talk that occurred not at the front door of the home but at a sliding door, on the side of the home, adjacent to a car port, was a warrantless entry into the curtilage of a home. Police initiated the encounter with the home's residents as they sought to find a man named Michael Zita. When told he was not in the home, they asked for consent to search, which was granted. The encountered ended when they did not find Zita. Subsequently the residents filed a civil suit claiming the police had conducted a warrantless entry into their home. The district court rejected the claim, arguing that the officer had qualified immunity. The Third Circuit reversed, citing one lower court decision that when conducting a knock and talk, police must conduct that at the front door, where they have an implied invitation to go. The Supreme Court reversed the decision, arguing that the Third Circuit's reliance on one precedent was in error, and cited several other lower court decisions (but no Supreme Court precedent) that were counter to the decision. Ultimately the Court never ruled on the substantive issue, but merely reversed the lower court and remanded the case for further proceedings.

Tolan v. Cotton (2014) is also a case in which the Court made a technical ruling concerning a motion for summary judgment in a qualified immunity case, but this time in favor of the injured citizen. This case involved a claim of excessive use of force from an encounter that itself was the result of a data entry error by an officer, who misread a license plate and believed a vehicle was stolen when it was not. Because of the error, police pursued two African American teenagers, Robert Tolan and Anthony Cooper, to Tolan's home, where he lived with his parents. The boys were treated as dangerous suspects and made to lie face down on the home's front porch at gunpoint. Despite the pleas of Tolan's parents that the car was not stolen, the confrontation escalated. Tolan objected to the treatment of his mother by the police and rose from the porch, at which time he was shot three times. While Tolan survived the gunshots, he suffered life-altering injuries. Tolan sued, claiming his Fourth Amendment rights had been violated. Officer Cotton moved for summary judgment, which was granted by the district court on the basis that the officer's actions were not unreasonable in light of the facts. Upon appeal, the Fifth Circuit agreed with the granting of summary judgment, but not the reasoning of the district court, holding that the officer was entitled to summary judgment because his actions did not clearly violate existing federal law. The Supreme Court granted certiorari and summarily held that the Fifth Circuit failed to follow the rule that courts faced with a motion for summary judgment to consider the evidence in a way that is most favorable to the party opposing the motion, in this case Robert Tolan. The Court dissected five specific elements of the facts and challenged them all. In the end, the decision was reversed, and remanded to reconsider the issues in light of the Supreme Court's interpretation of the legal standard to be applied when a police officer moves for summary judgment. The decision was highly technical, and did not rule on the substance of the claim of qualified immunity. Nor did the justices seem concerned at all by the tragic facts of the case.

Qualified immunity cases have become a regular part of the Court's Fourth Amendment caseload. They frequently serve to advance the jurisprudence of crime control, in that the precedents underlying the doctrine of qualified immunity are generally favorable to protecting government actors from liability.

This does not mean that the government actor will always be immune, but justices who are predisposed to not use the exclusionary rule are also highly likely to find reasons to spare law enforcement from claims of civil liability for its actions.

CONCLUSION

The jurisprudence of crime control certainly has some cracks in its foundation, but after 10 years in the Roberts Court, it remains the dominant approach to Fourth Amendment cases. Three-fifths of its decisions have favored the state, and most of those do so in a way that either reinforces police power or expands it at the expense of the individual's rights. The addition of Justice Sotomayor and Justice Kagan has certainly served to temper the enthusiasm for the crime control model, and Justice Scalia's newly discovered appreciation for "original" Fourth Amendment rights provided a fifth vote in cases where the prodefendant position would often be in dissent. Yet, there is little evidence to suggest that the underlying premises of the crime control jurisprudence are in jeopardy. Reasonableness, rather than the warrant requirement, remains the primary focal point for Fourth Amendment inquiry. The exclusionary rule is a shadow of its former self, and efforts by persons whose Fourth Amendment rights have been violated to obtain redress in an action for civil damages are severely limited by the doctrine of qualified immunity as interpreted generously by the Roberts Court. Even the protections provided to the home from warrantless intrusion have been whittled away. Justices Kennedy, Alito, and Thomas provide a solid core of support for crime control, and the chief justice is usually with them.

But to fully understand the Roberts Court's Fourth Amendment jurisprudence, we need to look at one more issue carefully. When the defendant wins in court, how much of a victory is there? To what degree do prodefendant (or liberal) decisions expand individual rights, and to what degree are they merely corrective measures, reining in the excesses of the system while reinforcing its crime control essence? It is to this question we turn in chapter 7.

7. Reining in the Excesses of Crime Control

After receiving an anonymous tip that a particular residence was a possible crack house, police in Tucson, Arizona, decided to visit the home and speak with the residents. They arrived at the house and knocked on the front door. Rodney Gant answered the door and identified himself, but said he did not live there. The officers left but ran Gant's name through the law enforcement database and discovered that he had a suspended driver's license and an outstanding warrant for his arrest. Later that evening they returned to the home, with the goal of making contact with a Mr. White. While they were there, a vehicle pulled up that the officer recognized from the prior visit, and Rodney Gant was behind the wheel. When he got out of the car, he was immediately arrested, handcuffed, searched, and locked in the backseat of the patrol car. The officers then proceeded to search the passenger compartment of Gant's vehicle and found both an illegal handgun and crack cocaine. At his trial, Gant moved to suppress the evidence from the search of the car, arguing that the search incident to arrest was an unreasonable search.

In many ways, the experience of Rodney Gant was no different from thousands of other cases. A person is arrested at or near a vehicle, the suspect is secured, and then the passenger compartment of the vehicle is searched. *New York v. Belton* (1981) permitted police to search the interior of the vehicle after any arrest, regardless of whether there was an officer safety issue or any belief that there was evidence of the crime to be found. The bright line rule provided maximum flexibility to law enforcement, but in doing so had become disconnected from the dual underlying rationales for a search incident to arrest, the concern for officer safety and the need to preserve evidence. Rodney Gant was arrested for driving under a suspended license, and for an active warrant for failure to appear in court. His person was searched. He was handcuffed and secured. He posed absolutely no officer safety issue. Moreover, his arrest for driving under a suspended license was such that there was no evidence to find. The officers saw him drive the car, and thus the crime was complete in itself. The officer who conducted the search admitted at trial that he had no specific reason to search the car, but that he did so "because the law says we can do it."[1]

This type of search had become a mainstay of police in fighting the war on drugs. When the police use a tactic for an extended period of time, they tend to become overzealous.

What is unusual about the case is that the defendant won at the Supreme Court. Even in the most crime control–dominated periods, defendants win in about 25 percent of cases. This does not mean that the Court is inconsistent or unpredictable. All of the cases that make it to the Court are hard cases that have been scrutinized repeatedly by the lower courts. Sometimes the defendant will win. In this chapter we will focus on the Roberts Court cases where the defendant wins. Most of these cases are not major departures from the dominance of crime control. Even though the defendant wins the case, the majority opinion usually focuses on fine-tuning an existing precedent. These are corrective measures, not fundamental changes in the law. By reining in excessive police behavior, the Court actually protects the legitimacy of itself as an independent, nonpartisan branch of government and legitimizes the hegemony of crime control in our society.

When *Arizona v. Gant* (2009) arrived at the Supreme Court, it seemed possible that there might be a majority willing to overturn or at least limit the *Belton* rule. Three members of the Court, Justices Stevens, O'Connor, and Scalia, had expressed doubts about the *Belton* bright line rule in separate opinions in *Thornton v. United States* (2004), which had expanded the reach of the doctrine to include arrestees who were not in the vehicle at the time of the arrest, but were recent occupants. O'Connor boldly stated that "lower court decisions seem now to treat the ability to search a vehicle incident to the arrest of a recent occupant as a police entitlement rather than as an exception justified by the twin rationales of *Chimel*."[2] Justice Scalia went even further, criticizing *Belton* searches as having little connection to the actual rationale for search incident to arrest. Justice Stevens, joined by Justice Souter, dissented: "Unwilling to confine the *Belton* rule to the narrow class of cases it was designed to address, the Court extends *Belton*'s reach without supplying any guidance for the future application of its swollen rule."[3]

Oral argument in *Gant* turned largely on the question of whether the two-pronged justification for search incident to arrest could support the bright line rule established by *Belton*. Justices Scalia, Stevens, Ginsburg, and Souter expressed disbelief that the officer safety rationale made sense as the justification for *Belton*, particularly given the facts involved in *Gant*. Justice Breyer, Justice Alito, and Chief Justice Roberts were the only justices to actively engage the respondent and make the case for continuing the *Belton* rule. Justice Thomas was typically silent; he virtually never participates in questioning during oral argument. The Court appeared divided. *Arizona v. Gant* ended up being a 5–4 decision for the defendant. As senior associate justice, John Paul Stevens assigned the decision to himself. Justices Ginsburg, Souter, Thomas, and Scalia joined the majority. Scalia opted to only concur with the outcome, writing a separate opinion, but in effect forcing Stevens to adopt his logic to provide the fifth vote.

Justice Stevens' opinion sought to return the law of search incident to arrest to its constitutional origins of officer safety and the preservation of evidence. When faced with the facts in *Gant*, it was clear that the *Chimel* reaching distance rule did not apply once a suspect had been handcuffed and secured outside of the vehicle. Moreover, the claim to search for evidence was equally flawed, when the arrest was for a traffic offense. Stevens repeated O'Connor's criticism from *Thornton* and argued that the bright line rule in *Belton* had been created to provide officers with maximum efficiency in conducting their work, but did so by ignoring the constitutional rationale for the search in the first place. Stevens held that the proper standard for search incident to arrest was found in *Chimel v. California* (1969), and that a vehicle search was only authorized when the suspect was unsecured and within reaching distance of the passenger compartment at the time of the search.

But in order to gain a fifth vote, Stevens conceded to Justice Scalia's argument for when it would be reasonable to search a vehicle incident to arrest. Scalia believed that a search of the passenger compartment was permissible if it was reasonable to believe that further evidence of the crime of the arrest would be found. Stevens added this second prong to his opinion, creating a two-part standard for vehicle searches. Steven's first prong held that if the suspect was unsecured, officers could conduct a *Chimel* reaching distance search. But since few officers leave an arrestee unsecured in a vehicle, this prong would rarely be used to justify a search. The second prong of *Gant* would, in effect, be the primary means by which a vehicle search incident to arrest would be justified. Instead of remaining a bright line rule, *Belton* had been turned into a conditional search. The passenger compartment could only be searched if it was reasonable to believe further evidence of the crime of arrest would be found in the vehicle.

Justices Alito and Breyer both dissented, criticizing the Court for overruling *Belton* when the rule had worked well in the field and had been taught to police for more than a quarter-century. The dissents read like a classic defense of crime control. The dissenters accused the majority of preventing the police from doing their jobs by making it more difficult to conduct searches and catch criminals. Alito argued that not only was the bright line rule workable, but circumstances had not changed to justify overturning it.

Arizona v. Gant raises two questions that are important for our analysis of the state of the Fourth Amendment: Why did the Court seemingly change course, after almost 30 years of expanding the doctrine permitting vehicle searches incident to arrest, and how significant of a shift was this decision? The first question is perhaps the easier of the two to answer. The composition of the Court had changed, but Justice Alito and Chief Justice Roberts shared the same ideology as their predecessors. If anything, Justice Alito is more conservative than Justice O'Connor. Justice Breyer had never been a strong proponent of individual rights in Fourth Amendment cases, so his dissent was not surprising. Nor were the votes of the three moderates on the Court, Justices Stevens, Ginsburg, and Souter. In the end, it was Justices Scalia and Thomas who provided the key fourth and fifth votes to end the *Belton* bright line rule. Thomas did not write in the case, or explicitly join Scalia's concurrence, so it is unclear what his rationale was, yet, with his prior history, and because he had been in the majority of all prior vehicle search cases since joining the Court, his vote is peculiar. Scalia, on the other hand, made it crystal clear why he was joining the majority, as he thought it better to avoid a 4–1–4 outcome, leaving the law unclear. More importantly, he had voiced his criticism of *Belton* four years earlier in *Thornton*, where he argued that given the diminished expectation of privacy in a vehicle, it was plausible, after an arrest, to search for further evidence of the crime. In *Gant* he went further, and was in the position as the fifth vote to force Stevens to accept his evidentiary argument. In a sense, Scalia was making a crime control argument for expanding warrantless searches of vehicles, not an argument about Gant's situation.

The question of the larger significance of the *Gant* decision is harder, but it is not too difficult to sort out. *Gant* initially sent shock waves through law enforcement, which was forced to scramble to find ways around the decision, including increasing use of consent searches, impounding vehicles to conduct inventory searches, and making greater use of K9 narcotics dog sniffs to trigger the automobile exception. While there is evidence that vehicle searches incident to arrest certainly have diminished since the decision, it is not clear that the decision was truly detrimental to law enforcement's crime control agenda.

We do not believe that the decision marks a rejection of the jurisprudence of crime control. What *Gant* most likely indicates is the effort by the Court to rein in the excesses of the crime control jurisprudence created by police behavior over time in the aftermath of the decision in *Belton*.

Over the years since *Belton* was decided, police had realized that they could make use of it in any arrest, and it became a convenient means of conducting investigatory searches for drugs and contraband without a warrant. As the war on drugs heated up in the 1980s and 1990s, vehicle searches became an extremely valuable tool. Stop someone for a minor traffic offense if the police had a hunch that they would find contraband through a search, arrest them for the traffic offense, and then conduct a *Belton* search. An empirical study of police tactics in methamphetamine enforcement found that these tactics were used time and again. A suspected drug user would be stopped for failure to use a turn signal properly or some other equally minor violation. The driver would not have proof of insurance, and instead of issuing a citation, the officer would arrest him, and then conduct a search incident to arrest, hoping to find drugs or other contraband. If the search turned up nothing, the driver would be unarrested and let off with a citation.[4]

The decision in *Arizona v. Gant* served as a corrective measure—one designed to curb the excesses of the crime control regime. Given that it still permitted vehicle searches when it was reasonable to believe that further evidence of the crime of arrest would be found, *Gant* did not eliminate vehicle searches; it merely limited them to those instances that were consistent with the underlying rationales for such searches. *Gant* did not create a bold new individual right against warrantless searches. Instead it created new parameters for vehicle searches that were in line with the law before *Belton* was stretched far beyond its original rationale. Many of the decisions favoring the defendant in both the Rehnquist and Roberts Courts have fit this model. The Rehnquist Court's decision in *Knowles v. Iowa* (1998) is a good example. In *Knowles*, the Court said that Iowa was not free to expand search incident to arrest to search incident to citation. The defendant won, but the decision did not broaden individual rights or expand Fourth Amendment protections. It simply constrained a law enforcement effort to expand *Belton* searches to any traffic stop where a citation was issued.

In what follows, we explore how many of the prodefendant decisions issued by the Roberts Court are actually consistent with the jurisprudence of crime control, and are a means by which the Court can maintain balance and accountability in the regime it has established. Of the 36 Fourth Amendment cases decided by the Roberts Court in its first decade, 14, or 39 percent, favored the defendant. All but 2 of those 14 cases, *United States v. Jones* (2012) and *Riley v. California* (2014), can be readily classified as corrective measures.

OTHER VEHICLE CASES

The Roberts Court has decided two other vehicle cases that have served as corrective measures. The first of these, *Brendlin v. California* (2007), permits a passenger in a stopped vehicle to challenge the legality of their seizure. Prior to this decision, only drivers could challenge the stop. In some ways, this reinforces prior Rehnquist Court decisions on the status of passengers in traffic stops, but the fact that the Court focuses on the ability of the passenger to challenge the legality of the seizure is a narrow corrective measure. This does not mean that the passenger will succeed in such a challenge, as we saw in the decision of *Arizona v. Johnson* (2009), but the very fact that he or she can make the challenge serves as a constraint in a body of law that until this point had consistently expanded the power of the police over passengers.

Missouri v. McNeely (2013) involved an involuntary blood draw from a driver suspected of being intoxicated. Tyler McNeely was stopped by a police officer who observed the vehicle speeding and repeatedly crossing the yellow center line. The officer noticed that McNeely had bloodshot eyes, slurred speech, and smelled of alcohol on his breath. McNeely performed poorly on a roadside sobriety check, and refused to take a portable Breathalyzer test. He was placed under arrest for driving under the influence. The officer began to transport McNeely to the police department, but when he indicated that he would still refuse a Breathalyzer test, the officer changed course and drove to a nearby hospital for blood testing. He did not seek a warrant for the blood draw. McNeely was once again asked if he would consent to a blood test, under the penalty of losing his driver's license for a year if he refused. McNeely held firm, and refused. His blood was drawn, and a blood alcohol content of .154 percent was measured, more than double the legal minimum for intoxication.

McNeely sought to have the warrantless blood draw suppressed as a violation of his Fourth Amendment rights. The trial court agreed, and held that the exigency exception to the Fourth Amendment's warrant requirement did not apply as there was no emergency that prohibited the officer from obtaining a warrant, even though the alcohol in McNeely's bloodstream was being metabolized by his liver. The Missouri Supreme Court affirmed, holding that the mere concern of the dissipation of blood alcohol content was not enough to merit a warrantless blood draw. The officer would need some special facts, like a delay to investigate an accident or the need to bring an injured suspect to the hospital for treatment, to merit an exigency. This was a routine DUI case, not an emergency. The Court's own precedent, *Schmerber v. California* (1966), had held that a warrantless blood draw was not unreasonable under the Fourth Amendment. The Supreme Court granted certiorari in order to resolve a conflict among the circuits about whether a warrantless blood draw always qualified as an exigency in a DUI case. In a 5–4 decision, the Court held that it did not.

Justice Sotomayor wrote the opinion of the Court, and was joined by Scalia, Ginsburg, and Kagan. Chief Justice Roberts concurred in part and dissented in part. In *McNeely*, the Court considered whether or not there should be a per se or bright line rule that treated every DUI case as an exigency that would permit a warrantless blood draw when a suspect refused a Breathalyzer test. Justice Sotomayor's opinion held that it did not. Her opinion reiterated that the standard to judge probable cause was the totality of the circumstances, and this same test is used to determine whether an exigency exists. She acknowledged that blood alcohol content dissipates in the body as it is metabolized, but argued that the totality of the circumstances does not mean that an exigency exists in every case. Moreover, technology had changed since the Court's decision in 1966. Telecommunications advances make it possible for a warrant to be issued much more quickly, and courts have permitted police to phone in a warrant in time-limited situations. While the natural dissipation of alcohol in the bloodstream might precipitate an exigency, it does not necessarily do so categorically in every case.

In a concurrence, the chief justice agreed that the Missouri rule was overbroad, but proposed an alternate per se rule, which would permit a blood draw if it weren't possible to get a warrant in the time it took to transport the suspect to the hospital. Sotomayor refused to adopt this standard, arguing that it would lead to odd results, by permitting warrantless blood draws in situations where the arrest occurred close to a hospital, even if the officer did not attempt to get a warrant. It would create incentives for police to find ways to avoid getting the warrant. Justice Thomas dissented, building on the chief justice's frustration that the majority's decision did not provide any guidance to officers in determining whether an exigency exists, and he saw no compelling reason to prevent an officer who possessed probable cause that a crime was committed to collect the necessary evidence. Justice Thomas' approach completely ignored any semblance of concern for individual rights. All that matters is prosecuting the crime.

Missouri v. McNeely does not create a broad new right for defendants against warrantless blood draws. It merely says that police cannot automatically claim exigency to justify a warrantless blood draw in routine DUI cases. The Court's decision serves as a corrective measure in that it refuses to establish a bright line rule permitting warrantless blood draws in every case. Yet, it does not reject warrantless blood draws. Each case should be evaluated on its own merits using the totality of the circumstances standard. Thus, the precedent from *Schmerber* was not overruled, but merely modified.

MODIFICATIONS TO THE DOG SNIFF DOCTRINE

The Rehnquist Court's decision in 2005 in *Illinois v. Caballes* provided an important tool for police in fighting the war on drugs. The Court held that a K9 narcotics sniff could be done at any traffic stop, with no requirement that an officer have any individualized suspicion beforehand. No one has an expectation of privacy in possessing contraband, and because narcotic dog sniffs only detected the presence or absence of contraband, the use of the dog was not even a search. But if the dog alerted, it triggered the automobile exception to the warrant requirement, providing probable cause to justify a full search of the vehicle. The Roberts Court has decided three cases involving the use of dog sniffs, all since 2013. All three have served to limit the application of *Caballes*, and are excellent illustrations of the notion of corrective measures. Yet, ironically, taken together, they also call into question the idea that a K9 sniff is not a search within the meaning of the Fourth Amendment.

Florida v. Jardines (2013) involved an effort by police to extend the logic of the dog sniff from the vehicle context to the home. After receiving an anonymous tip that marijuana was being grown in a home, a Florida detective joined forces with the Drug Enforcement Agency and put the home under surveillance. After watching the home for 15 minutes, and observing no signs that anyone was home, the detective approached the front door of the home, along with another detective and his drug-sniffing dog. The dog alerted on the front door, indicating that it had smelled contraband. After the dog alerted, one of the officers claimed to smell what they believed to be marijuana, a fact only mentioned in Justice Alito's dissent. The officers left the scene and sought a warrant for a search of the home based primarily on the dog's alert. The subsequent search uncovered several marijuana plants in the home, and its owner, Joel Jardines, was arrested. Jardines sought to have the evidence suppressed on the basis that the dog sniff on the front steps of his home was an unreasonable search and a violation of his privacy. The trial court agreed, suppressing the evidence. On appeal, the intermediate appellate court reversed the trial court, only to be reversed by the Florida Supreme Court, which reinstituted the original trial court order. The state of Florida sought certiorari and the Supreme Court granted it.

Justice Scalia wrote an opinion for a 5–4 majority, affirming the decision of the Florida Supreme Court. Scalia relied on the trespass doctrine he developed in *United States v. Jones* the year before, holding that the use of a dog sniff on the curtilage of a home was a physical intrusion of a constitutionally protected place, one's home, and thus was an unreasonable search under the Fourth Amendment. Scalia began his opinion by establishing that the curtilage, "the area immediately surrounding and associated with the home," is part of the home, and is subject to the same constitutional protections as the home, relying on *Oliver v. United States* (1984). With the curtilage established as part of the home, Scalia then turned to the question of whether it was reasonable to bring a narcotics dog to its front steps to perform a drug sniff. He cited an early Warren Court decision, *Silverman v. United States* (1961), to reiterate the often-repeated doctrine that the protections of the Fourth Amendment are strongest in the home: "At the Amendment's 'very core' stands 'the right of a man to retreat into his home and there be free from unreasonable governmental intrusions.'"[5] Scalia began by acknowledging that the Fourth Amendment does not prohibit police from conducting nonintrusive surveillance of a home from the street, nor does it prohibit an officer from walking up to the home and knocking on the door. There is an implicit license that permits a visitor to approach the home by the front path and knock and wait to be received. This is no different for a police officer than for a Girl Scout selling cookies or a Halloween trick-or-treater. Scalia then argued that no such common invitation exists when the police officer brings the narcotics dog to the same front step to conduct a search.

The argument then turns on distinguishing the use of the narcotics sniff at the front door with the vehicle search case law that held that there is no reasonable expectation of privacy against dog sniffs. Both *United States v. Place* (1983) and *Illinois v. Caballes* (2005) had treated the dog as being sui generis (or unique in itself) because the trained narcotics dog was specially trained to only alert on the presence of contraband. The consequence of this was that the Court held that since the dog only detected the presence of contraband, and no individual has a reasonable expectation of privacy in possessing contraband, the use of a narcotics sniff was not even a search under the Fourth Amendment, and as a result officers needed no suspicion to conduct a narcotics sniff. Scalia avoids the problem this creates for his argument by using the property law–based argument he had revived in *Jones*. The original understanding of the Fourth Amendment was based on a common law trespass. Just as prior cases did not hold that there was a reasonable expectation of privacy to be free from governmental surveillance by radio transmitters, the use of a GPS was still a search because it was a physical intrusion into a constitutionally protected area: "A person's Fourth Amendment rights do not rise and fall with the *Katz* formulation. The *Katz* reasonable-expectations test has 'been *added to*, not *substituted for*' the traditional property-based understanding of the Fourth Amendment."[6] Thus, he does not have to discern whether there is a reasonable expectation of privacy within the meaning of *Katz v. United States* (1967). It is enough that the dog conducts a search for evidence on the front step of the home. It is a physical intrusion into a constitutionally protected area.

Justice Kagan concurred, joined by Sotomayor and Ginsburg. In her opinion, she acknowledged that while she was willing to decide the case on a property-based approach, she could have just as easily decided it using *Katz*, and argued that in addition to being a trespass, the use of a dog sniff was also an invasion of privacy. She also asserted that this case is controlled by *Kyllo v. United States* (2001), in which the Court had invalidated police use of a thermal imaging device to measure the heat signature of a home. Kagan quoted Scalia's own words from the majority opinion in *Kyllo*: "Where, as here, the government uses a device not in general public use, to explore details of a home that would previously have been unknowable without physical intrusion, the surveillance is a 'search' and is presumptively unreasonable without a warrant."[7]

Justice Alito dissented, claiming that there is no basis in the history of common law to claim that bringing a dog to the front steps of a home is a trespass.

He argued that since dogs have been domesticated for more than 12,000 years, this case involves little more than the officer and his dog, Franky, walking up the front steps. Alito rejected both the trespass doctrine and reasonable expectation of privacy argument. In doing so, he assumed that all dogs are the same, and does not acknowledge that narcotics-sniffing dogs are highly trained in detecting contraband, and are not the same as a household pet. Instead, the narcotics dog was a very valuable tool for law enforcement. Moreover, Alito suggests that the fact that the dog was at the front step for a minute or two minimizes the intrusion. Just as he thought a short period of surveillance using GPS technology would not offend the Fourth Amendment in *Jones*, the quick sniff done by the dog here is not a Fourth Amendment violation in his view.

Florida v. Jardines is typical of corrective measure decisions. The Court had developed the law of K9 narcotics sniffs in such a way to enable police to utilize a dog without any individualized suspicion in any traffic stop. When the police attempted to extend the use of dog sniffs to a home, that was, in the eyes of the Court, one step too far. The very nature of the home had a level of constitutional protection that was dramatically different from a vehicle. As a result, in prohibiting warrantless use of narcotics sniffs at the outside of the home, the Court was restoring balance. It was not carving out a new right, but instead was holding the line. Dogs would continue to be used in vehicle searches with little limit, but their use would not be extended to the outside of a home.

Testing the Dog's Reliability

A second narcotics sniff case came from Florida in the same term. *Florida v. Harris* (2013) considered the issue of whether the reliability of a narcotics dog can be challenged. Clayton Harris' truck was pulled over for an expired license plate. Upon approaching the vehicle, Officer Wheetley noted that the driver appeared to be nervous, "unable to sit still, shaking, and breathing rapidly." There was also an open can of beer in the cup holder. The officer asked to conduct a consent search, but was denied. As a result, he retrieved his narcotics dog, Aldo, from the patrol car, and conducted an open-air sniff. The dog alerted on the driver's door. This provided probable cause for the officer to search the vehicle. While he did not find any drugs, he did find 200 pseudoephedrine pills, 8,000 matches, and other precursor chemicals that are used to manufacture methamphetamine. Harris was arrested and charged with possessing pseudoephedrine for manufacturing meth. While Harris was on bail, the same officer stopped him again and had Aldo conduct another search. Once again, the dog alerted, but this time the search found no drugs.

Clayton Harris sought to have the evidence from the first search suppressed, claiming that the dog's alert did not provide probable cause for a search. At trial, the officer described the training he and the dog had received in narcotics detection. Harris' attorney focused on how Aldo's narcotics certification had expired the prior year, and had not been updated. The trial court denied the motion, but on appeal, the Florida Supreme Court reversed, finding that the dog's training and certification were not enough to establish probable cause when the dog alerted. The Court instead insisted upon detailed records being kept of its performance in the field.

The Supreme Court granted certiorari, and Justice Kagan wrote the opinion for a unanimous court. In some ways, the decision appears to be a vindication of the jurisprudence of crime control, as the first part of Kagan's opinion focuses on how the Florida Supreme Court flouted the totality of the circumstances standard for probable cause established in *Illinois v. Gates* (1983), by insisting that the dog's reliability and alerts only be permitted if there were detailed data on its performance history. Kagan asserted that the totality of the circumstances was how probable cause was to be measured, and rejected the test offered by the Florida Supreme Court as counter to that. She held that "evidence of a dog's satisfactory performance in a certification or training program can itself provide sufficient reason to trust its alert."[8]

Yet, Kagan did not end with the reaffirmation of *Gates*' totality of the circumstances test. For the first time, the Supreme Court acknowledged that the reliability of a narcotics dog could be challenged in Court. She wrote, "A defendant, however, must have an opportunity to challenge evidence of a dog's reliability, whether by cross-examination, or by introducing his own fact or expert witnesses."[9] A probable cause hearing for the dog's reliability has to follow the totality of the circumstances standard as used in all other probable cause hearings, but the dog is not assumed to be reliable just because it conducts a narcotics sniff. While Harris lost his appeal, the decision created a possible limitation on drug dog sniffs that did not exist up until that point.

Kagan's holding that a defendant could challenge the reliability of a narcotics dog, even if it was measured by the state-friendly totality of the circumstances standard, was a limitation on the use of K9 narcotics sniffs. The decision was a corrective measure. It did not eliminate the use of narcotics sniffs or even mandate some justification for their use, but it served to put police on notice that they had to be ready to defend the reliability of their narcotics dogs in court.

Further Limiting the Dog Sniff

A third K9 case was decided in the 2014 term. *Rodriguez v. United States* (2015) considered the question of whether a narcotics sniff could extend the length of a traffic stop. Shortly after midnight on March 27, 2012, Dennys Rodriguez was observed by a police officer, Morgan Struble, as his vehicle veered onto the highway shoulder for a few seconds, before jerking back onto the highway. The officer pulled Rodriguez's vehicle over. Struble approached the car, and asked why he had veered onto the shoulder. Rodriguez replied that he did so to avoid a pothole. The officer took Rodriguez's license and registration and returned to his vehicle. After running a records check, he returned to the vehicle and asked the passenger in the vehicle, Scott Pullman, for his license, and questioned the pair as to where they were going. The officer returned to his vehicle, ran a records check on the passenger, and called for backup. He wrote Rodriguez a warning ticket for driving off the shoulder of the road. The traffic stop had taken about 22 minutes at this point, and at trial the officer acknowledged that at this time all of the reasons for the stop "were out of the way." He apparently did not believe that Rodriguez and Pullman were free to leave, however, as Rodriguez was asked to consent to a vehicle search, which he refused. Another five minutes passed until a second officer arrived, and then Officer Struble retrieved his K9 from the vehicle and proceeded to have the dog do a narcotics sniff. On the second walk around the vehicle, the dog alerted. Struble searched the vehicle and found methamphetamine. Approximately seven or eight minutes had transpired after issuing the traffic warning.

Rodriguez sought to have the evidence suppressed on the basis that the dog sniff was unreasonable, arguing that Struble had prolonged the traffic stop without reasonable suspicion to conduct the dog sniff. At trial, the district court agreed that there was no reasonable suspicion to support the detention once the traffic violation was completed, but upheld the search under the Eighth Circuit's rule that a seven- or eight-minute extension to the stop was a minimal intrusion. The court of appeals affirmed the district court's ruling. The Supreme Court granted certiorari to resolve a conflict between the Eighth and Tenth Circuits over whether a traffic stop could be extended without reasonable suspicion once the purpose of the stop was completed.

The Court reversed the Eighth Circuit's ruling, in a 6–3 decision, authored by Justice Ginsburg. Justices Kennedy, Alito, and Thomas dissented.

Ginsburg argued that a traffic stop is a relatively brief encounter, and is more "analogous to a *Terry* stop than a formal arrest."[10] The mission the police are conducting determines the length of a traffic stop, the time needed to address the traffic violation. Relying on the Burger Court's decision in *United States v. Sharpe* (1985), Ginsburg held that "authority for the seizure ends when the tasks related to the traffic infraction are—or reasonably should have been—completed."[11] This is based on an assumption that the police are acting diligently to pursue the investigation. Ginsburg pointed out that even in *Caballes*, which upheld the use of suspicion-less K9 narcotic sniffs, "a traffic stop can become unlawful if it is prolonged beyond the time reasonably required to complete the mission of issuing a warning ticket."[12] An officer can ask questions unrelated to the traffic violation, but may not do so in a way that prolongs the stop, absent the reasonable suspicion required by *Terry v. Ohio* (1968). This includes checking the driver's background for warrants. But a narcotics sniff is different; it is a measure "aimed at detecting evidence of ordinary criminal wrongdoing." A dog sniff is not part of the officer's traffic mission. Ultimately, the question for Ginsburg was whether the dog sniff extends the length of the stop: "As we said in *Caballes* and reiterate today, a traffic stop 'prolonged beyond' that point is 'unlawful.' The critical question, then, is not whether the dog sniff occurs before or after the officer issues a ticket, as Justice Alito supposes, but whether conducting the sniff 'prolongs'—*i.e.*, adds time to—'the stop.'"[13]

Justices Alito and Thomas both wrote dissents, challenging Ginsburg's rationale. Thomas was not persuaded that a 29-minute traffic stop was unreasonable. Moreover, he relied on *Caballes* to argue that there is no reasonable expectation of privacy against dog sniffs, and thus the use of a dog sniff does not change the character of the traffic stop, as long as it is executed in a reasonable manner. Thomas went to great lengths to explain why he believed the officer had reasonable suspicion to conduct the dog sniff, relying on his own opinion from *Navarette v. California* (2014). He questioned the explanation given by Rodriguez and Pullman for why they were out, having traveled to Omaha, from Norfolk, Nebraska, at night to look at a vehicle they were thinking about purchasing. Thomas was persuaded by Officer Struble's claim that it seemed suspicious to drive two hours to see a vehicle sight unseen, and was even more suspicious given that "usually people leave Omaha to get vehicles, not the other way around," due to Omaha's higher taxes. Thomas' dissent captured the diminished standard of reasonable suspicion that he had articulated in *Navarette*.

Justice Alito's dissent described the majority opinion as "unnecessary, impractical, and arbitrary" because it addressed what he considered to be a hypothetical question of whether "the traffic stop in this case would be unreasonable if the police officer, prior to leading a drug-sniffing dog around the exterior of petitioner's car, did not already have reasonable suspicion that the car contained drugs."[14] Alito viewed the majority's opinion as arbitrary because he did not think the Court actually determined the actual Fourth Amendment question of whether the stop was actually unreasonably prolonged. He then framed the issue as one of officer safety. To Alito, the Court's decision was perverse because the officer chose the sequence of when to do the dog sniff to protect his own safety. Alito claimed that Officer Struble was outnumbered at the scene, and wanted to wait for a second officer to arrive to conduct the sniff. Justice Kagan responded to this concern, arguing that in a traffic safety stop, the officer safety concern is tied to the mission of the traffic stop itself, and this permits the officer to take necessary precautions. But the choice to investigate other possible crimes "detours from that mission," and the choice to take precautions cannot be justified on the same basis—there needs to be some independent level of suspicion: "Highway and officer safety are interests different in kind from the Government's endeavor to detect crime in general or drug trafficking in particular."[15]

Rodriguez v. United States raises questions about the use of narcotics sniffs that will need to be addressed in future cases. The majority opinion insisting that traffic stops cannot be extended beyond the issuance of the citation or warning is a significant limit on the use of dog sniffs. Of course, Justice Alito points out one of the problems the decision will face. Officers will simply change their sequence of events and take longer to issue the citation:

> The rule that the Court adopts will do little good going forward. It is unlikely to have any appreciable effect on the length of future traffic stops. Most officers will learn the prescribed sequence of events even if they cannot fathom the reason for that requirement. (I would love to be the proverbial fly on the wall when police instructors teach this rule to officers who make traffic stops.)[16]

But the decision is a corrective measure. It is an effort to rein in the excesses of the law that has developed in the area of traffic stops and vehicle searches. Just as *Arizona v. Gant* narrowed the ability to conduct vehicle searches incident to arrest, *Rodriguez* places a small constraint on dog sniffs. It also creates tension with the decision in *Caballes*, which held that no suspicion is needed to conduct a sniff, but now if that sniff cannot be done within the time needed to write a ticket, then reasonable suspicion is required.

GEORGIA V. RANDOLPH AND COTENANT CONSENT

The Rehnquist Court decision in *Illinois v. Rodriguez* (1990) held that police could conduct a warrantless search when they received the consent of a person who shares, or reasonably is believed to share, common authority over a residence, even if the other tenant later objects to the search. *Illinois v. Rodriguez* was a typical crime control decision, where the police were held to an extremely lax standard. They did not make any effort to determine whether the person claiming to be a cotenant actually resided at the apartment, but instead held that the police simply had to reasonably believe that the person held common authority in the totality of the circumstances. The Roberts Court first dealt with a similar consent case in its first term, when it heard *Georgia v. Randolph* (2006). In this case, both tenants were present, and the police sought consent to search. The wife granted it, but the petitioner objected.

Scott and Janet Randolph were separated, and Janet had moved out of the family home to stay with her parents. A month later, she returned with her child. A domestic dispute occurred, and Scott removed the child from the home, bringing him to a neighbor's house, out of concern that his wife would take the child out of the country. Janet called the police and, in the process, told them that Scott was a cocaine user. The police came to the house and helped Janet to retrieve her child. She reiterated her claim that her husband was a drug user and stated that there was evidence of drug use in the home. The officer asked Scott for consent to search the home, which he refused. He asked Janet, and she readily agreed, and led the officer to a bedroom, where he found a straw with a powdery residue that he suspected was cocaine. He retrieved the straw and called the district attorney's office, who told him to cease the search and get a warrant. A search warrant was granted, further evidence was found, and Randolph was charged with possession of cocaine.

Randolph sought to have the evidence suppressed, claiming that he had objected to the consent search that provided probable cause for the search warrant. The motion to suppress was denied by the trial court, but the Georgia Court of Appeals reversed. The Georgia Supreme Court affirmed the lower appellate court. It held that consent given by one occupant is not valid in the face of the refusal of another occupant who is physically present at the time. It relied on *United States v. Matlock* (1974), which held that the "consent of one who possesses common authority over premises or effects is valid as against the absent, non-consenting person with whom that authority is shared,"[17] but held that *Matlock* was distinguished because Randolph was physically present.

The Supreme Court granted certiorari, and affirmed the Georgia Supreme Court. Justice Souter's majority opinion placed a consent search in the home in the context of a reasonable expectation of privacy, and argued that if Janet Randolph wanted to bring criminal behavior to light, she could have taken evidence from the home and brought it to the police. He pointed out that *Matlock* was based on an "absent non-consenting resident," whereas in this case the nonconsenting resident was physically present. He also acknowledged that the decision might undermine the Court's precedent in *Illinois v. Rodriguez*, in which the defendant was in the home, but sleeping, when the police entered. Souter acknowledged that "if those cases are not to be undercut by today's holding, we have to admit that we are drawing a fine line; if a potential defendant with self-interest in objecting is in fact at the door and objects, the co-tenant's permission does not suffice for a reasonable search, whereas the potential objector, nearby but not invited to take part in the threshold colloquy, loses out."[18] Souter acknowledged that while this rule might not be truly satisfying, the primary concern was that "there is no evidence that the police have removed the potentially objecting tenant from the entrance for the sake of avoiding a possible objection,"[19] and thus this distinction would be acceptable.

Georgia v. Randolph is a prototypical example of a corrective measures case. It does not carve out a broad new right, but merely makes a correction to a doctrine that had been in existence since the 1970s and was modified once before in 1990. *Randolph* answered the one remaining question: If both tenants are present and one objects over the other's consent, is that grant of consent valid? While protective of individual rights, the decision does not carve out a broad new right.

Nine years after *Randolph*, the Court decided *Fernandez v. California* (2014), which explored the very issue that Souter raised as a concern near the end of his opinion in *Randolph*—that the police do not remove the potentially objecting tenant for the sake of avoiding a possible objection. In *Fernandez*, Los Angeles police officers were in pursuit of a suspect in a gang-related assault. They arrived at an apartment where they heard the sounds of screaming and fighting. They knocked on the door, and Roxanne Rojas answered. She showed signs of having been injured, having a bruised nose and blood on her shirt. They asked if anyone else was home, and she said it was just her and her four-year-old son. When she was asked to allow the officers to conduct a protective sweep of the apartment, Walter Fernandez appeared and explicitly asserted his rights as a resident of the apartment to deny the officers access. At that point, he was arrested on suspicion of domestic violence and taken to the police station for booking. One hour later, the police returned to the apartment and received consent to search from Rojas, in part by suggesting that, if she refused, her fitness as a parent would be called into question. Fernandez had not been released from custody and was not present at the time. The police found clothes worn by the defendant in the robbery in question as well as a knife, sawed-off shotgun, and evidence of gang affiliation.

In an opinion by Justice Alito, the Court held that Fernandez's objection to the consent search was invalid since he was not physically present at the apartment. While not overruling *Randolph*, the decision limited it by requiring that an objection to a consent search come from one who was physically present to object. Justice Alito disregarded the fact that the only reason Fernandez wasn't physically present to object was because the police had removed him. Taken together, the *Randolph* and *Fernandez* cases suggest that in the jurisprudence of crime control, even if a cotenant can object to a consent search, the privacy right can be overridden easily, by simply removing the objecting tenant from the scene.

THE STRANGE CASE OF STUDENT STRIP SEARCHES AND QUALIFIED IMMUNITY

In October 2003, middle school administrators in Safford, Arizona, became suspicious that a 13-year-old girl, Savanna Redding, was giving other students drugs in violation of school policy. The drugs in question were nonnarcotic pain relievers, prescription-strength ibuprofen (the equivalent of two Advil pills), and over-the-counter naproxen (Aleve). The case began when a student, Jordan Romero, reported to the school principal that students were bringing drugs and weapons on campus. A week later, that same student turned over a pill to the principal he said had been given to him by another student, Marissa Glines. In the presence of an administrative assistant, Glines was told to go to the principal's office. Her teacher gave the principal a day planner that was in Glines' vicinity. She was questioned and asked to turn out her pockets and open her wallet. The search uncovered several white pills, a blue pill, and a razor blade. When questioned about the blue pill, Glines accused Savanna Redding, by saying, "I guess it slipped in when she gave me the IBU 400s." The blue pill was an anti-inflammatory over-the-counter medicine, naproxen. The day planner was searched and included additional contraband. Glines was then subjected to a search of her bra and underpants, but no other pills were found.

School officials then called Savanna Redding into the office. They had determined that the two girls were on friendly terms. Savanna claimed not to know anything about the contents of the day planner but admitted lending it to Glines. A statement from Jordan Romero that the two girls had been at a party where alcohol was served further strengthened the principal's suspicion. With Glines' accusation that the pills came from Redding, the principal decided that he had reasonable suspicion that Redding was involved in the distribution of the pills. The principal proceeded to search Redding's backpack and outer clothing. The girl was then instructed, under the watch of two female staff members, to pull out her bra and the elastic band on her underpants. This exposed her breasts and genital area. No pills were found.

Redding's mother filed a civil suit claiming that her daughter's Fourth Amendment rights had been violated by the strip search. The school officials claimed that they were acting under the law established by *New Jersey v. T.L.O.* (1985), a Burger Court decision that established that in the context of a school, administrators do not need probable cause to conduct a search of a student. The district court ruled in their favor, holding that they were immune from suit. The Ninth Circuit reversed, holding that a strip search was not permissible under the rule in *T.L.O.* and that her right was clearly established at the time of the search. The Supreme Court granted certiorari and, in a surprising decision, ruled in favor of Redding, in terms of her right against strip searches, but then decided that the law was not clear at the time, and thus the principal was immune from damages under the doctrine of qualified immunity. Redding won, in that future students would not be subject to strip searches by school officials, but she lost in seeking damages in the strip search conducted on her.

Of any Roberts Court case, *Safford Unified School District v. Redding* (2009) best illustrates the tension between curbing the excesses of crime control and the desire to protect government officials against suit. The decision makes a strong statement that Safford had a reasonable expectation of privacy against a strip search by a school official. Justice Souter's majority opinion held that while the search of her backpack and outer clothing was reasonable under *T.L.O.*, the strip search was not: "Savanna's subjective expectation of privacy against such a search is inherent in her account of it as embarrassing, frightening, and humiliating. The reasonableness of her expectation (required by the Fourth Amendment standard) is indicated by the consistent experiences of other young people similarly searched, whose adolescent vulnerability intensifies the patent intrusiveness of the exposure."[20] Souter then held that the search wasn't just an indignity; the suspicion did not match the level of the intrusion. The principal knew that the drugs in question were prescription-strength ibuprofen and over-the-counter naproxen. This was not a search for cocaine. There was no reason to believe large quantities of pills were being distributed. Nor could he have reasonably suspected her to be storing these pain relievers in her underwear. This would require some justification in suspected facts, not just a general belief that students hide drugs in their underwear: "A reasonable search that extensive calls for suspicion that it will pay off. But nondangerous school contraband does not raise the specter of stashes in intimate places, and there is no evidence in the record of any general practice among Safford Middle School students of hiding that sort of thing in underwear."[21]

After determining that the strip search was an unreasonable search under the Fourth Amendment, Souter then held that the two school administrators were immune from suit, for no other reason than that there was disagreement in the interpretation of *New Jersey v. T.L.O.* by a variety of lower courts. Justices Stevens and Ginsburg dissented from this part of the opinion, claiming that the school administrators were liable for their actions. Justice Thomas, to the contrary, concurred with the holding of qualified immunity, but dissented from the holding that Redding's rights had been violated. The case represents a conundrum of sorts. It can be thought of as a corrective measure, placing limitations on school officials (in the future) and clarifying the ruling in *T.L.O.*, while never clearly stating that strip searches of students were categorically prohibited, but limiting them to facts where there was reason to believe that such a search would result in finding contraband. Yet, the Court refused to hold the school officials accountable. The decision showed the power that the jurisprudence of crime control holds over the justices. Even where there is a constitutional violation, there is a strong pull to avoid using the exclusionary rule or holding government officials (in civil liability suits like this) responsible for their actions. For Savanna Redding, the victory in court was hollow. Yet, for future defendants, her case would serve to provide a precedent that would usually prevent such extremely intrusive searches from occurring.

HINTS ON HOW TO WIN ON REMAND?

It is easy to forget that the rulings at the Supreme Court level often do not determine the final outcome of a case. Although Antoine Jones won his case concerning the use of a GPS tracking device, on remand, a retrial occurred. During the new trial, the prosecution introduced tracking data from Jones' cell phone to establish his whereabouts during the key times in question.[22] He ultimately entered into a plea bargain and was sentenced to 15 years in a federal prison.[23] While the long saga of Antoine Jones is extreme, it is important to remember that defendants who win at the Supreme Court often get as their only reward a new trial and that they may remain in prison during the years of legal wrangling.

Often when the Roberts Court issues a search and seizure decision favoring the defendant, the opinion contains instructions to the lower courts on how they might find a way to uphold the search in further proceedings. For example, in *Brendlin v. California*, the Court ruled that a passenger in a motor vehicle does have standing to challenge the validity of the initial traffic stop, thus allowing the defendant to object to the introduction of evidence seized incident to that traffic stop. The majority opinion also contained the following statement near the end of the opinion: "It will be for the state courts to consider in the first instance whether suppression turns on any other issue."[24] On remand, the California attorney general successfully moved for the consideration of the issue of whether a subsequent discovery of a warrant for the arrest of the defendant affected the legality of the search. The California Supreme Court expressly cited to the United States Supreme Court's invitation to consider other issues in holding that the inadvertent finding of an outstanding warrant for the arrest of the defendant attenuated the effect of the unlawful seizure.[25]

The case of *Bailey a.k.a. Polo v. United States* (2013) offers an even more blatant example of the Court ruling in favor of a defendant while providing direction to the lower courts as to how the state can win on remand. *Bailey* involved the police detaining two men while they searched an apartment for which they had a warrant. The men were followed and detained some distance from the apartment, and the Court ruled that the right to detain while a search warrant is executed only applies to the immediate vicinity of the premises searched. In theory, this opinion was a corrective measure; it placed limits on the police, preventing them from detaining a suspect who is not at the location of the search. *Bailey* also contained a clear hint as to how to justify the stop under *Terry v. Ohio*. The Court suggested that there might be other ways to legitimately detain the suspect on an investigatory stop: "It must be noted that the District Court, as an alternative ruling, held that stopping petitioner was lawful under *Terry*. This opinion expresses no view on that issue. It will be open, on remand, for the Court of Appeals to address the matter and to determine whether, assuming the *Terry* stop was valid, it yielded information that justified the detention the officers then imposed."[26] On remand, the search was upheld as a legitimate *Terry* stop.[27]

CONCLUSION

The Roberts Court's Fourth Amendment jurisprudence is in flux. A decade of decisions has resulted in some cracks in the jurisprudence of crime control. While major decisions such as *Riley v. California* and *United States v. Jones* are rare, the Court has handed down several cases that are favorable to defendants. Many of the liberal outcomes are still quite narrow, and the Court is more likely to simply rein in the excesses of crime control than carve out new rights. That said, these corrective measure cases have been quite common, and since the arrival of Justices Sotomayor and Kagan, almost half of all Roberts Court Fourth Amendment decisions have been favorable to the defendant.

This does not mean that the Court has abandoned the crime control paradigm or that the Court is shifting to the left in fundamental ways on Fourth Amendment issues. The defendant might win in some cases, but even when the outcome is favorable, the state may still prevail on remand. The police may be forced to fine-tune their training and procedures, but not to alter them fundamentally. The rules of the game still favor the state in most criminal cases, but perhaps not as much since 2011. The Court still retains its desired public perception that it is ideologically neutral, that each case is decided on its own merits without preconception or partisanship, and that the Court still serves its constitutionally mandated role as a check on the executive and legislative branches. It will remain for another day to see if more cases like *United States v. Jones* and *Riley v. California* are decided. If that happens, perhaps one can argue more forcefully that the paradigm is shifting. In the concluding chapter, we return to assess the state of the Fourth Amendment and explore some of the issues the Court is likely to grapple with in the near future.

8. Toward the Future

When the Roberts Court began there were few expectations that the Court's approach to Fourth Amendment cases would differ significantly from that of the Rehnquist Court. Yet, in the decade that has passed since William Rehnquist's death, there have been numerous changes in the development of search and seizure law. From 1981 through 2005, Fourth Amendment decisions resulted in outcomes favorable to the state in 75 percent of cases. This trend continued during the first five years of the Roberts Court, with 73 percent of its first 15 decisions upholding law enforcement interests. In the five years since Justices Sotomayor and Kagan joined the Court, however, defendants won in almost half (47 percent) of 21 cases. In total, the Roberts Court's Fourth Amendment cases have only had conservative outcomes in 61 percent of cases. It is our argument that the Roberts Court's approach to the Fourth Amendment is in flux, and while the justices are still driven by the jurisprudence of crime control, the Court is less monolithic in its approach to search and seizure issues than it has been in the past 30 years.

We have sought not only to explain how Fourth Amendment law has changed since the early 1980s, but also to understand the consequence of those changes for the Court today. In chapter 1, we argued that four factors help explain the Roberts Court's Fourth Amendment decisions. First, and perhaps most important, we cannot understand the Roberts Court without placing it into the context of how the law of search and seizure has developed since the end of the 1960s. The backlash to the Warren Court's criminal procedure decisions resulted in the selection of new justices who were determined to place greater emphasis on crime control and less emphasis on the rights of the accused. The Burger and then Rehnquist Courts provided a counterrevolution of sorts to the liberal Warren Court and, in the process, created a jurisprudence of crime control that favors law enforcement discretion over individual rights. The focus on crime control has both minimized the role of the warrant requirement and significantly discouraged use of the exclusionary rule. The early 1980s were particularly important. In the two-year span between 1982 and 1984, the Court decided two-dozen cases, creating what Richards and Kritzer called a jurisprudential regime shift.[1] Major decisions on probable cause and the exclusionary rule resulted in a paradigm shift in how Fourth Amendment cases are evaluated. This, in turn, has influenced the philosophical approach of a generation of judges at all levels when evaluating Fourth Amendment claims. The jurisprudential regime shift defines the baseline for Fourth Amendment analysis today. It helps explain why the state won in 75 percent of all search and seizure cases through 2010.

Our second argument is that to make sense of the evolution of the Fourth Amendment on the Roberts Court, we have to take into account changes in the composition of the Court. The retirements of Justices Souter and Stevens, and their replacements by Justices Sotomayor and Kagan, have resulted in justices who are considerably more liberal in their approach to the Fourth Amendment. While Justices Souter and Stevens were quite moderate, their successors have voted for the defendant in every prodefendant or liberal decision. In addition to new justices, the shift in approach to decision making by Justice Scalia, one of the Court's leading conservatives, provided a voice for Fourth Amendment rights that was not present in his decisions throughout the Rehnquist Court years. Scalia was no longer a reliable conservative vote on search and seizure cases, although he was quite idiosyncratic and less predictable than the Court's liberal bloc of justices. He viewed the Fourth Amendment through a different set of perceptual lenses.

Third, we argue that while there are more liberal rulings from the Roberts Court, many of those are not carving out broad new Fourth Amendment rights, but instead serve as corrective measures that rein in the excesses of the jurisprudence of crime control. In a world where the Court has continually expanded police power, liberal decisions have often served to pull the Court back when law enforcement seeks to expand its discretion even beyond what the Court is willing to provide. These decisions serve to fine-tune the outer boundaries of what is allowed, as opposed to creating new precedent. In an ironic sense, these decisions actually serve to strengthen the legitimacy of the Court's crime control jurisprudence in that they increase the likelihood that the general public will perceive the judiciary as a nonpartisan, apolitical check on the actions of the executive and legislative branches.

Finally, we argue that some of the flux in the development of Fourth Amendment law has been precipitated by the challenges associated with the need to apply the Fourth Amendment to cases that involve modern information technology. The saliency of smartphones and GPS technology to the general public has put pressure on the Court to approach some Fourth Amendment issues differently than it would normally. The Court has struggled with this task, resulting in tension between the desire to preserve the jurisprudence of crime control and the need to recognize the threat to privacy that results from the ubiquitous gathering of all sorts of data about each and every one of us every single minute of our lives. In this chapter we will conclude our examination of the Roberts Court by engaging in the more speculative task of considering the future.

THE COURT AS A SMALL GROUP

It is unlikely that the Roberts Court will remain static in its membership for an extended period of time. While none of the justices has indicated a desire to retire, the odds are good that one or more justices will leave the Court in the next five years. Anticipating future changes in the composition of the Court is a risky business, as there are two unknowns that shape any vacancies. First, presidents almost always seek to appoint justices from their own party and who are sympathetic to their political views. We do not pretend to speculate on the outcome of the 2016 presidential election, but past history suggests that if a Republican wins the White House, he or she will appoint justices who are more conservative on many issues, including crime, than a Democrat would.

The second unknown is tied to the justices themselves. Supreme Court justices have life tenure, and unless serious illness or an untimely death occurs, as with Scalia, they choose when they leave the Court. The Roberts Court includes two justices who will be 80 years old or older by the time the next president takes office. Justice Ginsburg is already 82 years old, and is a cancer survivor. Justice Kennedy will be 80 in 2016, and will have served on the Court for 29 years. If a Republican wins the White House, and Justice Ginsburg retires, her replacement could significantly alter the balance of power in favor of crime control. Justice Alito, the safest of the crime control votes on the Court, would likely have three sure allies after such an appointment in Justices Thomas, Kennedy, and the new justice, with Chief Justice Roberts a likely fifth vote, except on digital privacy issues. Justices Kagan and Sotomayor, both Obama appointees, would lose a key ally and might find themselves isolated. By contrast, the replacement of Justice Kennedy with a more liberal Democrat could embolden the liberals on the Court. Justices Sotomayor and

Kagan would have two reliable votes in Justice Ginsburg and the new justice, and would need only to convince Breyer or Roberts to go along with them to secure a majority. Justices Alito and Thomas might find themselves alone in dissent on more occasions than they do now.

The consequences of replacing Justice Scalia are a bit harder to predict. Not only were his views on the Fourth Amendment unique among the justices, but his impact on the interpersonal dynamic of the Court was hard to foresee as well. He was well known for his intense questioning of attorneys during oral argument and for his biting and often caustic dissents that attacked his colleagues. Reports of how well the justices get along are hard to find, but the few that exist portray Scalia as sometimes difficult and abrasive.[2] What makes it even harder to predict the impact of his departure was his unique approach to some Fourth Amendment cases. Since 2010, he voted with the defendant half of the time and revived the long-overruled trespass doctrine. He used that theory to write the majority opinions in *United States v. Jones* (2012) and *Florida v. Jardines* (2013), both of which limit the powers of the police. Replacing him with a safe crime control conservative would certainly empower Justices Alito and Thomas, while replacing him with a more liberal justice would upset the balance of power in some cases. While we have no crystal ball for likely retirements or presidential election outcomes, the experience of the Roberts Court in the past five years has shown that the composition of the Court does matter, and we have every reason to believe that future changes in justices would affect how the Court approaches Fourth Amendment cases.

WHY IT MATTERS WHAT THE COURT DECIDES IN FOURTH AMENDMENT CASES

Fourth Amendment issues are often viewed as matters of the routine administration of justice, given that they apply primarily to those accused of or convicted of crimes. Law-abiding citizens may not see the relevance of such decisions. The issue of digital privacy provides a potential linkage between search and seizure law and the daily lives of almost all Americans. In the years since the September 11, 2001, attacks, the government has monitored electronic traffic in a variety of ways, with the gathering of bulk data by the National Security Agency being one of the most controversial. After Edward Snowden's revelations of the vast extent of the NSA's surveillance of the everyday lives of American people, the issue of governmental surveillance increased in saliency. When reauthorization of the USA Patriot Act came before Congress in June 2015, the Senate refused to reauthorize the bulk collection of such data, and a compromise was passed in the form of the USA Freedom Act.[3] This act provides for the collection and storage of such data by phone and Internet service providers, and requires the government to seek court approval to access the data. While the Court placed limits on the ability of police to search smartphones, there are several related Fourth Amendment issues that remain outstanding, and that the Court will have to address in future years.

The Fourth Amendment is also entangled with recent controversies concerning the police's use of deadly force against young, black males. Several high-profile instances of police use of deadly force in 2014 and 2015 against unarmed young males of color made national news and inspired protests both peaceful and violent. The deaths of Michael Brown in Ferguson, Missouri, and Eric Garner in New York City were the most widely reported of these incidents. In both cases, decisions by grand juries not to prosecute the officers involved have created significant public doubt about the ways in which the police exercise their discretion. The protests have reignited political debates over police use of racial profiling as well. Since its decision in *Whren v. United States* (1996), the Court has refused to even consider the constitutional implications of racial profiling. One of the consequences of the way the Fourth Amendment and criminal procedure law in general developed during the Burger and Rehnquist Courts is that the Court created a system in which law enforcement has become largely immune from claims of racial bias.[4] As civil and criminal cases arising out of incidents of police use of force against minorities make their way through the courts, litigators and the media will question the consequences of a jurisprudence of crime control that provides such vast discretion to police in combatting crime and frequently shields officers from legal liability for their actions. There will certainly be cases challenging the use of force by the police in the coming years. How the Court will eventually deal with these issues, however, remains uncertain.

In the 1960s, presidential candidates Barry Goldwater and Richard Nixon used rising crime and social disorder to target the Supreme Court for its decisions expanding the rights of the accused. The law and order movement that resulted played a significant role in President Nixon's selection of his four Supreme Court nominees. All four were pivotal in the development of a jurisprudence of crime control. The underlying motivations of law enforcement are not seen as relevant to Fourth Amendment issues, as long as there is some objective measure of probable cause present for the most minor of offenses. A long train of cases has made it such that the warrant exception has become the rule as opposed to the rare occurrence. This has fed into the vast expansion of police power and the belief that combatting crime control is far more important than protecting individual rights.

The criticism and backlash against police that have arisen in the past few years are different in many ways from what happened in the 1960s. Then, the Court was blamed for coddling criminals, and it was the focal point of criticism over both the rights of the accused and civil rights issues. Today, criticisms of excessive police use of force are focused on the police, with few commentators making a link between the decisions of the Supreme Court and the behavior of the police. While criticisms of mass incarceration and the racial disparity evident in the war on drugs have begun to raise questions about the fairness of the criminal justice system, the Court has managed to stay on the periphery of them. As a result, there has been no public push demanding change by the Supreme Court to its criminal procedure jurisprudence. This does not mean that the Court is not aware of the broader political issues surrounding its actions, but the degree to which the justices take them into account when deciding cases is uncertain.

Advocates for limiting the discretionary power of police have always faced the challenge that the very rules they favor objectively benefit individuals who have been accused of crimes. The relationship between protecting the rights of the accused and avoiding trampling the rights of the innocent is a tough one for many Americans to perceive. Digital privacy issues offer a unique opportunity to assert this relationship in a compelling way. If the government can monitor the way we use our smartphones, they have access to where we are, what we buy and sell, what questions we ask when we go to the doctor, and a whole host of personal activities. Similarly, if the police can scroll through our cell phones whenever they make a traffic stop, without a warrant, they have access to many of the intimate details of our lives. When you combine the power that access to digital information gives to the government with the large number of false positives produced by efforts to stop the flow of drugs on our highways, you get a situation wherein large numbers of law-abiding citizens involuntarily give up intensely private information to the police if cell phones can be searched incident to arrest. This connection is made even more salient by the general belief among many groups in our society that the police disproportionately target people of color. Whether it is questions of racial justice or concern about digital privacy, these issues are likely to result in cases that the Roberts Court will have to address in the coming decade.

COMING CASES: CELL PHONE TRACKING AND THE THIRD PARTY DOCTRINE

Perhaps no Roberts Court Fourth Amendment case has been as salient as *Riley v. California* (2014), requiring police to obtain a warrant before searching the digital contents of a cell phone. *Riley* is one of the few search and seizure decisions to do more than rein in the excesses of crime control, actually making a strong statement for digital privacy as a substantive individual right. But *Riley* does not determine the outcomes of all digital privacy cases that will likely come before the Court in the next few years. How will the Court rule when faced with a situation wherein a police officer seizes a cell phone from a driver who has just been involved in a collision where the officer has valid reason to suspect texting while driving? Will a limited search of the log of texts sent be allowed for the purpose of verifying whether the driver was texting at the time the accident occurred? Will *Arizona v. Gant*'s (2009) standard for search incident to arrest permit a search if it is reasonable to believe further evidence of the crime of arrest will be found, or will *Riley* force the officer to first get a warrant? Such a scenario is not far-fetched, and at least one case involving a celebrity accused of texting while driving and causing a fatal accident has already occurred.[5]

One type of case that has been the subject of significant litigation in the lower courts is the use of cell phone records to track the location of a particular device and, presumably, its user. Cell phones are radio transmitters and receivers, in frequent communication with the cellular towers that make up the network operated by cell service providers. This network makes it possible to calculate the approximate location of a cell phone through a process of triangulation based on the communication between the phone and the cell towers owned by the network. Today, all cell phones have a GPS device in them so that an even more precise location is possible. For modern smartphones, the GPS serves to make possible a huge range of applications, including navigation, finding restaurants, businesses, and other attractions, and monitoring the location of friends and family members. Commercial uses for locational data are numerous, and the GPS technology makes it possible to very precisely locate a phone as long as it is powered on. This is very important for police who can make use of a device called a stingray to mimic a cell phone tower and trick the phone in question into communicating its whereabouts and other information to the police.[6]

The data that allow the tracking of a cell phone, commonly called Cell Site Location Information, or CSLI, can provide both real-time and historical location data.[7] Law enforcement makes extensive use of these data, frequently accessing them without any judicial oversight at all. Over 1 million requests for data are made each year, often directly to cell service providers, who frequently provide the data voluntarily. If police use a stingray, they can gather CSLI without the involvement of the service provider at all. In the past decade, several federal courts have considered cases involving this technology. State courts have also been faced with these types of cases, and a few state legislatures have also enacted laws that provide protection to cell phone users for the digital records held by their service providers.[8]

Lower courts have been split on how to approach these cases. One way to do so is to merely assert that the data are business records held by a third party. As such, the defendant has no rights whatsoever to protest the use of the data, and they are easily allowed in despite being hearsay because of the business records exception to the rule against hearsay. This approach depends on the continuing validity of the ruling in *Smith v. Maryland* (1979). While some legal scholars see *Smith* as settling the matter, at least with regard to historical tracking through CSLI, others are not so sure.[9] Perhaps most importantly, Justice Sotomayor stated explicitly in her concurring opinion in *United States v. Jones* that the *Smith* precedent is "ill suited to the digital age." Similarly, when Chief Justice Roberts described the search of a cell phone as potentially more invasive than a search of the home, it raised the possibility that *Smith v. Maryland* could be reconsidered. At least two court of appeals decisions have challenged the continued use of *Smith* as it relates to CSLI.[10] In addition, the decision in *City of Los Angeles v. Patel* (2015) further calls into questions the validity of the third party doctrine as controlling precedent. Justice Sotomayor's majority opinion does not directly address the third party doctrine, but the implications of the holding that there must be some opportunity for review prior to the police gaining access to hotel registration information are clear. The holder of the data now has a good argument that there must be some procedure for review prior to the release of the data to the police. This review has the potential for allowing a criminal defendant the opportunity to participate in a proceeding that will determine whether the police can access the data.

When a cell phone tracking case does come to the Court, there will be two main issues: (1) the validity of the third party doctrine; and (2) the strength of the right to privacy with regard to one's location. The first issue is far from certain, but given that the justices have described cell phones as integral parts of our lives, close examination of the underlying justification for *Smith v. Maryland* is likely. With regard to the second issue, Justice Sotomayor's concurring opinion in *United States v. Jones* demonstrates that she believes that tracking a person over a period of time is a search within the meaning of the Fourth Amendment. Justice Alito's concurrence in the same case also voiced concern over long-term surveillance. One could certainly argue that taking Justice Sotomayor's opinion together with Justice Alito's creates a five-person majority for the proposition that the use of a cell phone as a tracking device is a search within the meaning of the Fourth Amendment. If so, the next logical step is an assertion that a person has a right to privacy in their location, meaning that real-time tracking of a person with any kind of digital technology is suspect without a warrant.

Police Access to Commercially Gathered Data

Edward Snowden's revelations that the National Security Agency was monitoring the cell phone and Internet usage of large numbers of Americans and others have resulted in a political controversy that has lasted two years. While the NSA made public attempts to assure the citizenry that no content is monitored without a warrant, skepticism abounds about the NSA's actions. Passage of the USA Freedom Act in 2015 shifts the issue from government collecting data on individuals to cellular phone companies and Internet service providers. The law requires judicial approval before such data from providers can be accessed by the government. Cases in which these data have been accessed will likely make their way through the courts over time, but the fact that judicial oversight is required before the data are accessed in the first place means that these kinds of cases will not be handled in ways that are different than most cases involving a motion to suppress evidence. There is ample evidence that corporations conduct intensive data collection about the habits of consumers.[11] Given the record of cooperation, either voluntarily or via court order, of phone service providers and the integration of phone and Internet service, the more likely scenario for cases challenging government use of data is that the government will gain access to data being collected by commercial search engines, commercial marketing firms, and Internet service providers. It is certainly plausible, for example, that the government could make use of location data gathered by a commercial firm in the process of providing safety services, such as General Motors' "OnStar" product.

The constitutional issues of information gained by the government from private parties are somewhat analogous to the old silver platter doctrine that allowed federal agents to use evidence gained via Fourth Amendment violations committed by state or local law enforcement during the time period between *Weeks v. United States* (1914) and *Elkins v. United States* (1960). Instead of state or local law enforcement being the conduit of information to the federal government, evidence is given to law enforcement by private entities. For example, in *United States v. Jacobsen* (1984), police were allowed to introduce cocaine into evidence that was discovered by Federal Express after a package was damaged in transit. Even though federal agents could not have opened the package without a warrant, the Court ruled that the sender and addressee of the cocaine had lost any reasonable expectation of privacy when the shipping company opened the package. As long as *Smith v. Maryland* remains good precedent, it is possible that data gathered via monitoring of Internet traffic by commercial marketing firms can be retrieved by the government and used in a criminal prosecution. The defendant would have no standing to challenge the use of the evidence since law enforcement agents did not gather the data via any violation of the defendant's rights. If cases like this occur, it is hard to believe that the Court would go so far as to limit the ability of commercial firms to gather data via monitoring of Internet traffic through that company's servers. It is more likely that the Court would attempt to limit the ability of the government to access such data if a pattern of widespread involvement by the government itself in such monitoring is demonstrated.

Drone Usage

Law enforcement use of drones is on the rise. Drones, or unmanned aerial vehicles, are robotically operated aircraft. They can be as small as a small bird or larger than a private plane. The small ones use rotors, like a helicopter, but usually employ multiple rotors for greater stability in flight. The larger ones are often fixed-wing aircraft. The smaller ones have to have an operator nearby, often within a few hundred yards, to work, but the biggest ones can be operated from halfway around the world. The types commonly used by law enforcement weigh just a few pounds and carry video cameras or other small imaging devices. The operator can see color video from the drone in real time.

The Supreme Court has not yet addressed whether evidence gathered by a drone is admissible in court, and only a small number of agencies are reportedly using them on a regular basis. There are credible reports, however, that local law enforcement has been able to borrow drones from federal agencies hundreds of times. North Dakota is the first state to directly address the issue of arming drones, passing a law in 2015 that forbids arming them with lethal weapons, but implicitly allowing nonlethal weapons.[12] While no appellate court cases have been found that involve a challenge to the use of evidence gathered via the use of a drone, at least two documented arrests have been made with the assistance of drones. The Obama administration was required by statute to issue safety rules regulating the use of drones in 2015, and made grant funds available to local law enforcement to help fund their use. It is safe to say that drone use by both private and public entities will likely increase dramatically over the next decade.

There are significant privacy concerns over the potential abuse of drones, prompting concern from privacy organizations such as the American Civil Liberties Union and the Electronic Frontier Foundation. The smallest ones could certainly be used for close, covert surveillance on private property, by private entities or a government agency. Drones could be used to create large-scale databases of the movement of individuals in a given area, much like the use of fixed-location cameras with license plate recognition software. The Court's plain view doctrine has long approved the use of manned overflights to gather evidence, without a warrant, as long as the aircraft is in navigable airspace.[13] If drones are treated like manned aircraft, then overflights by drones in navigable airspace would not require a warrant.[14] If the Court determines that drones themselves are a unique technology, and not simply a way to extend the reach of ordinary vision, then their legality becomes more questionable. It is uncertain whether the Court would apply the *Kyllo v. United States* (2001) standard for judging technological enhancements of the senses. *Kyllo* held that police cannot claim that a search falls under the plain view doctrine if they make use of technology that is not available to the general public without first obtaining a warrant. If the Court were to apply Justice Scalia's trespass doctrine, the use of drones over a home could also be challenged. As the range of sensors available to be deployed on drones grows, the Court will have to determine whether the use of these sensors will require the judicial oversight of a warrant. Additionally, as drone use by private entities is approved by the Federal Aviation Administration, data collected by private companies may well be sought and used by law enforcement agencies. The use of such data would likely be analyzed in the same way as the use of data from cell phone or Internet service.

IS THE WAR ON DRUGS WINDING DOWN?

The war on drugs, which has dominated America's politics of crime control for the past 40 years, is also under pressure. Critics argue that the war on drugs has resulted in a system of mass incarceration where more than 1 out of every 100 adults is under correctional supervision.[15] The economic costs of incarcerating more than 2,000,000 Americans have also resulted in calls for the end of the harsh sentences and single-minded focus on drugs that have continued even though by most counts, crime has been declining since the early 1990s. Critics such as Michelle Alexander have argued that the war on drugs has focused primarily on minorities and has decimated minority communities. Most of the complaints about racial profiling are tied to the war on drugs, as police disproportionately target minorities when making investigatory stops, and cities such as New York focus almost exclusively on minorities in aggressive stop and frisk policies, where minorities are stopped, frisked, and harassed, usually resulting in no criminal charges. In recent years the push for relaxing penalties for marijuana use has increased, as many states have made marijuana a petty offense, and four states have legalized recreational use of marijuana. Almost half of the states have adopted medical marijuana laws. The calls by both liberals and conservatives alike to end the war on drugs, claiming that the war has been lost and has had a destructive effect on minority and poor communities, are all evidence that the nation's obsession with illegal drugs is waning, although it is not clear that law enforcement shares that view. Police have made drug interdiction and investigatory stops one of the primary indicators of their effectiveness and productivity. Far too many political and economic pressures still exist to continue to vigorously prosecute those dealing in illegal drugs.

There is nothing in the language used by the Court in recent cases that indicates that the Court is affected in any way by the waning support for the war on drugs. The rhetoric used to justify the decisions made in favor of the defendant contains no hint that the crime control paradigm is waning with regard to drug or gang prosecutions. The Court has certainly reined in some of the excesses of the ways police use traffic stops to fight the war on drugs. *Rodriguez v. United States* (2015) has limited the use of suspicion-less K9 dog sniffs to the time it takes to complete the traffic stop. *Arizona v. Gant* effectively ended the *Belton* bright line rule for vehicle searches. But the Court has reinforced its claims that suspects can be arrested for any offense, and recent decisions have held that reasonable suspicion for a stop can be based on little more than an anonymous 911 call. While there are some limits on when a vehicle can be searched, the underlying ability of the police to stop pretty much anyone they want is still in place. Roberts Court decisions have placed some outer limits on the police toolbox for the war on drugs, but these decisions have not meaningfully limited the power of the police to aggressively seek out and arrest drug offenders.

Questioning the Logic of the K9 Dog Sniff

One of the key tools for law enforcement in the war on drugs is the use of K9 narcotics dog sniffs. Canine units are common in most agencies of any size, and they are used quite often in traffic stops. In *Illinois v. Caballes* (2005), the Rehnquist Court asserted that sniffs by a trained drug dog were not a search within the meaning of the Fourth Amendment. The logic was that the dog's sniff could only detect the presence of contraband, and no one has a legitimate expectation of privacy in possessing contraband. Personal or private information was not considered at risk of detection. The narcotics dog was considered to be sui generis (or unique in itself) and was treated as if it was infallible in its ability to only detect contraband. The dissents in *Caballes* challenged this argument, pointing to evidence of false alerts, where the dog alerts, but no contraband is found. In some traffic stop K9 studies, as many as half of dog sniffs result in no contraband being found even though the dog had alerted.[16] Police often claim that the dog's acute sense of smell is simply detecting residue of drugs that had been present at one point in time, but those arguments are hard to take seriously, given the frequency that dog alerts come up empty.

The first of the three Roberts Court dog sniff cases, *Florida v. Harris* (2013), addressed the issue of the reliability of the dog. While the Court accepted the reliability of the dog in question, it also made it clear that the lower courts must give the defendant the opportunity to introduce evidence regarding the training and field performance record of the dog, effectively removing the presumption of its infallibility. While a small step, it calls into question one of *Caballes*' underlying principles, that the dog sniff is unique in itself. *Caballes* also held that police did not need reasonable suspicion to conduct a dog sniff because no individual had an expectation of privacy in possessing contraband. *Rodriguez v. United States* now requires that if a dog sniff is to be done after a citation or warning is issued, and a traffic stop's purpose is completed, then the officer needs to have reasonable suspicion to extend the length of the stop. This questions the assertion that the dog sniff is not a search. The logic of *Rodriguez* implies that if a dog sniff is done after a traffic ticket is issued, it is a search and requires reasonable suspicion. But if the sniff is done before a ticket is issued, it isn't a search, and thus no suspicion is needed. The dog sniff appears, for all practical purposes, to be a search, justified by the lower standard of reasonable suspicion, but only some of the time.

The trespass doctrine cases raise even more questions for the legitimacy of dog sniffs. Both *United States v. Jones* and *Florida v. Jardines* used the trespass doctrine to hold that the government had physically intruded on a constitutionally protected area. In *Jones*, the placement of the GPS device on the vehicle was a physical intrusion on a constitutionally protected area. In *Jardines*, the use of the dog to conduct a narcotics sniff on the front step of the home was an intrusion into the home. If the vehicle is an effect and is protected against physical intrusions, and the Court has held that dog sniffs into the interior of other constitutionally protected areas (the home) are unreasonable searches and seizures, then it holds that a dog sniff of a vehicle is also a physical intrusion into a constitutionally protected area. Scalia's trespass doctrine could unravel the entire logic of the *Caballes* dog sniff. Moreover, if Scalia's argument is taken seriously, it calls into question the very notion of the diminished expectation of privacy in the vehicle that has defined the Court's approach to vehicles for 75 years, by making the privacy of the vehicle irrelevant. Yet, it is unclear whether or not the justices would agree with this, or be willing to follow the logic in the decisions to its conclusion. Still, it is likely that there will be more dog cases before the courts, as a result of *Florida v. Harris*. Such cases will force the Court to decide how far to take Justice Scalia's trespass doctrine.

If the Court continues to give credence to the trespass doctrine, it could result in significant changes in the law of dog sniffs. But, given how deeply embedded the jurisprudence of crime control is on the Court, it is just as likely that the justices would ignore the logic that we have laid out, and instead apply the totality of the circumstances approach to both probable cause and reasonable suspicion. The relative nonintrusiveness of a dog sniff will be a factor that may very well lead the Court to uphold many of these searches.

THE FUTURE OF THE TRESPASS DOCTRINE

The trespass doctrine causes problems for more than dog sniffs. The Court has used it in three cases since 2012. Its most recent application came in the per curiam *Grady v. North Carolina* (2015), in which the Court held that the attachment of a GPS tracking device to the person of a sex offender was a search. The trespass doctrine provides a narrow way to decide Fourth Amendment cases, and comes into tension with the *Katz* reasonable expectation of privacy test that the Court has repeatedly stated is the proper standard to determine the constitutionality of searches. Yet, as we have seen in our review of the Burger and Rehnquist Courts, *Katz* claims are only successful a small proportion of the time. When the Court decided *Riley v. California*, Chief Justice Roberts based his decision on the defendant's interest in digital privacy, but never once mentioned *Katz* or the reasonable expectation of privacy standard. Nor, for that matter, did he even broach the subject of the trespass doctrine.

In many ways, the *Katz* standard has become less and less relevant. The jurisprudence of crime control has shifted the Court to make the reasonableness of a search the first question that is answered, and as it has done with the standard of probable cause, the totality of the circumstances has become the means by which most Fourth Amendment analysis is done. Witness how Justice Thomas used it in *Navarette v. California* (2014) to hold that an anonymous 911 call provided reasonable suspicion for a stop. The totality of the circumstances is malleable enough to serve the ends of all of the justices, whether liberal or conservative. If *Riley* is a guide, the Court will perhaps seek a third way, relying on neither the trespass doctrine nor the reasonable expectation of privacy standard to define searches. While *Riley* makes a strong statement for digital privacy, it does so in a way that appears to be guided by no standard at all. While the presence of an issue of digital information in a case might increase the likelihood that the Court will be more deferential to claims of individual privacy, it remains to be seen what the Court will do in future cases. While *Grady v. North Carolina* used the trespass doctrine, that case seemed to be a pure application of *United States v. Jones*. None of the other cases decided since *Riley* has provided a clear test to see where the Court will go in framing the issues of the proper standard for judging the privacy interests in a search.

CONCLUSION

We have argued that the Roberts Court's approach to the Fourth Amendment is in flux. The jurisprudence of crime control that developed in the 1970s and 1980s provides the foundation by which the Court approaches the Fourth Amendment, but changes in the Court's membership as well as shifting approaches to decision making by Justice Scalia created tensions in the law that did not exist throughout the Rehnquist Court years. Ten years into the Roberts Court, while much is still the same in terms of how search and seizure issues are decided, the Court today seems to be more open to reining in the excesses of the crime control model and, for some issues, willing to advance privacy interests. There is little likelihood that the Roberts Court will transform into a new Warren Court in its approach to Fourth Amendment rights. The foundation for a crime control approach that replaced the warrant requirement with reasonableness as the touchstone of Fourth Amendment analysis has become deeply rooted. We see this in the reluctance of the justices to use the exclusionary rule, in the willingness to permit exigent circumstances to breach the privacy of the home, and in the desire to protect government officials, even when they have violated the law, through the doctrine of qualified immunity. In spite of this, we cannot discount the fact that in the area of the Fourth Amendment at least, Roberts Court decisions look different, in many ways, from those of its predecessors. When the Court decides almost half of its decisions in ways favorable to the defendant, as it has done in the past five years, that is a real shift.

The tensions in the jurisprudence of crime control are certainly exacerbated by the changes in the broader political issues that have been such a part of American politics in recent years. After expanding police discretion for more than a generation, today there is a political backlash building in response to excesses of the use of that power, focusing on claims of racial profiling, excessive use of force, and growing frustration over the way police use their powers on the highways through traffic stops. As the late William Stuntz wrote in his critique of the criminal justice system, "Because nearly all drivers violate traffic laws, those laws have ceased to function on the nation's highways and local roads. Too much law amounts to no law at all: when legal doctrine makes everyone an offender, the relevant offenses have no meaning independent of law enforcers' will. The formal rule of law yields to the functional rule of official discretion."[17] These concerns are certainly greater for minority populations than for middle- and upper-class Caucasians, who often do not experience the same encounters that African Americans and Hispanics do with law enforcement, but the issues have gained saliency and are a real part of the political agenda. It is unclear how responsive the Court will be to these concerns in future cases, but the very fact that these issues are a part of the political landscape makes them more likely to result in litigation that could end up at the Court. The ways that the Supreme Court applies the doctrine of qualified immunity to protect police officers from lawsuits by injured suspects and citizens could potentially put it into direct conflict with those who are so frustrated with the seeming lack of police concern for the safety of people of color.

Recent years have also seen a complete transformation in how ordinary citizens make use of digital technology. The heightened role of technology by ordinary citizens in the forms of numerous handheld devices and the extensive use of cloud storage and computer technologies have changed the way people live. Social media are embedded in American life, and they serve to make people more aware of possible privacy issues, as well as generating a new set of issues for the Court. As technology becomes embedded in our lives, criminals are also able to make better use of it, and law enforcement has been quick to take advantage of the same technologies in targeting criminal activity. Increasingly, law enforcement will come to rely on access to digital content of all types in its prosecutions, if for no other reason than the criminals, like the rest of us, are living in a connected world. The Court will ultimately be forced to grapple with issues that arise in appeals, from police access to data stored in commercial archives, or from regulatory action, or even from adverse employment decisions, that will require the courts to think carefully about the meaning of privacy in a digital, information age. Government desire for access to emails and other data stored in a cloud or on service provider servers will become so great that the courts will ultimately be forced to directly confront the third party doctrine and determine whether Americans have a protected privacy interest in their movements or location, whether the creation of databases of the movements of individuals implicates privacy rights, whether a drone itself is the type of technology not commonly available to the general public, and what kinds of sensors can be deployed on a drone without violating the Fourth Amendment.

There are no clear answers to how the Roberts Court will address these issues, but the *Riley* opinion provides an important indicator. There is little doubt that the Court will face many more cases involving information technology in the near future. Confronting issues of privacy in a digital age will force fundamental conflicts between the more conservative justices' preference for originalism as a means of constitutional interpretation and the necessity of resolving issues with reference to a rapidly changing pattern of use. Eighteenth-century constitutional language and concepts are poorly suited to the resolution of these issues. While the trespass doctrine seems to provide a simple approach for Fourth Amendment cases, it diminishes all concerns for privacy beyond the person, home, papers, and effects. Moreover, it risks creating inconsistencies in the Court's overall approach to search and seizure law, and threatens to cause more problems than it solves. It would be very helpful to the police, to citizens, and to scholars seeking to make sense of the decisions of the Court if the language used to frame these issues was more consistent. How that will develop remains uncertain, yet it remains an interesting time to study the Fourth Amendment. Constitutional questions involving search and seizure are at the heart of the criminal justice system and the law of criminal procedure. The Roberts Court will certainly play a significant role in how concerns about criminal justice policy play out in the next decade.

Notes

CHAPTER 1: EXPLAINING THE ROBERTS COURT'S FOURTH AMENDMENT JURISPRUDENCE

1. See American Civil Liberties Union, Amicus Curiae Brief, *Maryland v. King* (2013), 32–33, www.aclu.org/files/assets/aclu_amicus_brief_1.pdf.

2. Lynn Langton and Matthew Durose, *Police Behavior during Traffic and Street Stops, 2011* (Washington, DC: Bureau of Justice Statistics, September 24, 2013), www.bjs.gov/index.cfm?ty=pbdetail&iid=4779.

3. Herbert Packer, *The Limits of the Criminal Sanction* (Palo Alto, CA: Stanford University Press, 1968).

4. Jan Crawford Greenberg, "Interview with Chief Justice Roberts," *ABC News*, November 28, 2006, http://abcnews.go.com/Nightline/story?id=2661589; Will Oremus, "Elena Kagan Admits That Justices Haven't Quite Figured Out E-Mail Yet," *Slate*, August 20, 2013, www.slate.com/blogs/future_tense/2013/08/20/elena_kagan_supreme_court_justices_haven_t_gotten_to_email_use_paper_memos.html.

5. *Navarette v. California*, 572 U.S. ___, 134 S. Ct. 1683 (2014).

6. Mark J. Richards and Herbert M. Kritzer, "Jurisprudential Regimes in Supreme Court Decision Making," *American Political Science Review* 96, no. 2 (June 2002): 305–320.

7. Ibid., 308.

8. Herbert M. Kritzer and Mark J. Richards, "The Influence of Law in the Supreme Court's Search-and-Seizure Jurisprudence," *American Politics Research* 33, no. 1 (January 2005): 33–55.

9. Harold J. Spaeth, Lee Epstein, Andrew D. Martin, Jeffrey A. Segal, Theodore J. Ruger, and Sara C. Benesh, 2014 Supreme Court Database, Version 2014 Release 01, http://supremecourtdatabase.org.

10. The Supreme Court Database includes an online codebook. The "decision direction" variable description can be found at http://scdb.wustl.edu/documentation.php?var=decisionDirection.

11. See, for example, Andrew Dugan, "Americans' Approval of Supreme Court Near All Time Low: After Historic Term Less Than a Third of Republicans Approve of the Court," *Gallup.com*, July 19, 2013, www.gallup.com/poll/163586/americans-approval-supreme-court-near-all-time-low.aspx; and Rasmussen Reports, "Supreme Court Update: 26% Rate Supreme Court Performance Positively," June

24, 2014, www.rasmussenreports.com/public_content/politics/mood_of_america/supreme_court_update.

12. William Stuntz, *The Collapse of American Criminal Justice* (Cambridge, MA: Harvard University Press, 2012).

13. Charles H. Sheldon, *A Century of Judging: A Political History of the Washington Supreme Court* (Seattle: University of Washington Press, 1988), 9–12.

14. Antonin Scalia, October 1, 2014, speech at Colorado Christian University, *Washington Times*, www.washingtontimes.com/news/2014/oct/1/justice-antonin-scalia-defends-keeping-god-religio/.

15. Antonin Scalia, "Mullahs of the West: Judges as Moral Arbiters," speech to North Carolina Bar Association," *USA Today*, June 21, 2013, www.usatoday.com/story/news/nation/2013/06/21/scalia-speech-judges-morality/2446569/.

16. See, for example, Steven G. Calabresi, "A Critical Introduction to the Originalism Debate," *Harvard Journal of Law and Public Policy* 31, no. 3 (June 2008): 875–897.

17. "Antonin Scalia Says Constitution Permits Court to Favor Religion over Non-Religion," *Huffington Post*, www.huffingtonpost.com/2014/10/02/antonin-scalia-religion-government_n_5922944.html.

18. "An Illegal Search, by GPS," *New York Times*, October 5, 2010, www.nytimes.com/2010/10/05/opinion/05tue2.html.

CHAPTER 2: SETTING THE STAGE

1. Entick v. Carrington *and Three Other King's Messengers*, 19 Howell's State Trials 1029 (1765).
2. *Weeks v. United States*, 232 U.S. 383, 391 (1914).
3. *Olmstead v. United States*, 277 U.S. 438, 474 (1928).
4. *Olmstead v. United States*, at 474–475.
5. *Olmstead v. United States*, at 478.
6. *Olmstead v. United States*, at 485.
7. Kenneth M. Murchison, "Prohibition and the Fourth Amendment: A New Look at Some Old Cases," *Journal of Criminal Law & Criminology* 73, no. 2 (Summer 1982): 471–532.
8. Fred Graham, *The Due Process Revolution: The Warren Court's Impact on Criminal Law* (New York: Hayden, 1970).
9. *Draper v. United States*, 358 U.S. 307, 309, footnote 2 (1959).
10. *Draper v. United States*, at 314.
11. *Draper v. United States*, at 315.
12. *Mapp v. Ohio*, 367 U.S. 643, 655 (1961).
13. *Mapp v. Ohio*, at 672.

14. *Katz v. United States*, 389 U.S. 347, 351 (1967).
15. *Katz v. United States*, at 352–353.
16. *Katz v. United States*, at 361, Harlan concurring.
17. *Terry v. Ohio*, 392 U.S. 1, 38 (1968).
18. *Terry v. Ohio*, at 39.
19. See James Allen Fox and Marianne W. Zawitz, "Homicide Trends in the United States," 2007, www.bjs.gov/content/pub/pdf/htius.pdf; Patrick A. Langan and Matthew R. Durose, "The Remarkable Drop in Crime in New York City," paper prepared for the International Conference on Crime, Rome, December 3–5, 2003, www.scribd.com/doc/322928/Langan-rel; and Andrew V. Papchristos, "48 Years of Crime in Chicago: A Descriptive Analysis of Serious Crime Trends from 1965 to 2013," Institute for Social and Policy Studies, Yale University, December 9, 2013, http://images.politico.com/global/2013/12/15/48yearsofcrime_final_ispsworkingpaper023.pdf.
20. Graham, *The Due Process Revolution*, was originally titled "The Self-Inflicted Wound."
21. William Stuntz, *The Collapse of American Criminal Justice* (Cambridge, MA: Harvard University Press, 2012).
22. Kevin McMahon, *The Nixon Court* (Chicago: University of Chicago Press, 2011), 27, citing Richard Nixon, "Toward Freedom from Fear," May 8, 1968, published in Nixon for President Committee, New York.
23. Graham, *The Due Process Revolution*, 306.

CHAPTER 3: THE BURGER COURT AND THE RISE OF A JURISPRUDENCE OF CRIME CONTROL

1. See Henry J. Abraham, *Justices, Presidents, and Senators: A History of the U.S. Supreme Court Appointments from Washington to Bush II*, 5th ed. (Lanham, MD: Rowman and Littlefield, 2007).
2. *People v. Defore*, 242 N.Y. 13 (1926); see, for example, *Davis v. United States*, 131 S. Ct. 2419, 2434 (2011).
3. Tracey Maclin, *The Supreme Court and the Fourth Amendment's Exclusionary Rule* (New York: Oxford University Press, 2012), 139.
4. *Coolidge v. New Hampshire*, 403 U.S. 443, 498 (1971).
5. Papers of Harry A Blackmun, *Coolidge v. New Hampshire*, Box 128, Manuscript Division, Library of Congress.
6. Bob Woodward and Scott Armstrong, *The Brethren: Inside the Supreme Court* (New York: Simon and Schuster, 1979).
7. Summer Memorandum for *United States v. Calandra*, Papers of Lewis F. Powell, July 30, 1973, Box 13. Washington and Lee Law School.

8. Craig M. Bradley, "The Fourth Amendment: Be Reasonable," in *The Rehnquist Legacy*, ed. Craig M. Bradley (New York: Cambridge University Press, 2006), 83–85.

9. Memo from Rehnquist to Burger, Papers of Harry A. Blackmun, March 30, 1984, *New Jersey v. T.L.O.*, Box 414.

10. *United States v. Calandra*, 414 U.S. 338, 347 (1974).

11. *United States v. Calandra*, 347–348.

12. *United States v. Janis*, 428 U.S. 433, 448–449 (1976).

13. Maclin, *The Supreme Court and the Exclusionary Rule*, 234.

14. Memorandum from Stewart to Burger, Blackmun Papers, March 5, 1979, Box 288.

15. Michael C. Gizzi and Craig Curtis, "What Is a Landmark Case? Ranking Search and Seizure Cases Using Shepard's Citations," *Criminal Law Bulletin* 49, no. 2 (Summer 2013): 236–273.

16. Herbert M. Kritzer and Mark J. Richards, "The Influence of Law in the Supreme Court's Search-and-Seizure Jurisprudence," *American Politics Research* 33, no. 1 (January 2005): 33–55.

17. *United States v. White*, 401 U.S. 745, 752 (1971).

18. *United States v. White*, 753.

19. *United States v. Miller*, 425 U.S. 435, 439 (1976), citing *Boyd v. United States*, 116 U.S. 616, 622 (1886).

20. Stephen J. Schulhofer, *More Essential Than Ever: The Fourth Amendment in the Twenty-First Century* (New York: Oxford University Press, 2012), 123.

21. *Smith v. Maryland*, 442 U.S. 735, 749 (1979).

22. *California v. Carney*, 471 U.S. 386 (1985); *United States v. Villamonte-Marquez*, 462 U.S. 579 (1983).

23. See Charles R. Epp, Steven Maynard-Moody, and Donald P. Haider-Markel, *Pulled Over: How Police Stops Define Race and Citizenship* (Chicago: University of Chicago Press, 2014), 50–51; Michelle Alexander, *The New Jim Crow: Mass Incarceration in the Age of Colorblindness* (New York: New Press, 2012), 89–91; New York Times, "U.S. Wrote Outline for Race Profiling, New Jersey Argues," *New York Times*, November 29, 2000, www.nytimes.com/2000/11/29/nyregion/29FEDS.html.

24. See Michael C. Gizzi, "Pretextual Stops, Vehicle Searches, and Crime Control: An Examination of Strategies Used on the Frontline of the War on Drugs," *Criminal Justice Studies: A Critical Journal of Crime, Law & Society* 24, no. 2 (June 2011): 139–152.

25. *Cardwell v. Lewis*, 417 U.S. 583, 590 (1974); *United States v. Knotts*, 460 U.S. 276, 281 (1983).

26. *United States v. Knotts*, 282.

27. *United States v. Karo*, 486 U.S. 705, 711 (1984).

28. *United States v. Karo*, 714.

CHAPTER 4: THE WAR ON DRUGS AND
THE TRIUMPH OF THE REHNQUIST COURT

1. Craig M. Bradley, "Introduction," in *The Rehnquist Legacy*, ed. Craig M. Bradley (New York: Cambridge University Press, 2006), 3.
2. The percentage of people who expressed fear of walking alone in their neighborhood remained mostly constant, in the neighborhood of 34 percent from 1965 to 2013: Gallup, "Crime," www.gallup.com/poll/1603/crime.aspx.
3. Elliot Currie, *Reckoning: Drugs, the Cities, and the American Future* (New York: Hill and Wang, 1993).
4. TRACDEA, "DEA and Overall Trends in Federal Drug Expenditures," http://trac.syr.edu/tracdea/findings/aboutDEA/drugBudget.html; Drug Policy Alliance, *The Federal Drug Control Budget: New Rhetoric, Same Failed Drug War*, February 2015, www.drugpolicy.org/sites/default/files/DPA_Fact_sheet_Drug_War_Budget_Feb2015.pdf.
5. *United States v. Sokolow*, 490 U.S. 1, 8–9 (1989).
6. Ibid.
7. *United States v. Sokolow*, at 4.
8. *United States v. Sokolow*, at 13.
9. See, for example, Brandon Garrett, "Remedying Racial Profiling," *Columbia Human Rights Law Review* 33 (Fall 2001): 41–147, at 44n7. See also Illinois Traffic Stop Data Collection Act (625 ILCS 5/11–212), passed in 2003, and New Jersey Executive Order no. 29, signed by Governor Corzine in 2006, both of which created mandated data collection during traffic stops.
10. Michael C. Gizzi, "Pretextual Stops, Vehicle Searches, and Crime Control: An Examination of Strategies Used on the Frontline of the War on Drugs," *Criminal Justice Studies: A Critical Journal of Crime, Law & Society* 24, no. 2 (June 2011): 139–152, at 140; Marcus Dirk Dubber, "Policing Possession: The War on Crime and the End of Criminal Law," *Journal of Criminal Law and Criminology* 91, no. 4 (Summer 2001): 829–996; David A. Harris, *Profiles in Injustice: Why Racial Profiling Cannot Work* (New York: New Press, 2003).
11. Gizzi, "Pretextual Stops."
12. *Thornton v. United States*, 541 U.S. 615, 624 (2004).
13. *United States v. Place*, 462 U.S. 696 (1983).
14. *Illinois v. Caballes*, 543 U.S. 405, 410–411 (2005).
15. Charles Epp, Steven Maynard-Moody, and Donald Haider-Markel, *Pulled Over: How Police Stops Define Race and Citizenship* (Chicago: University of Chicago Press, 2014), chap. 2.
16. Stephen J. Schulhofe, *More Essential Than Ever: The Fourth Amendment in the Twenty-First Century* (New York: Oxford University Press, 2012).

17. Robin Shepard Engel and Jennifer M. Calnon, Jr., "Examining the Influence of Drivers' Characteristics during Traffic Stops with Police: Results from a National Survey," *Justice Quarterly* 21, no. 1 (March 2004): 49–90; Angela J. Davis, "Race, Cops, and Traffic Stops," *University of Miami Law Review* 51 (January 1997): 425–443.

18. Michelle Alexander, *The New Jim Crow: Mass Incarceration in the Age of Colorblindness* (New York: New Press, 2010).

19. See *Skinner v. Railway Labor Executives' Association*, 489 U.S. 602 (1989); *National Treasury Employees Union v. Von Raab*, 489 U.S. 656 (1989); *Veronia School District 47J v. Acton*, 515 U.S. 646 (1995); and *Board of Education of Independent School District No. 92 of Pottawatomie County v. Earls*, 536 U.S. 822 (2002).

20. *California v. Hodari D.*, 499 U.S. 621, 623, footnote 1 (1991).

21. Proverbs 28:1.

22. *California v. Hodari D.*, at 647.

23. Ibid.

24. *Illinois v. Wardlow*, 528 U.S. 119, 122 (2000).

25. *Illinois v. Wardlow*, at 124.

26. *Illinois v. Wardlow*, at 125.

CHAPTER 5: THE ROBERTS COURT IN FLUX

1. Jeffrey Toobin, *The Nine: Inside the Secret World of the Supreme Court* (New York: Anchor, 2007), 337–345.

2. Michael C. Gizzi and Craig Curtis, "The Impact of *Arizona v. Gant* on Search and Seizure Law as Applied to Vehicle Searches," *University of Denver Criminal Law Review* 1, no. 1 (Spring 2011): 30–50.

3. Ryan J. Owens and Justin P. Wedeking, "Justices and Legal Clarity: Analyzing the Complexity of U.S. Supreme Court Opinions," *Law & Society Review* 45, no. 4 (December 2011): 1027–1061.

4. Antonin Scalia, "Originalism: The Lesser Evil," *University of Cincinnati Law Review* 57 (1989): 849–865; Richard H. Seamon, "*Kyllo v. United States* and the Partial Ascendance of Justice Scalia's Fourth Amendment," *Washington University Law Review* 79, no. 4 (2001): 1013–1033; Jack N. Rakove, "Joe the Ploughman Reads the Constitution, or, the Poverty of Public Meaning Originalism," *San Diego Law Review* 48, no. 2 (Spring 2011): 575–600.

5. *United States v. Knotts*, 460 U.S. 281 (1983) and *United States v. Karo*, 468 U.S. 705 (1984).

6. *United States v. Knotts*, at 281, quoting *Cardwell v. Lewis*, 417 U.S. 583, 590 (1974).

7. See *United States v. McIver*, 186 F.3d 1119 (9th Cir. 1999).

8. *State v. Jackson*, 150 Wn.2d 251 (2003).
9. *People v. Weaver*, 12 N.Y.3d 433, 909 N.E.2d 1195 (2009).
10. *United States v. Maynard*, 615 F.3d 544, 563 (D.C. Cir. 2010).
11. "GPS and Privacy Rights," *New York Times*, editorial, November 23, 2009; "An Illegal Search, by GPS," *New York Times*, editorial, October 5, 2010.
12. "The Court's GPS Test," *New York Times*, editorial, November 6, 2011.
13. Kim Zetter, "FBI Gets Caught Tracking Man's Car: Wants Its GPS Device Back," *Gizmodo*, October 7, 2010, http://gizmodo.com/5658661/fbi-gets-caught-tracking-mans-car-wants-its-gps-device-back.
14. *United States v. Jones*, 132 S. Ct. 945, 950 (2012).
15. *United States v. Jones*, at 958.
16. *United States v. Jones*, at 954.
17. *United States v. Jones*, at 956.
18. Ibid.
19. *United States v. Jones*, at 957.
20. Ibid.
21. *Riley v. California*, 134 S. Ct. 2473, 2491 (2014).
22. *Riley v. California*, at 2489.
23. Ibid.
24. *Riley v. California*, at 2490.

CHAPTER 6: THE JURISPRUDENCE OF CRIME CONTROL ON THE ROBERTS COURT

1. See, for example, *Alabama v. White*, 496 U.S. 325 (1990); *Florida v. J. L.*, 529 U.S. 266 (2000).
2. *Navarette v. California*, 134 S. Ct. 1683, 1697 (2014).
3. *Scott v. Harris*, 550 U.S. 372, 384 (2007).
4. *Herring v. United States*, 555 U.S. 135, 143 (2009).
5. *Herring v. United States*, at 152.
6. *Herring v. United States*, at 155.
7. *Florida v. Jardines*, 563 U.S. 452, 473 (2013).
8. *Brigham City v. Stewart*, 547 U.S. 398, 407 (2006).
9. *Kentucky v. King*, 131 S.Ct. 1849, 1864 (2011).
10. *Samson v. California*, 547 U.S. 843, 856 (2006).
11. Michelle Alexander, *The New Jim Crow: Mass Incarceration in the Age of Colorblindness* (New York: New Press, 2010); Marie Gottschalk, *Caught: The Prison State and the Lockdown of American Politics* (Princeton, NJ: Princeton University Press, 2015).

12. Gottschalk, *Caught*, 101–107.
13. *Maryland v. King*, 133 S. Ct. 1958, 1980 (2013).
14. *Florence v. Board of Chosen Freeholders of the County of Burlington*, 132 S. Ct. 1510, 1515 (2012).
15. *Florence v. Board of Chosen Freeholders*, at 1527.
16. Civil Act for Deprivation of Civil Rights, U.S. Code 42 (1996), § 1983.

CHAPTER 7: REINING IN THE EXCESSES OF CRIME CONTROL

1. *Arizona v. Gant*, 556 U.S. 332, 337 (2009).
2. *Thornton v. United States*, 541 U.S. 615, 624 (2004).
3. *Thorton v. United States*, at 636.
4. Michael C. Gizzi, "Methamphetamine and Its Impact on the Criminal Justice System: A Three Year Examination of Felony Drug Filings," *Journal of Crime and Justice* 34, no. 2 (July 2011): 103–123.
5. *Florida v. Jardines*, 133 S. Ct. 1409, 1414 (2013).
6. *Florida v. Jardines*, at 1417.
7. *Florida v. Jardines*, at 1419.
8. *Florida v. Harris*, 133 S. Ct. 1050, 1057 (2013).
9. Ibid.
10. *Rodriguez v. United States*, 135 S. Ct. 1609, 1614 (2015).
11. Ibid.
12. *Rodriguez v. United States*, at 1614–1615.
13. *Rodriguez v. United States*, at 1616.
14. *Rodriguez v. United States*, at 1623.
15. *Rodriguez v. United States*, at 1616.
16. *Rodriguez v. United States*, at 1625.
17. *United States v. Matlock*, 415 U.S. 164, 170 (1974).
18. *Georgia v. Randolph*, 547 U.S. 103, 121 (2006).
19. Ibid.
20. *Safford Unified School District v. Redding*, 557 U.S. 364, 375 (2009).
21. Ibid.
22. *United States v. Jones*, 918 F. Supp. 2d 1 (D.D.C. 2013).
23. Nick Anderson and Anne E. Marimow, "Former D.C. Nightclub Owner Antoine Jones Sentenced on Drug Charge," *Washington Post*, May 1, 2013, www.washingtonpost.com/local/antoine-jones-pleads-guilty-to-drug-charge/2013/05/01/1109c268-b274-11e2-bbf2-a6f9e9d79e19_story.html. Jones also challenged this outcome, albeit unsuccessfully; *United States v. Jones*, 2014 U.S. Dist. LEXIS 95395 (D.D.C. 2014).

24. *Brendlin v. California*, 551 U.S. 249, 263 (2007).

25. *People v. Brendlin*, 45 Cal. 4th 262; 195 P.3d 1074; 85 Cal. Rptr. 3d 496 (2008); Cal. LEXIS 13631 (2008).

26. *Bailey a.k.a. Polo v. United States*, 568 U.S. ___, 133 S. Ct. 1031, 1043 (2013).

27. *United States v. Bailey*, 743 F.3d 322; 2014 U.S. App. LEXIS 3320 (2nd Cir 2014).

CHAPTER 8: TOWARD THE FUTURE

1. Mark J. Richards and Herbert M. Kritzer, "Jurisprudential Regimes in Supreme Court Decision Making," *American Political Science Review* 96, no. 2 (June 2002): 305–320.

2. Jeffrey Toobin, *The Nine: Inside the Secret World of the Supreme Court* (New York: Anchor, 2007).

3. USA Freedom Act, Public Law 114-23, June 2, 2015.

4. See Michelle Alexander, *The New Jim Crow: Mass Incarceration in the Age of Colorblindness* (New York: New Press, 2010).

5. Tami Abdollah, "Bruce Jenner Texting While Driving? No, Says His Publicist (+video)," *Christian Science Monitor*, February 9, 2015, www.csmonitor.com/USA/Latest-News-Wires/2015/0209/Bruce-Jenner-texting-while-driving-No-says-his-publicist-video.

6. Julia Angwin, *Dragnet Nation: A Quest for Privacy, Security, and Freedom in a World of Relentless Surveillance* (New York: Times Books, 2014).

7. See Craig Curtis, Michael C. Gizzi, and Michael J. Kittleson, "Using Technology the Founders Never Dreamed Of: Cell Phones as Tracking Devices and the Fourth Amendment," *University of Denver Criminal Law Review* 4 (Summer 2014): 61–106, for a detailed treatment of the technical issues and a list of cases from 2004 to 2013 in which the use of CSLI was at issue.

8. Ibid.

9. John Yoo, "The Legality of the National Security Agency's Bulk Data Surveillance Programs," *Harvard Journal of Law and Public Policy* 37, no. 3 (Summer 2014): 901–933. But see Curtis, Gizzi, and Kittleson, "Using Technology"; and Laura K. Donahue, "Bulk MetaData Collection: Statutory and Constitutional Considerations," *Harvard Journal of Law and Public Policy* 37, no. 3 (Summer 2014): 757–900.

10. See, for example, *United States v. Moreno-Nevarez*, 2013 U.S. Dist. LEXIS 143900 (SD Cal 2013); and *In re: Application of the United States of America for Historical Cell Site Data*, 724 F.3d 600 (5th Cir. TX).

11. Julia Angwin, *Dragnet Nation*.

12. All Things Considered, "North Dakota Law Aims to Set Parameters for Police Use of Drones," National Public Radio, August 31, 2015, www.npr.org/2015

/08/31/436377494/north-dakota-law-aims-to-set-parameters-for-police-use-of-drones.

13. *California v. Ciraolo*, 476 U.S. 207 (1986); *Florida v. Riley*, 488 U.S. 445 (1989).

14. *Administrator v. Pirker*, NTSB Order No. EA-5730 (Nov. 18, 2014).

15. Marie Gottschalk, *Caught: The Prison State and the Lockdown of American Politics* (Princeton, NJ: Princeton University Press, 2015).

16. See, for example, Illinois Department of Transportation, "Illinois Traffic Stop Studies, 2004–2014," www.idot.illinois.gov/transportation-system/local-transportation-partners/law-enforcement/illinois-traffic-stop-study.

17. William Stuntz, *The Collapse of American Criminal Justice* (Cambridge, MA: Harvard University Press, 2011), 3.

Cases

Administrator v. Pirker, NTSB Order No. EA-5730 (Nov. 18, 2014).
Aguilar v. Texas, 378 U.S. 108 (1964).
Alabama v. White, 496 U.S. 325 (1990).
Arizona v. Evans, 514 U.S. 1 (1995).
Arizona v. Gant, 556 U.S. 332 (2009).
Arizona v. Johnson, 555 U.S. 323 (2009).
Arkansas v. Sanders, 442 U.S. 753 (1979).
Atwater v. City of Lago Vista, 532 U.S. 318 (2001).
Bailey a.k.a. Polo v. United States, 568 U.S. ___, 133 S. Ct. 1031 (2013).
Bivens v. Six Unidentified Federal Narcotics Agents, 403 U.S. 388 (1971).
Board of Education of Independent School District No. 92 of Pottawatomie County
    v. Earls, 536 U.S. 822 (2002).
Bond v. United States, 529 U.S. 334 (2000).
Boyd v. United States, 116 U.S. 616 (1886).
Brendlin v. California, 551 U.S. 249 (2007).
Brigham City v. Stuart, 547 U.S. 398 (2006).
Brown v. Board of Education, 347 U.S. 483 (1954).
California v. Carney, 471 U.S. 386 (1985).
California v. Ciraolo, 476 U.S. 207 (1986).
California v. Hodari D., 499 U.S. 621 (1991).
Cardwell v. Lewis, 417 U.S. 583 (1974).
Carroll v. Carman, 574 U.S. ___, 135 S. Ct. 348 (2014).
Carroll v. United States, 267 U.S. 132 (1925).
Chambers v. Maroney, 399 U.S. 42 (1970).
Chimel v. California, 395 U.S. 752 (1969).
City of Indianapolis v. Edmond, 531 U.S. 32 (2000).
City of Los Angeles v. Patel, 576 U.S. ___, 135 S. Ct. 2443 (2015).
City of Ontario v. Quon, 560 U.S. 746 (2010).
Coolidge v. New Hampshire, 403 U.S. 443 (1971).
Davis v. United States, 564 U.S. 229, 131 S. Ct. 2419 (2011).
Delaware v. Prouse, 440 U.S. 648 (1979).
Draper v. United States, 358 U.S. 307 (1959).
Elkins v. United States, 364 U.S. 206 (1960).
Entick v. Carrington, 19 Howell's State Trials 1029 (1765).
Escobedo v. Illinois, 378 U.S. 478 (1964).

Ferguson v. City of Charleston, 532 U.S. 67 (2001).
Fernandez v. California, 571 U.S. ___, 134 S. Ct. 1126 (2014).
Florence v. Board of Chosen Freeholders of the County of Burlington, 566 U.S. ___, 132 S. Ct. 1510 (2012).
Florida v. Bostick, 501 U.S. 429 (1991).
Florida v. Harris, 568 U.S. ___, 133 S. Ct. 1050 (2013).
Florida v. Jardines, 569 U.S. ___, 133 S. Ct. 1409 (2013).
Florida v. J. L., 529 U.S. 266 (2000).
Florida v. Riley, 488 U.S. 445 (1989).
Florida v. Wells, 495 U.S. 1 (1990).
Georgia v. Randolph, 547 U.S. 103 (2006).
Gideon v. Wainwright, 372 U.S. 335 (1963).
Gooding v. United States, 416 U.S. 430 (1974).
Grady v. North Carolina, 575 U.S. ___, 135 S. Ct. 1368 (2015).
Heien v. North Carolina, 574 U.S. ___, 135 S. Ct. 530 (2015).
Herring v. United States, 555 U.S. 135 (2009).
Hester v. United States, 265 U.S. 57 (1924).
Hudson v. Michigan, 547 U.S. 586 (2006).
Illinois v. Caballes, 543 U.S. 405 (2005).
Illinois v. Gates, 462 U.S. 213 (1983).
Illinois v. Lidster, 540 U.S. 419 (2004).
Illinois v. Rodriguez, 497 U.S. 177 (1990).
Illinois v. Wardlow, 528 U.S. 119 (2000).
In re: Application of the United States of America for Historical Cell Site Data, 724 F.3d 600 (5th Cir. TX 2013).
Katz v. United States, 389 U.S. 347 (1967).
Kentucky v. King, 563 U.S. 452 (2011).
Knowles v. Iowa, 525 U.S. 113 (1998).
Kyllo v. United States, 533 U.S. 27 (2001).
Los Angeles County v. Rettele, 550 U.S. 609 (2007).
Mapp v. Ohio, 367 U.S. 643 (1961).
Maryland v. King, 569 U.S. ___, 133 S. Ct. 1958 (2013).
Michigan v. Clifford, 464 U.S. 287 (1980).
Michigan v. DeFillippo, 443 U.S. 31 (1979).
Michigan v. Fisher, 558 U.S. 45 (2009).
Michigan v. Sitz, 496 U.S. 444 (1990).
Michigan v. Tyler, 436 U.S. 499 (1978).
Mincey v. Arizona, 437 U.S. 385 (1978).
Minnesota v. Olson, 495 U.S. 91 (1990).
Miranda v. Arizona, 384 U.S. 436 (1966).

Missouri v. McNeely, 569 U.S. ___, 133 S. Ct. 1552 (2013).
National Treasury Employees Union v. Von Raab, 489 U.S. 656 (1989).
Navarette v. California, 572 U.S. ___, 134 S. Ct. 1683 (2014).
New Jersey v. T.L.O., 469 U.S. 325 (1985).
New York v. Belton, 453 U.S. 454 (1981).
O'Connor v. Ortega, 480 U.S. 709 (1987).
Ohio v. Robinette, 519 U.S. 33 (1996).
Oliver v. United States, 466 U.S. 170 (1984).
Olmstead v. United States, 277 U.S. 438 (1928).
Payton v. New York, 445 U.S. 573 (1980).
Pennsylvania v. Mimms, 434 U.S. 106 (1977).
People v. Brendlin, 45 Cal. 4th 262, 195 P.3d 1074, 85 Cal. Rptr. 3d 496 (2008).
People v. Defore, 242 N.Y. 13 (1926).
People v. Weaver, 12 N.Y.3d 433; 909 N.E.2d 1195 (2009).
Plumhoff v. Rickard, 572 U.S. ___, 134 S. Ct. 2012 (2014).
Riley v. California, 573 U.S. ___, 134 S. Ct. 2473 (2014).
Rodriguez v. United States, 575 U.S. ___, 135 S. Ct. 1609 (2015).
Ryburn v. Huff, 565 U.S. ___, 132 S. Ct. 987 (2012).
Safford Unified School District v. Redding, 557 U.S. 364 (2009).
Samson v. California, 547 U.S. 843 (2006).
San Francisco v. Sheehan, 575 U.S. ___, 135 S. Ct. 1765 (2015).
Schmerber v. California, 384 U.S. 757 (1966).
Schneckloth v. Bustamonte, 412 U.S. 218 (1973).
Scott v. Harris, 550 U.S. 372 (2007).
Silverman v. United States, 365 U.S. 505 (1961).
Skinner v. Railway Labor Executives' Association, 489 U.S. 602 (1989).
Smith v. Maryland, 442 U.S. 735 (1979).
Spinelli v. United States, 393 U.S. 410 (1969).
Stanton v. Sims, 571 U.S. ___, 134 S. Ct. 3 (2013).
State v. Jackson, 150 Wn.2d 251 (2003).
Steagald v. United States, 451 U.S. 204 (1981).
Terry v. Ohio, 392 U.S. 1 (1968).
Thompson v. Louisiana, 469 U.S. 17 (1984).
Thornton v. United States, 541 U.S. 615 (2004).
Tolan v. Cotton, 572 U.S. ___, 134 S. Ct. 1861 (2014).
United States v. Arvizu, 534 U.S. 266 (2002).
United States v. Bailey, 743 F.3d 322; 2014 U.S. App. LEXIS 3320 (2nd Cir. 2014).
United States v. Calandra, 414 U.S. 338 (1974).
United States v. Chadwick, 433 U.S. 1 (1977).
United States v. Drayton, 536 U.S. 194 (2002).

United States v. Grubbs, 547 U.S. 90 (2006).
United States v. Jacobsen, 466 U.S. 109 (1984).
United States v. Janis, 428 U.S. 433 (1976).
United States v. Jones, 565 U.S. ___, 132 S. Ct. 945 (2012).
United States v. Jones, 918 F. Supp. 2d 1 (D.D.C. 2013).
United States v. Jones, 2014 U.S. Dist. LEXIS 95395 (D.D.C. 2014).
United States v. Karo, 468 U.S. 705 (1984).
United States v. Knights, 534 U.S. 112 (2001).
United States v. Knotts, 460 U.S. 276 (1983).
United States v. Leon, 468 U.S. 897 (1984).
United States v. Matlock, 415 U.S. 164 (1974).
United States v. Maynard, 615 F.3d 544 (D.C. Cir. 2010).
United States v. McIver, 186 F.3d 1119 (9th Cir. 1999).
United States v. Miller, 425 U.S. 435 (1976).
United States v. Moreno-Nevarez, 2013 U.S. Dist. LEXIS 143900 (SD Cal 2013).
United States v. Peltier, 422 U.S. 531 (1975).
United States v. Place, 462 U.S. 696 (1983).
United States v. Robinson, 414 U.S. 218 (1973).
United States v. Ross, 456 U.S. 798 (1982).
United States v. Sharpe, 470 U.S. 675 (1985).
United States v. Sokolow, 490 U.S. 1 (1989).
United States v. Villamonte-Marquez, 462 U.S. 579 (1983).
United States v. White, 401 U.S. 745 (1971).
United States v. Wurie, 728 F. 3d 1 (1st Cir. 2013).
Veronia School District No. 47J v. Acton, 515 U.S. 646 (1995).
Virginia v. Moore, 553 U.S. 164 (2008).
Weeks v. United States, 232 U.S. 383 (1914).
Whren v. United States, 517 U.S. 806 (1996).
Wilson v. Arkansas, 514 U.S. 927 (1995).
Winston v. Lee, 470 U.S. 753 (1985).
Wolf v. Colorado, 338 U.S. 25 (1949).
Wyoming v. Houghton, 526 U.S. 295 (1999).

Index

1960s, 6, 9–10, 13, 25, 38, 39–40, 143, 147–148
1970s, 6, 8, 9, 13, 42, 43, 47, 67, 84, 136, 158
1980s, 6, 9, 11, 13, 22, 23, 43, 78, 81, 91, 124, 143
1990s, 23, 78, 91, 124, 154

Administrator v. Pirker, 170n14
Aguilar, Nick Alford, 34
Aguilar and *Spinelli* standards, 35, 48–50, 60
Aguilar v. Texas, 34, 35, 48
Alabama v. White, 167n1
Alexander, Michelle, 154, 164n23, 166n18, 167n11, 169n4
Alito, Associate Justice Samuel, 12, 87, 93, 94–96, 98, 100, 107, 110, 114, 115, 122–123, 128, 129–130, 133–134, 137, 146, 151
   appointment of, 8, 18, 82
   ideology, 8, 19–20, 82, 88, 123
   participation in oral argument, 121–122
   views on crime control, 100, 111, 119, 137, 145, 146
American Bar Association, 42, 62
American Civil Liberties Union, 153, 161n1
Angwin, Julia, 169n6, 169n11
ankle monitor, 87, 96
anonymous informant, 101
   911 call, 8, 84, 90, 102, 155, 157
   letter, 48
   tip, 48, 49, 76, 87, 101, 120, 127

antiwar movement, 10, 39
Arizona v. Evans, 77, 85, 105
Arizona v. Gant, 8, 14, 16, 21, 23, 67, 83, 86, 89, 98, 121–124, 134, 149, 155, 166n2, 168n1
   "further evidence of the crime of arrest" prong, 16, 98, 122–124, 149
   reaching distance prong, 122
Arizona v. Johnson, 86, 104, 125
Arkansas v. Sanders, 53
Armstrong, Scott, 45
arrest, search incident to, 15, 16, 55–56, 67, 85, 89, 97–98, 100, 107, 109, 120–123, 124, 149
Atwater, Gail, 67, 104
Atwater v. City of Lago Vista, 67, 85, 104, 105, 115
automobile, 7, 30, 44, 53, 54–56, 57, 63–64, 68, 89, 92, 94, 123, 127
   car, 3, 16, 30, 44, 48, 51, 55, 56, 57, 63, 64, 68, 69, 70, 72, 73, 74, 89, 91–95, 97, 102, 103, 117, 118, 120, 130, 132, 134
   exception to the warrant requirement, 30, 44, 55–56, 63–64, 68, 89, 123, 127
   motor home, 55
   vehicle, 3–4, 7–8, 11–12, 15, 16–17, 21, 30, 44, 48, 49, 53, 54–58, 63–70, 86, 87, 91–94, 97, 101–103, 104, 105, 107, 109, 115, 118, 120–124, 125, 127, 129, 130, 132–134, 140, 152, 155, 156

Bailey a.k.a. Polo v. United States, 87, 141, 169n26

balancing test, 71
beeper, 56–58, 91, 92
   radio transmitter, 51, 56, 91–92, 129, 149
Bill of Rights, 5, 25, 29
Bivens v. Six Unknown Federal Narcotics Agents, 44, 45
Black, Associate Justice Hugo L., 34, 42, 44, 45
Blackmun, Associate Justice Harry, 10, 42, 44, 45, 47, 54, 59, 62
   papers of, 163n5, 164n8
blood alcohol content, 125–126
blood alcohol evidence, 84, 87
blood draw
   forced, 84
   warrantless, 87, 125–127
Board of Education of Independent School District No. 92 of Pottawatomie County v. Earls, 72, 166n19
Bond v. United States, 76
border, 64, 70
   illegal aliens, 76
Bork, Robert, 61, 82
Boyd v. United States, 25–28, 53
Brandeis, Associate Justice Louis D., 27–29, 33, 34, 35
   "right to be let alone," 28
Breathalyzer, 125–126
Brendlin v. California, 85, 104, 125, 140, 168n24
Brennan, Associate Justice William, 19, 43, 50, 60, 61
Breyer, Associate Justice Stephen, 18, 20, 23, 93, 103, 114, 115, 122, 146
   appointment of, 20, 62, 82
   ideology, 20, 62
   participation in oral argument, 121–122
   views on crime control, 88, 123

Brigham City v. Stuart, 14, 84, 109–110, 167n8
Brown, James, 65–66
Brown, Michael, 75, 147
Brown v. Board of Education, 40
Burger, Chief Justice Warren, 46, 48, 61
   appointment of, 10, 42
   ideology, 42, 59
   views on crime control, 42, 44, 45, 46, 59
Burger Court, 8–9, 11, 12, 14, 22, 36, 41, 45, 53, 61, 62–63, 67, 71, 72, 77, 86, 103, 105, 106, 133, 138, 143, 147, 157
   beepers, 56–58
   good faith exception, 47–50, 105
   jurisprudence of crime control, 7, 9, 11, 22, 41, 43, 59–60, 81, 83
   jurisprudential regime shift, 11, 13, 23, 42–43, 59–60
   reasonable expectation of privacy standard, 36, 51–52, 54, 60, 91
   third party doctrine, 53–54
   traffic stops, 55
Bush, George H. W., 18, 61, 62, 63, 78
Bush, George W., 18, 82, 83
bus stops, 70

Caballes, Roy, 68
California v. Carney, 164n22
California v. Ciraolo, 170n13
California v. Hodari D., 72–73, 89, 166n20
Cardozo, Associate Justice Benjamin, 33, 43
Cardwell v. Lewis, 57, 164n25, 166n6
Carroll v. Carman, 88, 117
Carroll v. United States, 30, 32, 54
cell phone, 3–5, 7, 21–22, 54, 88, 92, 96–100, 140, 148, 149–151, 154
   applications, 98–99, 149
   data storage, 99

data storage capacity, 98–99
    as smartphones, 21, 87, 90, 95, 97, 98, 99, 144, 147, 148, 149
    service providers, 54, 95, 96, 149, 150, 151
    towers, 149, 150
    use as a tracking device, 96, 149–151
Cell Site Location Information (CSLI), 21, 54, 150–151
Chambers v. Maroney, 55
Chicago, 31, 39, 48, 74
Chimel v. California, 55, 121–122
City of Indianapolis v. Edmond, 76
City of Los Angeles v. Patel, 87, 150
City of Ontario v. Quon, 86
civil rights, 10, 31, 40, 116, 148
civil rights movement, 39
Clark, Associate Justice Tom C., 33–34, 46
Clinton, William J., 18, 20, 62, 78
closed containers, 55
cloud storage, 98, 159
cocaine, 58, 63, 64, 65, 73, 78, 89, 92–93, 110–111, 120, 135, 139, 152
    crack, 63, 73, 78, 89, 120
CODIS. *See* Combined DNA Index System
Combined DNA Index System, 113
commercial data collection, 151–152, 159
Congress, 44, 100, 147
constitutional toolbox, 10, 63, 66, 69, 77, 155
Coolidge, Edward, 43–44
Coolidge v. New Hampshire, 43–45, 47, 50, 59, 163n4
Cooper, Anthony, 118
corrective measures, 14–17, 21, 22, 75–77, 81, 119, 121, 125, 127, 136, 144
Corzine, Jon, 165n9
counterculture, 39

Crime control, 16, 18, 23, 24, 25, 29, 49, 51, 54, 81, 86, 87, 98, 100, 113, 119, 120–121, 123, 135, 139, 141, 143, 145, 146, 148, 149, 158
    balance against privacy rights of individuals, 29, 87, 113, 139, 148, 149
    jurisprudence of, 10–11, 12, 13–14, 16, 20, 21, 22–24, 25, 32, 41, 42–43, 49, 50, 59–60, 61–63, 72, 75, 77–78, 81, 83, 85, 91, 101–105, 108, 115, 118, 119, 124, 131, 137, 140, 141, 143–145, 147, 157, 158
    narrative of, 12, 41
    Packer, Herbert, 5–6
    politics of, 9–12, 23, 38–39, 78, 154
    war on drugs, 62–63, 155
CSLI. *See* Cell Site Location Information
curtilage, 96, 117, 128

Day, Associate Justice William R., 26
DEA. *See* Drug Enforcement Agency
deadly force, 147
Delaware v. Prouse, 53
deterrence of police misconduct, 34, 43, 46–47, 50, 85, 106
digital privacy, 3, 6, 20, 23, 24, 84, 95, 96–98, 145, 146, 148–149, 157
DNA, 4–7, 21, 84, 87, 90, 97, 113–114
    buccal swab, 114
    cheek swab, 4
Dog sniff, 8, 67–68, 123, 127–131, 133–135, 155–157
    narcotics sniffs, 12, 90, 130–131, 134
    presumption of infallibility, 156
    reliability, 68, 87, 130–132, 156
    sui generis, 129, 155
    technology not available to the general public, 129

Douglas, Associate Justice William O., 32, 37–38
Draper, James, 31–32
Draper v. United States, 31–32, 34, 35, 37, 49, 60, 162n9
drones, 152–154
    arming of, 153
    law enforcement use, 152, 153
    plain view doctrine, 153
    sensors, 153, 154, 160
    state laws concerning, 153
    technology not available to the general public, 153, 160
drug courier profile, 64–65
Drug Czar. *See* Office of National Drug Control Policy
Drug Enforcement Agency, 48, 52, 56, 58, 64–65, 69, 92, 127
drug testing, 70–72, 76
    of public sector employees, 71–72
    in schools, 71–72
    as a search, 71
drunk driving, 69, 84, 87, 101, 102, 126–127
due process, 5–6, 9, 12, 25, 29, 31, 33, 38, 40
Due Process Revolution, 30–33, 40
    backlash against, 10, 13, 23, 25, 38–41, 158
DUI. *See* drunk driving

E. A. Boyd and Sons, 25
Eisenhower, Dwight D., 30
Electronic Frontier Foundation, 153
Elkins v. United States, 152
Entick v. Carrington, 28, 162n1
Equal Employment Opportunity Commission, 62
Escobedo v. Illinois, 38, 39
excessive force, 85, 103

exclusionary rule, 6, 9, 11–12, 14, 22–23, 25, 27, 29, 31, 33–34, 42, 43–47, 49–50, 59, 77, 83, 84, 85, 105–107, 108, 109, 119, 140, 144, 158
    cost benefit approach, 106
    empirical evidence, 47
    good faith exception to, 12, 14, 47–50, 59, 77, 83, 85, 103, 105–106, 109, 117
    judicially created remedy, 34, 43, 47, 50, 106
    silver platter doctrine, 27, 152
    social cost of, 46, 47, 50
exclusionary rule, justifications for
    deterrence, 34, 43, 46–47, 50, 85, 106
    judicial integrity, 33, 46, 106
    protecting rights of the accused, 9, 10, 25, 31, 34, 36, 38, 39, 40, 143, 147
    protecting rights of the innocent, 32, 69, 74, 97, 148
    principled basis for, 106
exigency, 7, 86, 87, 109–111, 125–127
exigent circumstances, 7, 14, 22, 23, 84, 86, 103, 109–111, 158

FAA. *See* Federal Aviation Administration
faraday bag, 99
FBI. *See* Federal Bureau of Investigation
Federal Aviation Administration, 154
Federal Bureau of Investigation, 4, 35, 93, 113
Ferguson v. City of Charleston, 76
Fernandez, Walter, 87, 137
Fernandez v. California, 8, 87, 136–137
fingerprinting, 4, 113, 114
firearms, 37
    gun, 3, 25, 37, 71, 97, 105
    gunpoint, 108, 118
    gunshots, 118

handgun, 3, 74, 105, 120
shotgun, 4, 43, 113, 137
Florence, Albert, 115
Florence v. Board of Chosen Freeholders of the County of Burlington, 115, 168nn14–15
Florida v. Bostick, 70
Florida v. Harris, 68, 87, 90, 130–131, 156, 168nn8–9
Florida v. Jardines, 19, 21, 86, 89, 96, 107, 111, 127–130, 146, 156, 167n7, 168nn5–7
Florida v. J. L., 76, 167n1
Florida v. Riley, 170n13
Florida v. Wells, 15, 75
Ford, Gerald, 17
Fortas, Associate Justice Abe, 40–41, 42
Frankfurter, Associate Justice Felix, 29

Gant, Rodney, 16, 120, 123
Garner, Eric, 75, 147
Gates, Lance, 48
Georgia v. Randolph, 8, 16, 83, 85, 87, 89, 135–137, 168n18
Gideon v. Wainwright, 18, 38, 39
Ginsburg, Associate Justice Ruth Bader, 18, 88, 93, 104, 111, 122, 126, 129, 133, 139, 145, 146
    appointment of, 62
    ideology, 20, 22, 62, 123
    participation in oral argument, 121
    views on crime control, 106
Gizmodo, 93
Glines, Marissa, 138
Global Positioning System (GPS), 21, 54, 88, 90, 91–92, 144, 149–150, 156, 157
    in cell phones, 92, 95, 144, 149–150
    Grady v. North Carolina, 157
    state laws on use of, 92

United States v. Jones, 4, 21, 58, 86, 91–96, 129, 140, 156
    use in police surveillance, 21, 84, 90, 92, 97
Goldwater, Barry, 10, 39, 147
Gooding v. United States, 55
Gottschalk, Marie, 167nn11–12, 170n15
GPS. *See* Global Positioning System
Grady v. North Carolina, 87, 96, 157, 158
Graham, Fred, 40

Harlan, Associate Justice John M., 34, 36, 42, 44, 45
Harris, Clayton, 130–131
Harris, Victor, 103
hearsay evidence, 31, 35, 150
Heien v. North Carolina, 87
Herring, Bennie Dean, 85, 105–106
Herring v. United States, 14, 85–86, 105–106, 167nn4–6
Hester v. United States, 30
highway checkpoints, 69–70
    sobriety checkpoints, 69
Hodari D., 72–73
home, 8, 48, 51, 52–53, 54, 77, 83–90, 118, 127–130, 135, 136, 150, 153, 156, 158, 160
    cotenant consent, 85, 135–136
    curtilage of, 96, 117, 128
    exigent circumstances, 83, 86, 109, 110, 158
    Fourth Amendment protections, 19, 77, 103, 107, 128
    knock and announce rule, 15, 84, 108, 117
    motor home, 55
    sanctity of, 28, 58, 76, 77, 107–112
    warrantless entry into, 14, 22, 26, 52, 58, 84, 86, 109, 112, 117, 119
homicide rate, 39

Hudson, Booker T., Jr., 108
Hudson v. Michigan, 84, 108
Huff, Vincent, 111–112

ideology, 123
    conservative, 10, 12, 13, 17, 18–20, 22, 23, 41, 46, 61–62, 76, 82–83, 88, 90, 105, 123, 143, 144, 145, 146, 154, 157
    decision direction variable, 13, 14, 18
    ideological neutrality, 22, 142
    liberal, 13, 14, 16, 17, 18, 20, 22, 41, 59, 61–62, 86, 89, 119, 141, 143, 144, 145, 146, 154, 157
Illinois v. Caballes, 67–68, 127, 129, 133, 135, 155–156, 165n14
Illinois v. Gates, 48–50, 59, 63, 131
Illinois v. Lidster, 70
Illinois v. Rodriguez, 85, 89, 135, 136
Illinois v. Wardlow, 74–75, 166nn24–26
impound, vehicle, 3, 7, 97, 105, 123
incorporation, Bill of Rights, 29, 34
    selective, 29
    total, 29
incremental approach, 59
incremental change in the law, 42, 59
information technology, 21, 81, 90, 144, 160
In re: Application of the United States of America for Historical Cell Site Data, 169n10
Internet, 95, 97, 147, 151–152, 154
Internet search histories, 97
Internet service providers, 95, 147, 151
inventory searches, 3, 7, 15, 97, 123

Jackson, Harvey, 51
Johnson, Lyndon, 10, 39, 40
Jones, Antoine, 4, 21, 92–93, 140
judicial neutrality, 4, 16

judicial remedy, 34, 43, 47, 50, 106
jurisprudence. *See* crime control
jurisprudential regime, 11, 22, 23, 50, 59, 69
    shift, 11, 13–14, 22, 23, 59, 143–144

K9, 7, 12, 68, 84, 87, 90, 96, 123, 127, 130–133, 155
    and sniffs, 7, 12, 84, 87, 90, 96, 123, 127, 130–133, 155
    sui generis, 129, 155
Kagan, Associate Justice Elena, 86, 88, 93, 119, 126, 129, 131, 134, 141, 143, 146
    appointment of, 8, 17, 18, 83–84, 144
    ideology, 18, 20, 22, 144
    views on crime control, 18, 86, 119, 131, 143, 145–146
Katz, Charles, 35–36
Katz v. United States, 15, 19, 35–36, 50–51, 54, 56, 60, 90, 91, 93–96, 98, 100, 129, 157
    legitimate expectation of privacy, 36, 52, 58, 68, 100, 155
    reasonable expectation of privacy standard, 19, 36, 50–51, 54, 56, 90, 91, 93, 95, 98, 129, 157
    subjective expectation of privacy, 36, 51, 56, 91, 139
Kennedy, Associate Justice Anthony, 4, 18, 20, 23, 87, 88, 93, 114, 115, 133, 145
    appointment of, 61
    ideology, 19, 61, 145
    views on crime control, 62, 114, 115, 119, 145
Kennedy, John F., 39
Kentucky v. King, 14, 86, 110, 167n9
King, Alonzo, 4–5, 113–115
King, Hollis, 110

King, Rodney, 116
Knowles, Patrick, 15
Knowles v. Iowa, 15, 75, 124
Kritzer, Bert, 11, 14, 50, 59, 143
Kyllo, Danny, 77, 89
Kyllo v. United States, 76–77, 89, 93, 111, 129, 153, 166n4

legitimacy, 16, 17, 22, 121, 144, 156
　Supreme Court, 17, 121, 144
Leon, Alberto, 49
locational data, 21, 149
Los Angeles County v. Rettele, 85, 108, 116

manned aircraft, over flights by, 153
Mapp, Dollree, 33
Mapp v. Ohio, 9, 10, 15, 32–34, 38, 39, 40, 44–47, 106, 162nn12–13
marijuana, 48, 68, 77, 101, 110, 111, 127–128
　legalization of, 154
　medical, 154
　recreational, 154
Marshall, Associate Justice Thurgood, 43, 50, 60, 62, 65
Maryland v. King, 4, 6, 7, 21, 87, 90, 96, 97, 113–114, 161n1, 168n13
Mason, Pamela, 43
mass incarceration, 60, 148, 154
McMahon, Kevin, 40
McNeely, Tyler, 125–126
methamphetamine, 105, 112, 124, 130, 132
Michigan v. Clifford, 52
Michigan v. DeFillippo, 47–48
Michigan v. Fisher, 86, 110
Michigan v. Sitz, 70, 76
Michigan v. Tyler, 52
Miers, Harriet, 82

Mincey v. Arizona, 52
Minnesota v. Olson, 76
Miranda v. Arizona, 10, 38–40
Miranda warnings, 42
Missouri v. McNeely, 87, 125–127
Moore, David Lee, 104
motion for summary judgment, 115, 118

narcotics dog, 8, 67–68, 123, 128–131, 155–156
　presumption of infallibility, 156
　reliability, 68, 130–132, 156
　sui generis, 129, 155
National Security Agency (NSA), 146, 151
National Treasury Employees Union v. Von Raab, 71
Navarette, Jose Prado, 101
Navarette, Lorenzo, 101
Navarette v. California, 76, 79, 90, 101–103, 115, 133–134, 157, 161n5, 167n2
navigable airspace, 153
neutral magistrate, 26, 44, 88, 111
New Jersey v. T.L.O., 46, 71, 138–139, 164n9
New York City, 39, 75, 147, 154
New York Times, 93
New York v. Belton, 11, 15–16, 55–56, 63, 66–67, 86, 120–124, 155
Nixon, Richard, 6, 10, 13, 40–41, 42, 45–46, 47, 59, 61, 147
NSA. *See* National Security Agency

O'Connor, Associate Justice Sandra Day, 8, 59, 62, 67, 71, 82, 83, 121–123
O'Connor v. Ortega, 71
Office of National Drug Control Policy, 63

Ohio v. Robinette, 70
Oliver v. United States, 128
Olmstead, Roy, 27
Olmstead v. United States, 27, 34, 35, 86, 91, 94, 162n3
open field, 30
Operation Pipeline, 56, 65
oral argument, 3, 44, 48, 49, 82, 93, 96, 98, 121, 122, 146
originalism, 19, 22, 90, 96, 115, 119, 160
originalist, 19, 90

Packer, Herbert, 5
  crime control model, 5–6
  due process model, 5–6
Payton v. New York, 52
Pennsylvania v. Mimms, 104
pen register, 54, 92, 99
People v. Brendlin, 169n25
People v. Defore, 163n2
People v. Weaver, 92, 167n9
physical surveillance, 21, 57
Plumhoff v. Rickard, 117
police, 3–12, 13–17, 21–23, 26, 30–40, 42–44, 46–70, 72–75, 77–78, 81, 84–92, 97, 99–113, 116–121, 123–137, 141, 144, 146–156, 158–160
  deterrence of misconduct by, 34, 43, 46–47, 50, 85, 106
  discretion, 5–6, 13–14, 31, 38, 43, 49, 63, 67–70, 74–75, 81, 102, 113, 143, 144, 147–148, 158–159
  misconduct by, 7, 43, 46–47, 50, 85, 106
  use of deadly force, 147
Police Chief magazine, 69
political backlash, 10, 13, 23, 25, 38–40, 143, 148, 158
Powell, Associate Justice Lewis F., 10, 42, 45–47, 48–49, 52, 53, 59, 61

precedent, 6, 11–12, 16, 42–43, 58, 75, 86, 91, 94, 100, 104, 118, 126, 127, 136, 140, 144, 150, 152
  corrective measures, 144
  departures from, 9, 86
  incremental change, 43, 121, 127
  jurisprudential regime, 11
  qualified immunity, 118
  reliance on, 15, 26, 90, 92, 117
  retroactive application, 106–107
presidency, 6
  appointment of Supreme Court justices, 6, 20, 40, 42, 59, 61–62, 82–83, 145, 147
  president, 20, 30, 40, 41, 42, 45, 59, 61–62, 63, 78, 82–83, 145, 147
  presidential, 10, 39, 146, 147
privacy, 4, 24, 27–29, 33, 67, 76, 89, 107, 112, 129, 153, 160
  balanced against crime control, 7, 29, 51, 60, 71, 77, 96
  bodily integrity, 76
  digital, 3, 6, 20–23, 24, 84, 95, 96–100, 145–146, 148–149, 151, 157, 159–160
  dog sniffs, 67–68, 127–130, 133, 155–157
  home, 52, 89, 107–112, 128, 136–137, 158
  individual right of, 15, 18, 22, 27, 28, 60, 77, 92, 158
  Katz v. United States, 19, 35–38, 50–58, 90–91, 93, 95, 98, 100, 129, 157
  motor vehicles, 54–56, 57, 91, 92, 123, 156
  reasonable expectation of, 11, 19, 23, 35–36, 43, 50–58, 60, 76, 90–100, 129–130, 133, 136, 139, 152, 157
  strip search, 139

subjective expectation of, 4, 36, 51, 56, 139
third party doctrine, 53–54, 95, 151
probable cause, 4, 7, 11, 30, 34, 54–58, 77, 84, 111, 135, 138, 143, 148
  Aguilar and *Spinelli* test, 35, 48–50, 60
  anonymous tip, 48–49
  dog sniffs, 68, 127, 130–131, 157
  Draper v. United States, 31–32, 34, 60
  Illinois v. Gates, 49, 131
  Terry v. Ohio, 36–37, 72, 102
  totality of circumstances test, 35, 49, 60, 64, 101–102, 126–127, 131, 157
  traffic stops, 65–66, 68–69, 85, 89, 104
Pullman, Scott, 132–133

qualified immunity, 16, 86–88, 103, 116–119, 137–139, 158, 159

racial profiling, 65–66, 69, 77, 147, 154, 158
  bias, 147
  false positives, 148
radio transmitters, 51, 56, 91–92, 129, 149
Randolph, Janet, 135–136
Randolph, Scott, 135–136
rape kit, 113, 114
Reagan, Ronald, 18, 61–62, 63, 70, 78, 82, 88
Redding, Savanna, 137–140
Rehnquist, William, 7, 8, 15, 143
  appointment of, 10, 42, 45, 61
  Associate Justice, 10, 42, 45, 46, 49, 57, 59, 61, 91
  Chief Justice, 15, 61–65, 67–72, 74–78, 82–83
  ideology, 62
  originalism, 19
  participation in oral argument, 82
  views on crime control, 10–11, 42, 45–46, 49, 57, 59, 61, 64–65, 70, 74, 77–78, 83
Rehnquist Court, 13, 16, 18, 19, 20, 82–83, 88, 89, 102, 103, 104, 105, 112, 135, 143, 144, 147, 155, 157, 158
  corrective measures, 15, 22, 75–77, 124
  drug courier profile, 64–65
  drug testing, 71–72
  good faith exception, 12, 77
  jurisprudence of crime control, 7–9, 11, 22, 23, 63, 72, 77–78, 106, 143
  traffic stops, 11, 64, 69–70, 72, 125
  war on drugs, 11, 61–70, 127
remand, 50, 96, 118, 140–141
retroactivity, 86, 106–107
Rettele, Max, 108–109
Richards, Mark, 11, 50, 59, 143
Riley, David Leon, 3–5, 97, 99, 100
Riley v. California, 3–4, 6–7, 21, 81, 87–88, 90–91, 96–97, 99–100, 125, 141, 142, 149, 157–158, 160, 167nn21–24, 170n13
roadside checks, 53, 76, 125
Roberts, Chief Justice John, 12, 87, 88, 109, 114, 115, 126
  appointment of, 7–8, 18, 82
  digital privacy, 3–4, 98–99, 145, 150, 157
  ideology, 8, 19–20, 82, 123
  participation in oral argument, 121–122
  views on crime control, 85, 105–106, 145–146
Roberts Court, 6–9, 18–20, 23–24, 67, 81–90, 93, 96, 100, 107, 135, 141, 143–145, 149, 158, 160
  corrective measures, 15, 16, 22, 121, 124–125, 127, 139–140, 144

Roberts Court, *continued*
   digital privacy, 8, 20–22, 54, 58, 149, 160
   dog sniffs, 127, 155–156
   exigent circumstances, 14, 22–23, 83, 109–113
   first five years, 8, 13, 16, 17, 83, 84–86, 89, 143
   good faith exception, 83, 105–107
   group dynamics, 18, 20, 144, 145–146
   jurisprudence of crime control, 12, 14, 22, 78, 81, 83, 101–105, 119
   last five years, 8, 14, 17, 20, 84, 86–88, 89, 143
   qualified immunity, 116–119
   traffic stops, 85, 103–105
Rodriguez, Dennys, 132–133
Rodriguez v. United States, 8, 87, 90, 132, 134–135, 155–156, 168nn10–16
Rohleder, Alex, 112
Rojas, Roxanne, 137
Romero, Jordan, 137–138
Ryburn v. Huff, 86, 111

Safford Unified School District v. Redding, 8, 83, 85, 116, 139, 168n20
Samson, Donald Curtis, 112
Samson v. California, 112, 167n10
San Francisco v. Sheehan, 88
Scalia, Associate Justice Antonin, 66, 77, 95, 98, 100, 103–105, 121–123, 126, 146
   appointment of, 18, 61, 88
   dissents, attacks on other justices, 88, 90, 102, 114, 115, 144–145, 146
   evolution of views of the Fourth Amendment, 18, 19, 22–23, 81, 84, 88–90, 102, 115, 144, 158
   ideology, 17, 18, 20, 23, 88, 144
   idiosyncratic view of the Fourth Amendment, 23, 88

oral argument, 98, 121, 146
originalism, 19, 22, 90, 96, 119, 145
sanctity of the home, 107–108, 111
trespass standard, 19, 86, 90, 93–94, 96, 98, 114, 128–129, 153, 156–158
views on crime control, 62, 73–74, 84, 89–90, 96, 108, 123
Schmerber v. California, 126–127
Schneckloth v. Bustamonte, 46
school(s), 16, 71–72, 85, 86, 111–112, 116, 137–139
   administration, 16, 85, 116, 137–139
   qualified immunity of, 86, 116, 138
Schulhofer, Stephen J., 164n20
science, 27–28, 57
Scott, Timothy, 85, 103
Scott v. Harris, 85, 103, 116–117, 167n3
search
   administrative, 71
   consent, 8, 16, 58, 68, 70, 84, 85, 87, 89, 117, 123, 125, 130, 132, 135–137
   cotenant consent, 8, 16, 85, 87, 89, 135–137
   dog sniff, 8, 67–68, 87, 123, 127–135, 155–157
   drug test, 70–72, 76
   exigent circumstances, 7, 14, 22, 23, 83, 84, 86, 87, 103, 109–111, 125–127, 158
   incident to arrest, 15–17, 21, 44, 55–56, 67, 85–87, 89, 96, 97–98, 100, 107, 109, 120–124, 148–149
   inventory, 3, 7, 15, 97, 123
   K9, 7, 12, 68, 84, 87, 90, 96, 123, 127, 130–133, 155
   parolees, 103, 112–113
   pat down, 37, 74, 104
   plain view, 44, 57, 63, 68, 77, 91, 109, 153
   probationers, 103, 112–113

stop and frisk, 37, 72, 154
strip search, 16, 85, 115–116, 137–139
vehicle, 8, 11–12, 15–17, 21, 30, 44, 48, 55–56, 63, 67–70, 86, 103, 107, 109, 120–124, 127, 129, 130, 132, 134, 155
warrantless, 3, 7, 14, 15, 21, 22, 26, 29, 32, 33, 37, 51–58, 64, 75–77, 84–88, 90, 91–93, 96, 98, 100, 107, 109–112, 114, 117, 119, 123–127, 130, 135, 148, 151, 153
search warrant, 33, 35, 44, 48–50, 54, 57–58, 85, 87, 92, 97, 108, 109, 135, 141
anticipatory warrant, 84, 107
administrative warrant, 52
automobile exception of warrant requirement, 30, 44, 55–56, 63, 68, 89, 123, 127
good faith exception of warrant requirement, 12, 14, 16, 47–50, 59, 77, 83, 85, 103, 105–107, 109, 117
knock and announce requirement, 15, 84, 108, 117
murder scene exception, 52
warrant requirement, 6, 30–31, 36, 60, 63, 119, 125, 127, 143, 158
segregation, 39
Sheldon, Charles, 17, 162n13
Silverman v. United States, 128
Silver Platter Doctrine, 27, 152
Sixth Amendment, 10
Skinner v. Railway Labor Executives' Association, 71, 166n19
smartphone, 21, 87, 90, 95, 97, 98, 99, 144, 147, 148, 149
apps, 98–99, 149
cell phone, 3–5, 7, 21–22, 54, 88, 92, 96–100, 140, 148, 149–151, 154
use as a tracking device, 96, 149–151

Smith v. Maryland, 53–54, 95, 150–152, 164n21
third party doctrine, 53–54, 96, 99–100, 149–151, 159
Snowden, Edward, 146, 151
Sotomayor, Associate Justice Sonia, 86, 87, 88, 96, 98, 126, 129, 145
appointment of, 8, 17, 18, 83–84, 144
digital privacy, 95–96, 151
ideology, 18, 20, 22, 144
third party doctrine, 95, 100, 150
United States v. Jones, 93–96
views on crime control, 20, 84, 95, 119, 141, 143, 145–146
Souter, Associate Justice David, 18, 20, 61, 62, 67–68, 83, 121–123, 136, 139, 144
Spinelli, William, 35
Spinelli v. United States, 35, 48–50, 60
Stanton, Mike, 117
Stanton v. Sims, 87, 117
stare decisis, 34
State v. Jackson, 167n8
Steagald v. United States, 52
Stevens, Associate Justice John Paul, 50, 67–68, 73, 75, 83, 109, 112, 139
appointment of, 17, 46
Arizona v. Gant, 121–12
ideology, 18, 20, 123, 144
views on crime control, 43, 60, 122
Stewart, Associate Justice Potter, 36, 44, 48, 52, 55, 59, 94
stingray device, 150
Struble, Morgan, 132–134
Stuntz, William, 17, 159, 162n12, 163n21, 170n17
Supreme Court
Arizona, 52
California, 73, 140
Florida, 70, 128, 131

Supreme Court, *continued*
  Georgia, 136
  Illinois, 48, 68, 74
  Kentucky, 111
  Louisiana, 52
  Missouri, 126
  New Hampshire, 44, 61
  Washington, 92
  United States, 3–8, 10–12, 14, 20, 25–26, 39–40, 44, 48, 51, 57, 63, 66–69, 74, 88, 92–93, 107–109, 112, 117–118, 121, 126, 128, 131–132, 136, 138, 140, 145, 147–148, 153, 159
Supreme Court, United States
  legitimacy of, 16, 17, 22, 121, 144
  membership on, 17–18, 82, 145, 158
  oral argument, 3, 44, 48–49, 82, 93, 96, 98, 121–122, 146
  political check, 14, 16, 21, 24, 41, 121, 142, 144
  small group dynamics of, 17–18, 145–146
Supreme Court Database, 12–13, 18, 161nn9–10
  decision direction variable, 13, 18, 161n10

technology, 8, 20–22, 27, 56–57, 100, 126, 153, 159–160
  cloud, 98, 159
  digital, 7, 151, 159
  digital privacy, 3, 6, 20, 23–24, 84, 95, 96, 98, 145–146, 148, 149, 157
  global positioning, 4, 21, 54, 58, 84, 86, 88, 90, 91–97, 129, 130, 140, 144, 149–151, 156–157
  information, 21, 81, 90, 144, 160
Terry v. Ohio, 36–37, 67, 72, 76, 102, 133, 141

reasonable, articulable suspicion standard, 37, 53, 69, 72–73, 102
stop and frisk, 37, 72, 74
Terry stop, 37, 76, 102, 133, 141
thermal imaging device, 77, 89, 94, 129
third party doctrine, 53–54, 77, 84, 95–96, 99–100, 149–151, 159
Thomas, Associate Justice Clarence, 15, 88, 90, 93, 114, 122–123, 126–127, 139
  appointment of, 18, 62
  ideology, 19–20, 62
  oral argument, 122
  originalism, 19
  views on crime control, 62, 101–102, 112, 119, 127, 133–134, 145–146, 157
Thompson v. Louisiana, 52
Thornton v. United States, 67–68, 121–123, 168n2
Tolan, Robert, 118
Tolan v. Cotton, 87, 118
Toobin, Jeffrey, 166n1, 169n2
totality of circumstances standard, 35, 49, 60, 64, 93, 101–102, 126–127, 131, 135, 157
traffic stop, 5, 8, 11, 56, 63–69, 85–87, 89–90, 101–104, 124–125, 127, 130–134, 140, 148, 155–157, 159
  citation stop, 8, 15, 85, 87, 124, 134, 156
  pretextual stop, 11, 63, 65–68
  vehicle stop, 53, 56, 64, 66–67, 87, 103–104, 115, 125
trespass doctrine, 35–36, 98, 100, 114, 153, 156–157, 160
  Florida v. Jardines, 19, 86, 89–90, 96, 128–130, 146, 156
  Grady v. North Carolina, 96, 157, 158
  Maryland v. King, 114
  Olmstead v. United States, 27–29, 86

overruled by *Katz v. United States*, 19, 29, 35, 90, 91, 94
United States v. Jones, 19, 90, 93–96, 98, 128, 146, 156, 158

United States v. Arvizu, 70
United States v. Bailey, 169n27
United States v. Calandra, 46, 163n7, 164nn10–11
United States v. Chadwick, 52–53
United States v. Drayton, 70
United States v. Grubbs, 84, 107
United States v. Jacobsen, 152
United States v. Janis, 47, 164n2
United States v. Jones, 4, 81, 96–100, 125, 141, 142, 167nn14–20, 168nn22–23
  GPS surveillance, 21, 58, 86, 91–94, 130, 156
  Justice Alito's concurrence, 93, 94
  Justice Sotomayor's concurrence, 93, 150–151
  originalism, 19, 90, 96
  third party doctrine, 150
  trespass doctrine, 86, 89–90, 93–94, 98, 128–129, 146, 156
  unanimous ruling, 4, 21, 88, 93, 98, 100
United States v. Karo, 57–58, 91, 164nn27–28, 166n5
United States v. Knights, 112
United States v. Knotts, 57–58, 91–94, 164nn25–26, 166nn5–6
United States v. Leon, 49–50, 59, 85, 105
United States v. Matlock, 136, 168n17
United States v. Maynard, 92, 167n10
United States v. McIver, 166n7
United States v. Miller, 53–54, 95, 164n19
United States v. Moreno-Nevarez, 169n10
United States v. Peltier, 59
United States v. Place, 67, 129, 165n13

United States v. Robinson, 15, 55
United States v. Ross, 55
United States v. Sharpe, 133
United States v. Sokolow, 64–65, 165nn5–8
United States v. Villamonte-Marquez, 164n22
United States v. White, 51, 54, 164nn17–18
unprovoked flight, 72–75
USA Freedom Act, 147, 151
USA Patriot Act, 147

vehicle identification number (VIN), 55
Veronia School District No. 47J v. Acton, 71, 166n19
Virginia v. Moore, 8, 85, 104

Wardlow, William "Sam," 74
war on drugs, 9–11, 14, 70, 86, 93, 121, 148
  constitutional toolbox, 10, 11, 56, 62–63, 66–69, 77, 155
  dog sniffs, 67, 127, 155
  George H. W. Bush, 78
  impact on minorities, 113, 154
  impact on the poor, 113, 154
  mass incarceration and, 60, 148
  politics of, 23, 154–155
  racial profiling, 65–66, 69, 77, 147, 154
  Richard Nixon, 6
  Ronald Reagan, 61, 63, 70, 78
  traffic stops and, 55–56, 67, 69, 120–121, 124, 155
Warren, Chief Justice Earl, 30–31, 38, 40, 42
  political backlash against, 10, 13, 23, 25, 38–41, 143, 148, 158

Warren Court, 5, 42–43, 59–60, 72, 128, 158
   backlash against, 9, 10, 23, 25, 38–41, 43, 59, 143
   due process revolution, 10, 25, 30–38
   early cases, 13, 31–32
   jurisprudential regime change, 12, 13, 14, 143
Weeks, Fremont, 26
Weeks v. United States, 26–27, 30, 152, 162n2
White, Associate Justice Byron, 45–48, 50, 51, 58–59, 62
White, James, 51
Whittaker, Associate Justice Charles E., 31
Whren, James, 65–66
Whren v. United States, 65–67, 89, 105, 147
Wilson v. Arkansas, 15, 75
Winston v. Lee, 53
wiretapping, 8, 27, 91, 100
Wolf v. Colorado, 29, 33–34
Woodward, Bob, 45
Woodward, Bob, and Scott Armstrong, 163n6
Wurie, Brima, 3, 97
Wyoming v. Houghton, 89

Zita, Michael, 117